Open Innovation Strategies

Smart Innovation Set

coordinated by
Dimitri Uzunidis

Volume 39

Open Innovation Strategies

Camille Aouinaït

WILEY

First published 2022 in Great Britain and the United States by ISTE Ltd and John Wiley & Sons, Inc.

Apart from any fair dealing for the purposes of research or private study, or criticism or review, as permitted under the Copyright, Designs and Patents Act 1988, this publication may only be reproduced, stored or transmitted, in any form or by any means, with the prior permission in writing of the publishers, or in the case of reprographic reproduction in accordance with the terms and licenses issued by the CLA. Enquiries concerning reproduction outside these terms should be sent to the publishers at the undermentioned address:

ISTE Ltd
27-37 St George's Road
London SW19 4EU
UK

www.iste.co.uk

John Wiley & Sons, Inc.
111 River Street
Hoboken, NJ 07030
USA

www.wiley.com

© ISTE Ltd 2022

The rights of Camille Aouinaït to be identified as the author of this work have been asserted by her in accordance with the Copyright, Designs and Patents Act 1988.

Any opinions, findings, and conclusions or recommendations expressed in this material are those of the author(s), contributor(s) or editor(s) and do not necessarily reflect the views of ISTE Group.

Library of Congress Control Number: 2022941074

British Library Cataloguing-in-Publication Data
A CIP record for this book is available from the British Library
ISBN 978-1-78630-708-8

Contents

Preface ix

Introduction xi

Part 1. Static and Descriptive Innovation 1

Chapter 1. Definition of Open Innovation and Collaborative Innovation 3

    1.1. Definition of open and collaborative innovation 3
    1.2. Basic characteristics. 9
        1.2.1. From closed innovation to open innovation 9
        1.2.2. Serendipity. 13
        1.2.3. Creativity. 15
        1.2.4. The absorption capacity of firms 16
        1.2.5. The various degrees of innovation 18
        1.2.6. Exploration versus exploitation in innovation processes 22
    1.3. The creation of innovation and associated partnerships 24
        1.3.1. Dynamics of collaborative innovation production. 24
        1.3.2. Forms of partnerships and degree of openness of innovation 25
        1.3.3. Collaborative models: from the triple helix to mode 2, via the NSI. 30

Chapter 2. History of the Evolution of Collaboration Between Actors, and Creation of Innovation Networks. 33

    2.1. Genesis of collaboration and its evolution through different innovation models 33
        2.1.1. History of collaboration 33
        2.1.2. Evolution of the innovation models used 35

2.1.3. Top-down and bottom-up approaches	37
2.1.4. Location of actors for collaboration and impact on the type of innovation	42
2.2. Business ecosystems	42
2.3. Partnership experience	45
2.3.1. Creation of innovation networks	45
2.3.2. Profiles of the partners involved in the collaboration	48
2.3.3. Importance of the territorial level for the governance of innovation	52
2.3.4. Emergence and use of collaborative platforms	54
2.3.5. Intellectual property rights: license exchange and other notable examples of collaboration	57

Part 2. Dynamic and Causal Innovation … 63

Chapter 3. The Reasons Behind Open Innovation and its Evolution … 65

3.1. Evolution of the use of collaborative innovation: from classical to new models	65
3.1.1. FabLabs	66
3.1.2. The Artlab	68
3.1.3. Coworking spaces	69
3.1.4. Hacker spaces and maker spaces	71
3.1.5. Living Labs	72
3.1.6. Creative Labs	73
3.2. Diversity of collaborative forms: an organized space of actors based on geographical, social and organizational proximity	74
3.2.1. The spatial organization of actors in the form of clusters	74
3.2.2. Industrial districts	81
3.2.3. National Innovation Systems and Local Innovation Systems	82
3.3. The intermediaries of innovation	83
3.4. Innovation jointly created with users	89

Chapter 4. Advantages, Disadvantages and Issues Related to Collaborative Innovation … 99

4.1. Benefits of collaborative innovation for the actors involved	99
4.1.1. The modes of knowledge transfer and their implications on collaborative innovation	106
4.1.2. The role of collaborative innovation at the economic, social, societal and environmental levels	108
4.1.3. Sectors conducive to open innovation	122
4.2. Limitations of the open innovation paradigm	124

4.2.1. Actors' levels of organization, between small and large firms . . . 124
  4.2.2. Intellectual property: a sensitive point in the collaboration 125
  4.2.3. Clarification of monetary benefits 126
  4.2.4. Restricting access to protected results and impacts on science . . . 127
  4.2.5. Actors' cognitive skills 127
  4.2.6. What value does the innovation bring? 128
 4.3. Questions related to collaborative innovation. 133
  4.3.1. The various paradoxes inherent in collaborative innovation. 133
  4.3.2. Role of governance and actors 138

Conclusion 143

References 151

Index 181

Preface

The elements dealt with in this book come from a literature review carried out over several years on the theme of innovation, notably as an end to processes involving various resources and stakeholders, and also as a means used to meet increasingly complex challenges.

My youthful experience and expertise in innovation management is generally focused on the agricultural sector. Thanks to the opportunity offered to me by Dimitri Uzunidis, Honorary President of the Research Network on Innovation, I was able to write this book, which is intended to be easy to read and useful for those who have questions about the use of open innovation. Several sectors are covered in the chapters, because of the universality of innovation and the open innovation paradigm.

Through my experience in the agricultural and agri-food sector, I have been able to observe that innovation is a source of dynamism for companies and at the heart of research and development projects, whether public or private. This sector and more particularly the production of traditional products can be dominated by informal collaborations that can lead to innovations, satisfying the interests of each stakeholder. The consumer or customer must, and wants to, be at the heart of the concerns of the actors proposing innovative solutions.

However, for several years now, environmental and societal challenges have been added to the development ambitions of many projects to remedy, in the most efficient and sustainable way possible, the problems that are multiplying on a territorial and global scale. This book takes up the links of collaborative innovation with these general challenges and attempts to identify levers of action on which to act to fuel research and development of collaborative projects. The educational, economic, political, social and environmental systems still have much to do, and their collaboration is crucial in a highly globalized world. Responsible innovation and elements related to corporate social and societal responsibility is a line of thought already understood and undertaken by actors. Interesting publications and events related to this topic have also led to the writing of this book.

July 2022

Introduction

This book investigates innovation from the perspective of collaborations, partnerships, cooperation or any other term referring to the openness of innovation. Having mainly done my research on innovation in the agricultural and agri-food sector, I have observed that many innovations come from collaborations, whether formal or informal, whether the innovation is radical or incremental. In short, adopting collaborative strategies can condition innovative results, in varying contexts. The profiles of the actors involved in this type of strategy are important, as is their location. Geographical proximity can be a determining factor and correlate with a propensity for innovation. Other proximities such as institutional, cognitive, social and organizational proximity are also significant and substantial aspects. The type of sector can explain the use of such proximities.

The type of innovation and the degree of innovation are also characteristics to be defined before any collaborative process. Indeed, the degree of innovation is important for the economy because of the possible spin-offs. Radical or disruptive innovations often have the particularity of leading to a paradigm shift, such as the adoption of new consumption patterns. Several sectors can be impacted, and these changes take place over time. We can cite many examples such as the use of the Internet in the organization of our professional and private days, the hybrid and electric car, mobile or contactless payments and also the numerous applications allowing us to book train or plane tickets and make appointments. These examples all include technological innovations. However, social, organizational or marketing innovations are not left out. Promoting brands or products via end-users, rethinking a mode of food consumption based on social and local links with local distribution channels or developing workplaces where break areas, sports facilities and childcare facilities are available to facilitate the organization of employees' days are all examples of new implementations that are interdisciplinary and concern many areas of activity. As far as the changes brought about by the adoption of innovations are concerned, it can generally be said that radical innovations have a major impact on consumers, while incremental innovations have a minor impact.

An incremental innovation will not be developed with the same actors or in the same partnerships as a radical innovation. The involvement of actors may differ in terms of participation (resources and information transferred) and also in terms of the time of the innovation process. These aspects are developed mainly in the first chapter.

On the contrary, serendipity or chance leading to innovation is an interesting element of new products and services that have been developed or historical discoveries such as the Lascaux cave. According to several accounts, it was discovered by pure chance by teenagers walking their dog in Montignac, Dordogne, on September 8, 1940. They discovered a cavity in the ground under an uprooted tree. After an exploration with basic equipment a few days later, the young men finally discovered the paintings present on several walls and in several underground rooms. Similarly, Teflon was discovered in April 1938 by Roy Plunkett. This doctor was working on the manufacture of a refrigerant. The freezing and compression of tetrafluoroethylene led to its polymerization, giving a waxy white solid, then called polytetrafluoroethylene (PTFE). This solid is insoluble in almost all solvents, resists a temperature of 260°C and has non-stick properties. Thus, many sectors use it, such as aerospace, communications, electronics or architecture. This demonstrates the need to keep a space for creativity and the unexpected in any innovation process. Collaborations can play a role in bringing together actors who would not have seen themselves working together without the opportunities they can then seize.

Academic articles, publications and scientific books on the subject of innovation and open innovation and collaboration are numerous and have abounded for several decades now. Henry Chesbrough's pioneering work on open innovation in the early 2000s paved the way for research on this subject. The definition of open innovation, which has been used in all the works related to the use of different partners for innovative activities, has attracted the interest of both the academic and private sectors. The objective of this book is to review open innovation from the perspective of collaboration and specifically the strategies that result from established partnerships and collaborations, both public and private. This theme concerns a diversity of disciplines such as social sciences, business management, economic management, among others.

Innovation is seen as a process and no longer as a fact. For Drucker (2014), innovation "is the specific instrument of entrepreneurship. It is the act that endows resources with a new capacity to create wealth. Innovation, indeed, creates a resource."

Innovation is then a tool at the service of the entrepreneur who is in a constant quest for change and maximizes its exploitation to accomplish new goals and move forward. The seven sources of innovation defined by Drucker include the unexpected (success, failure and unexpected external events), incongruities, process needs, changes in industry and market structure, demographic changes, changes in perception and mindset, and new knowledge. All of these sources should be studied to create innovation, although some of them are not predictable.

Open and collaborative innovation is not new; it has been practiced by companies, in a rather informal way. Collaborative innovation did not benefit from a regular and structured vision, but diffused in a tacit, non-formalized way. Before Chesbrough and Tidd (1995) discusses the more effective open networks as opposed to closed networks (Dekkers et al. 2019). The role of external sources in value creation has been reported by many other authors such as Herstad et al. (2008) with a mention of open innovation at the beginning of the 20th century, Schumpeter (1934), Pavitt (1984), von Hippel (1986), Cohen and Levinthal (1990), Freeman (1991) and Langlois (2003). Finally, Dekkers et al. (2019) point out that Trott and Hartmann (2009) refer to the conceptualization of open innovation as "old wine in new bottles". What has changed over the last 20 years is the formalization and structuring of the innovation process, first of all by clearly looking for actors who can become partners at key moments in the innovation process and who can bring specific expertise. Also, it is less and less common to establish innovation strategies by relying only on resources, knowledge and services within a firm. Knowledge that is useful for generating innovations comes from sources external to the company. Innovation is an integral part of the model of our society in the 21st century, and will be implemented with various actors, outside the boundaries of the firm.

Innovation is present everywhere, at all scales and in all sectors. It is a key factor in the knowledge economy and is increasingly important in society. It offers added value to citizens and consumers, as well as increases the competitiveness of companies through differentiation, access to niche markets or markets that are difficult to access. Innovation can create jobs and thus promote the well-being and integration of people in society. Moreover, it serves global issues such as environmental protection and the ecological transition on a large scale. Through the development of easy-to-use, accessible and affordable tools, the digital revolution is transforming many sectors. In the European Union, the innovation policy makes it possible to link research and technological development with businesses. Programs developed at the European level, such as the H2020 program or the Horizon Europe program, have defined themes that involve stakeholder participation to define the needs of stakeholders and work to find innovative solutions. The cooperation is essential to better target the expectations of citizens and propose innovations that are relevant to their daily lives. Horizon Europe has the particularity to increase the openness of data, making them accessible to any interested person. This novelty goes in the direction of sharing knowledge and results of projects initiated at the international level and that can be interesting to apply in different contexts and at a local level, for example.

Joseph Schumpeter described the economy as a cyclical process whose source is innovation. In other words, innovation was defined as one of the driving forces of the economy. It spreads in clusters, in which several innovations are linked to a major innovation. It took on its economic value when it was commercialized, as in the case of the steam engine (innovation) which valued the discovery of pressure (invention). Drucker described seven sources of innovation, while Schumpeter categorized five types of innovation: (i) product innovation, (ii) process innovation or production methods, (iii) new outlets such as new markets from new consumer trends, (iv) new sources of raw materials such as the reduction in the use of fossil fuels to meet environmental pressures and requirements, and (v) new work organizations. These cycles are accompanied by creative destruction where new innovations entering the market replace old innovations that have become obsolete, and weaker players make way for new ones. The innovations that are developed can trigger other innovations and thus appear in clusters and not in isolation. The destruction of certain economic activities is done in parallel with the creation of other economic activities. This notion has been taken up many times in works studying innovation since then.

In addition, cooperation has increased through the multiplicity of forms of partnerships, whether contractual or not. General interests such as the fight against diseases (cancer, diabetes, cardiovascular diseases, infectious diseases, among others), the fight against global warming, demographic pressure and related issues (housing, infrastructure, public transport, food, land use planning, etc.), and changing lifestyles (data security, citizen freedom, intelligent transport) are a playground for the implementation of innovation, in the sense that it can take many forms. All these challenges require investment in research and innovation on a global scale. It is through collaboration that innovative solutions are developed and disseminated for widespread adoption, where possible. Interactions between companies and universities, as established in the Triple Helix model of Etzkowitz and Leydesdorff (2000), in addition to government, are the vehicles for an innovation process that is more open and offers broader solutions.

Interactions between the different actors of the value chains can be seen as driving forces for innovation generation, which is ultimately a by-product of collaborative activities (Knickel et al. 2009). Interactions are crucial throughout the innovation process. They take place vertically between the buyer and the seller, or suppliers and customers, and also horizontally between several companies, public sector actors, citizens, scientists, etc. (Roy 2004). The advantage of the openness of innovation is the possibility of soliciting the various partners at different stages of the innovation process. Customers can be an important source of information and play a role in innovation performance when solicited at the introduction stage of the innovation process (Johnsen et al. 2006; Codini 2015). According to Gangloff-Ziegler (2009), collaboration makes it possible to overcome the "hierarchical structures" that are traditionally structured, based on transfers and exchanges of knowledge and resources. Collaborative innovation allows us to find convincing solutions to complex problems for which several actors have shared interests. For Drucker (1985), collaboration has the identity of "collective intelligence united around a project and reconfigurable according to the evolution of the objectives".

As a result, the significant development of coworking spaces around the world and particularly in France and the United States between 2012 and

2017 demonstrates the popularity and demand of this type of space, which offers the possibility to collaborate in a neutral environment. In 2012, about 60 coworking spaces were counted in France; this number climbed to more than 600 in 2017 (Sandulache 2019). The layout of these environments encourages the establishment of informal relationships between users. Coworking spaces implement collaborative tools, create events to facilitate interpersonal interactions and encourage creativity. Moreover, financial and human resources are needed to promote these collaborative opportunities, which no longer occur spontaneously by chance, as Sandulache studied in his empirical analysis.

Collaborative innovation strategies have the particularity of being able to be implemented for a wide range of possible actors. Innovations do not only come from companies and economic actors who use it to differentiate themselves on the market. For many years, the users of innovations have become a very important source for the development of these innovations. A reappropriation of the uses has enabled the introduction of disruptions into the market. The users who innovate are few, but learning-by-using is nevertheless developing. After a paradigm of innovation centered on the producers of goods and services (Schumpeterian vision), innovation becomes centered on the users (customer-driven). The latter are partly educated by the producers and take over the innovation. The lead-users are taking an increasingly important place in society, by acting on the demand and therefore the supply of novelties.

Open and collaborative innovation plays an important role in providing answers to the challenges that people, governments and society in general face. On the environmental front, the use of diverse resources through the involvement of several types of actors and forms of partnerships is a major asset in proposing innovative solutions, whether in the reduction of greenhouse gas emissions, in the use of agricultural tools that optimize water resources and inputs (e.g. pesticides) or in the development of green energy applied to individual and collective transport. At the social level, the ease and speed of communication possible to meet financial, temporal and also environmental requirements has developed in part with a form of open innovation. The information and communication technologies sector is at the heart of environmental challenges. This sector has the opportunity to play a leading role in the development of sustainable solutions that meet the requirements and expectations of society. Moreover, it can also propose solutions to facilitate the implementation of innovative solutions in different fields and at several scales (Liénart and Castiaux 2012).

Companies engaged in collaborative innovation processes can benefit from value creation resulting from the activities they carry out. Through the joint development of products and services, companies can enhance the value of innovations in their respective network. Thus, this value creation can be achieved internally and externally. Furthermore, customer satisfaction and loyalty are important objectives for companies, and can be supported in collaborative processes. Fostering and developing a collaborative management culture can allow customers to enjoy a positive experience, increasing the likelihood of a future purchase due to the positive emotions felt during the first purchase experience.

Innovations that are now an integral part of our daily lives can quickly become obsolete. All sectors innovate, to different degrees, following the laws of the market and trying to stand out. The collaborative practices that are put in place by project stakeholders, as well as by actors at the local, regional, national and even international level are diversifying in order to satisfy several interests. These interests cover the individual level of economic agents and the collective level. Actors can thus find innovative solutions to their challenges, while taking advantage of being inserted in a network that allows them to have access to various resources (human, financial, infrastructure, knowledge, for example). In addition, at a more general level, societal challenges concerning the environment, education, health, food, energy, transportation and many other sectors can benefit from innovations developed in collaboration between several actors, individuals or institutions of various profiles, such as farmers, researchers, political decision-makers and consumers.

This book seeks to analyze and present innovation and the collaborative strategies that gravitate around it, according to two axes: static and dynamic. The book begins with a descriptive part of innovation, and sets out to present a definition of open innovation, its emergence and its characteristics. Its use through different examples and its structuring at the level of actors and territories are part of this presentation.

Figure I.1. *Collaboration between several actors. For a color version of this figure, see www.iste.co.uk/aouinait/innovation.zip*

Then, the reasons for its evolution and dynamics complete the description. The limits and benefits of such a model of innovation, at different levels, close this book. This book is intended for a wide audience, including entrepreneurs, research and development managers of small and medium-sized enterprises or large companies, managers of other departments of these companies, consumers and users of products and services developed by these companies. The public sector with representatives of state or regional institutions, as well as researchers may also be interested in the content of this book.

PART 1

Static and Descriptive Innovation

1

Definition of Open Innovation and Collaborative Innovation

1.1. Definition of open and collaborative innovation

Innovation is a term defined by the Oslo Manual. This manual presents guidelines for the collection of data related to innovation. One of the goals is to be able to compare data at the international level and thus measure innovation across different contexts (OECD and Eurostat 2019). The definition of innovation in this manual is as follows:

> An innovation is the implementation of a new or significantly improved product (good or service), or process, a new marketing method, or a new organizational method in business practices, workplace organization or external relations (OECD and Eurostat 2005).

The different models of the innovation process that have been defined in the literature have evolved through research and empirical results. The linear model was first recognized to explain how innovations move from scientific research to practitioners and firms. This model has been criticized, and the nonlinear model with different sources of innovation reported the use of different agents included in iterative feedback loops to constantly innovate (Biggs and Clay 1981). The innovation process is iterative, from discovery and invention to commercialization with several possible feedback loops and modifications. Indeed, the linear nature of innovation has for some time been superseded by the participatory nature of innovation. The different departments and services of a company or the actors who are involved and solicited in the innovation creation processes can give feedback on the product, process, organization or service under development, depending on the structure and management of the process. The chain-link model of technological change by Kline and Rosenberg (1986) takes up this concept. Feedback is possible through interactions with external partners (Kline and Rosenberg 1986; Evangelista et al. 1997; Arbo and Benneworth 2007).

Innovation induces radical or slight changes. Radical or disruptive innovations and incremental innovations are generally opposed (Afuah and Bahram 1995). Consequently, the adoption of innovation is conditioned by the ability of firms to adapt to change. As Pavitt (1984) has argued, the diffusion of innovation is important for its success. For example, agriculture is a supplier-dominated industry; innovation comes primarily from input suppliers and research, but the needs of users are a growing source of concern for innovators (Rossi and Rosli 2013). Therefore, if the disclosed innovation does not target an appropriate audience, the diffusion and implementation of the innovation will fail. Thus, targeting the challenges of the value chain is fundamental to the success of the innovation.

Moreover, innovation is the result of a combination of factors such as new techniques, new knowledge and new organizations. Leeuwis and Aarts (2011) refer to it in terms of hardware, software and orgware respectively. Innovation therefore has several facets (Faure et al. 2018). The basic resources that are necessary for the proper development and use of an innovation are multifactorial and require knowledge and know-how that the agents developing the innovations do not have. This is where the intervention of external agents (individual or aggregated under the type of company) is crucial. Collaboration thus has the function of providing gaps that cannot be filled elsewhere.

Nevertheless, the opening of companies to their external environment does not ensure that internal R&D activities will cease. The latter is necessary so that companies can work on their absorption capacity (Loilier and Tellier 2011; Chesbrough 2012). Indeed, to be able to use the resources, information and knowledge collected outside the boundaries of the company, the latter must be able to reuse them internally.

However, the definition of innovation has not been agreed upon for years. Its multidimensional, nonlinear aspect, involving different actors, the degree of innovation and its stakes have been debated since the 1940s. The notion of creative destruction proposed by Jospeh Schumpeter is an example. Moreover, Baregheh et al. (2009) have reported on more than 60 definitions of innovation from several disciplines: from management, economics, science and marketing. The definitions can be adapted to the sector or field in which they are used. In the field of knowledge management, the object of study is knowledge. This key element is crucial for any development of novelties, which are to be commercialized. Nevertheless, the criterion of novelty in innovation remains a fixed and common element in all fields.

In addition to the type of innovation (i.e. product, process, service, organization, or marketing), the unit of analysis is important. The scale at which the innovation is developed and disseminated is important for its success and adaptation in different environments. Indeed, an innovation may be new for one company, but not for another (e.g. the implementation of a new production line). It is then very localized at the industrial level. It can be new for a sector (e.g. the digitization of agricultural tasks), an ecosystem or more broadly at the level of a region, a country or the world.

The production of knowledge differs between sectors. In supplier-dominated sectors such as agriculture and transport, firms develop innovations mainly through other firms such as their suppliers, customers or research departments. Scale-intensive sectors such as paper mills and telecommunications are characterized by process development via in-house production or capital goods suppliers. Specialized suppliers (e.g. software or professional services) develop new products in collaboration with customers. Finally, science-based producers (e.g. pharmaceuticals or biotechnology) collaborate more with universities to develop new products and processes (Lundvall 2008; Pavitt 1984). Not all of these sectors approach innovation with the same strategies and do not rely on the same resources.

One of the founding principles of open innovation concerns the interactions between the agents involved in the innovation creation process. By way of comparison, the interactions between supplier and customer or seller and buyer in industrial supply chains (Roy et al. 2004). The relationship is different according to the stage of the innovation's life cycle. Indeed, in the upstream stages of innovation creation, the innovator–customer relationship is critical to the performance and success of the final product, in contrast to the downstream stages, where the innovation reaches maturity (Johnsen et al. 2006; Codini 2015). Innovation is a by-product of networked collaborative network activities (Knickel et al. 2009). Thus, they are one of the driving forces of innovation generation.

In Figure 1.1, the different stages of the product life cycle in the innovation process are graphically presented. Several stages can then be identified.

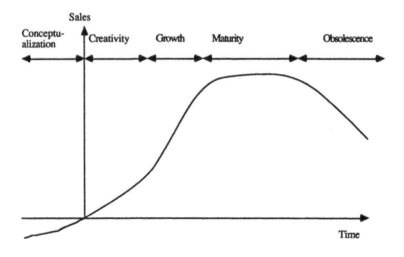

Figure 1.1. *Stages of the product life cycle (Karlsson 1988)*

The first stage of the product life cycle occurs before the product is launched on the market. The product is in development. Once the product is conceptualized, it is launched to penetrate the target market. The costs inherent in its promotion and production do not allow it to be profitable. The growth of the product's sales occurs as soon as it is diffused and adopted by users. Thanks to economies of scale, the product becomes profitable for the company, and gradually gains market share. This growth stage should be as long as possible because it brings value to the company. Communication and marketing strategies are used to promote the product and keep it in the best possible position in the market. Slowdown and stagnation occur during the maturity stage. Growth is stopped, and even if profitability is significant, it stagnates. Production costs remain low, but it must be promoted further to stay in the market. However, the costs related to this expense are difficult to bring down. It makes more economic sense to invest in the benefits of the product's profitability in another innovation, which has room for growth. Then, the end of the product's life occurs when profitability and market share decrease. This is the decline or obsolescence stage. Consumers turn to similar products or other types of products because of a lack of interest.

Roy et al. (2004) suggest that internal factors such as trust in information technology, adoption and commitment, as well as external factors such as the stability of connections in the network and implicit knowledge about the technology can have a moderating impact on the generation of innovations.

Figure 1.2 shows the number of scientific articles published on open innovation between 2000 and 2020. The growth of these publications is explained by the shared interest in collaborative innovation in several types of fields. Moreover, the work of Chesbrough in the early 2000s highlights the concept of open innovation. Open innovation is a 2003 concept that comes from the work of Henry Chesbrough, notably through the book entitled *Open Innovation: The New Imperative for Creating and Profiting from Technology*.

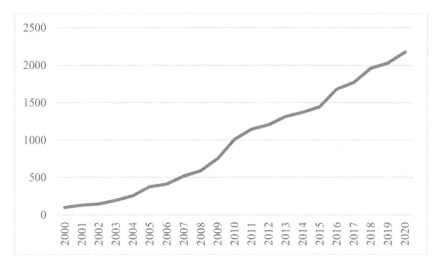

Figure 1.2. *Number of papers published on open innovation from 2000 to 2020. For a color version of this figure, see www.iste.co.uk/aouinait/innovation.zip*

In special issues of journals such as *R&D Management, Industry and Innovation, Research Policy and Management Science*, open innovation and open source have enabled this notable growth. Dahlander and Gann (2010) listed the top 10 journals by number of articles published on the topic of open innovation through to 2010. They are presented in Table 1.1.

Publications cited	Type of publications	Number of citations
von Hippel, E. (1988). *The Sources of Innovation*. Oxford University Press, New York.	Book	37
Lerner, J. and Tirole, J. (2002). Some simple economics of open source. *Journal of Industrial Economics*, 52, 197–234.	Book	35
Cohen, W.M. and Levinthal, D.A. (1990). Absorptive capacity: A new perspective on learning and innovation. *Administrative Science Quarterly*, 35(1), 128–152.	Book	33
Lakhani, K.R. and von Hippel, E. (2003). How open source software works: "Free" user-to-user assistance. *Research Policy*, 32(6), 923–943.	Book	30
von Hippel, E. and von Krogh, G. (2003). Open source software and the "private-collective" innovation model: Issues for organization science. *Organization Science*, 14(2), 209–223.	Book	30
Hertel, G., Niedner, S., Herrmann, S. (2003). Motivation of software developers in Open Source projects: An Internet-based survey of contributors to the Linux kernel. *Research Policy*, 32 1159–1177.	Book	29
von Hippel, E. (2005). *Democratizing Innovation*. The MIT Press, Cambridge, MA.	Book	26
Teece, D. (1986). Profiting from technological innovation: Implications for integration collaboration, licensing and public policy. *Research Policy*, 15, 285–305.	Article	25
Chesbrough, H.W. (2003). *Open Innovation: The New Imperative for Creating and Profiting from Technology*. Harvard Business School Press, Boston, MA.	Book	25
March, J. (1991). Exploration and exploitation in organizational learning. *Organization Science*, 2(1), 71–87.	Article	24
Chesbrough, H.W. (2003). The era of open innovation. *MIT Sloan Management Review*, Spring, 35–41.	Article	21
Laursen, K. and Salter, A.J. (2006). Open for innovation: The role of openness in explaining innovation performance among UK manufacturing firms. *Strategic Management Journal*, 27, 131–150.	Article	20

Table 1.1. *Numbers, types and details of publications related to open innovation (Dahlander and Gann 2010)*

These figures date from the early 2000s, so it is notable that they must have increased significantly since the work of Dahlander and Gann (2010). Furthermore, in the CIS-4 (4th Community Innovation Survey)[1], several results highlight the importance of the open innovation model. Although 75% of the companies that responded to the survey spend 80% of their R&D budget on internal R&D, half of these companies spend 5% of their R&D budget on external research activities; in other words, they spend more than 10% of their budget on internal R&D. At the French level, 4 out of 10 companies are engaged in an OI model through more sustained relationships with suppliers (65% of the companies surveyed), with customers (50% of the companies surveyed), with competitors (36% of the companies surveyed), with universities and higher education institutions (26% of the companies surveyed) and with public research (18% of the companies surveyed) (Isckia and Lescop 2011). At the sectoral level, it is the financial and insurance sector that stands out with one out of two companies having carried out at least one form of cooperation. The scientific and technical sector also shows a propensity for collaboration, with 43% of companies collaborating for the period 2014–2016. Moreover, almost all firms that cooperate do so with a partner (97%); 40% have created partnerships at the regional or national level and 23% at the international level (Europe or worldwide) (Duc 2018). These data correspond to companies with 10 or more employees located in France.

1.2. Basic characteristics

1.2.1. *From closed innovation to open innovation*

Initially, closed innovation (Figure 1.3) is opposed to open innovation (Figure 1.4). The closed model reflects a pattern of vertical integration where Research and Development (R&D) activities are internal to the firm[2]. The

---

[1] The community innovation survey was carried out at the request of the European Union, by all member countries.

[2] Vertical integration is opposed to horizontal integration. It is a way of managing activities. By integrating the different processes (production, transformation, logistics, marketing of products), the firm can see its overall performance or by activities, as well as its costs concerning various expense items optimized. Some sectors are more marked by vertical integration than others, such as the agri-food sector on the American continent. The fruit and vegetable or dairy industry is traditionally vertically integrated, in contrast to the cereal sector (Dufeu 2011).

boundaries of the firm with its external environment (other firms in the immediate environment, competitors, customers, suppliers) are closed and the firm can produce innovative solutions that will be diffused on the market classically used (Chesbrough 2012).

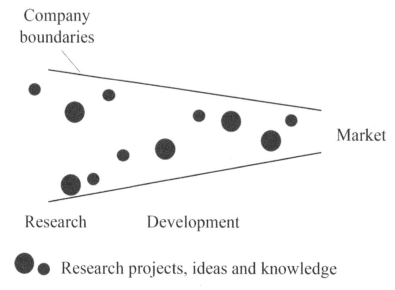

Figure 1.3. *Closed innovation paradigm defined by Chesbrough (based on Chesbrough 2003). For a color version of this figure, see www.iste.co.uk/aouinait/innovation.zip*

Open innovation is a model of collaborative innovation where "the use of purposive inflows and outflows of knowledge to accelerate internal innovation and to expand the markets for external use of innovation" (Chesbrough 2006a). This model relates the flows of and outflows of knowledge in order to improve internal innovation (Chesbrough and Appleyard 2007; Vrande et al. 2009). One of the driving forces of this innovation is cooperation through external partners to complement the internal resources of firms (Gallaud and Nayaradou 2012). Collaboration and the exploitation of new sources of ideas are at the heart of this open model.

Figure 1.4 shows the various flows of information, knowledge and of exchange of information, knowledge and other inputs that exist with the outside world thanks to a greater or lesser porosity of boundaries.

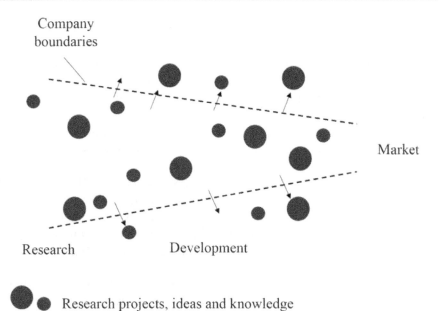

Figure 1.4. *Open innovation paradigm defined by Chesbrough (based on Chesbrough 2003). For a color version of this figure, see www.iste.co.uk/aouinait/innovation.zip*

Innovation can benefit from the feedback of the innovation's end-users, their experiences and suggestions. This aspect is dealt with in Chapter 3 of this book. In addition, von Hippel's (1988) "functional fixedness" favors incremental innovation as opposed to radical innovation. This notion refers to the fact that it may be difficult to envisage the use of a product other than that for which it was initially designed. It is therefore necessary to include external partners in order to get a comprehensive view and a fresh perspective on the innovation concerned (Enkel et al. 2005).

Through the openness of the innovation process, new opportunities can emerge for the actors involved. The results of the whole process are distributed through the usual channels used by the company. However, new markets may be accessible, due to the increased visibility of the firms or the contacts and partnerships established. This new arrangement characteristic of open innovation brings about new possibilities to create collaborations with actors with different profiles (e.g. competitors such as companies positioned on the same market, suppliers, universities or research laboratories) (Aouinaït 2021).

Research and Development (R&D) services, which companies have included in their innovation strategy, is a complementary service to the open innovation activities. This internal R&D is not a substitute for an open innovation strategy. However, the literature also discusses the advantageous effects that the substitution of R&D by an open innovation process could have on the companies practicing it. In the case where firms can rationalize their R&D activities and engage in external interactions in order to compensate for a more limited internal R&D orientation (Chesbrough 2003).

Many authors have discussed the openness of innovation (Dahlander and Gann 2010). There are different types of openness referred to in the literature. As research on the topic of open and collaborative innovation has progressed, the binary classification model of open innovation has eroded. Openness versus closure is no longer appropriate (Chesbrough 2003).

The emergence of OI is to be seen in parallel with "open source", initially used for the software supply sector. Open source software is free for all to use. This type of software has been developed by communities of users for users. Thus, many projects and communities have been developed on a global scale since their creation in the 1960s–1970s (von Hippel 2001, 2003). Intellectual property rights (IPRs) are an important stake in the strategies of companies that want to gain a competitive edge in the results of innovation processes. One of the main purposes of IPRs is to protect the innovator from the potential fraudulent use of the innovation. The other purpose is to confer an exclusive but temporary right on the innovation concerned (on average, 20 years in France and 17 years in the United States, for example). Finally, IPRs confer income to the holders of these rights. The dissemination and commercialization of information relating to the protected product or service is the innovator's responsibility. The best known and most widely researched IPR is the patent. Other examples include licenses, copyrights and trademarks (Liotard 1999).

To return to the emergence of the open innovation model, it is necessary to understand the decline of the closed innovation model. According to Chesbrough, several factors have contributed to this, such as the mobility and availability of skilled workers. In addition, the knowledge and material and immaterial inputs useful for innovation are redistributed differently among actors. Finally, the new capacities of suppliers to undertake R&D precipitate the paradigm of closed innovation (Isckia 2011).

To conclude on the definition of open and collaborative innovation, it is useful to specify that this paradigm has been sought, investigated and used indisputably in many different disciplines. Henri Chesbrough (2012) attests to 483 million links when searching for "Open innovation" in the Google search engine. Since the last decade, this number has certainly increased. According to the author, one of the key factors in innovation is the business model. He explores these characteristics in his book "Open Business Models: How To Thrive In The New Innovation Landscape" in 2006. As an example, the service sector benefits from bringing together a wide range of players with different profiles to create positive spin-offs for many companies. These actors complement each other and bring their own knowledge and expertise to create value and generate interesting economic spin-offs for the companies concerned. An example of a failure due to an unsuitable entrepreneurial business model is that of the Xerox firm and its Palo Alto Research Center.

Chesbrough highlights the opportunities for companies to optimize their research and development process by drawing on multiple sources of innovation in the environment. The platforms in this OI can be used according to the degree of openness desired (Boudreau and Hagiu 2009; Boudreau 2010; Isckia 2011).

1.2.2. Serendipity

Serendipity is a factor that has been studied by various disciplines, from the social sciences, to the so-called hard sciences, to the arts and humanities. In the humanities and social sciences, serendipity plays an important role in revealing connections that would be hidden between different parts. "The hidden analogies are revealed through serendipitous links between information sources" (Foster and Ford 2003).

One example of a serendipitous discovery was the cookie, or chocolate chip cookie. Ruth Wakefield and her husband Kenneth created it by accident, when Ruth Wakefield added chocolate and cut it into pieces because she had run out of baking chocolate, thinking it would melt and mix with the rest of the ingredients. But the pieces remained independent of each other in the form of chips and the cookie was created.

> **Serendipity or chance: the origin of its emergence**
>
> Serendipity or chance was defined in 1754 by Horace Wapel in a letter to Sir Horace Mann on January 28, 1754 (Remer 1965, p. 20):
>
> This discovery is almost of a kind which I call serendipity, a very expressive word.... I once read a silly fairy tale called "The three Princes of Serendip"... as their highnesses travelled, they were always making discoveries, by accidents and sagacity, of things which they were not in quest of... (Foster and Ford 2003).
>
> Serendipity is a "faculty or phenomenon of finding valuable or pleasant things not sought after". In this tale, three princes of Serendip travel to distant lands in an attempt to find a secret poem line that would pacify a band of menacing dragons. However, on their journey, the princes have such fantastic and unexpected encounters that they almost forget the original reason for their journey (Kakko and Inkinen 2009).

Box 1.1. *Definition of serendipity*

Moreover, serendipity also has a role in scientific research. One of the best-known examples to describe what serendipity is includes the discovery of penicillin by Alexander Fleming (André et al. 2009). Alexander Fleming wanted to disinfect bacterial cultures before going on vacation but was indeed unsuccessful. After his return, Penicillium molds had contaminated the cultures until they killed the bacteria present. Other more recent examples are cited by Thagard and Croft (1999), with the probable role of bacteria in peptic ulcers, discoveries in the field of paleontology with the discovery of the extinction of dinosaurs following a collision with an asteroid, as well as the telecommunications sector with the development of the Java programming language by James Gosling and Patrick Naughton. This program was initially established for a specific application such as interactive television and game consoles. The program created then called Oak could then be suitable for many Internet browsers. The language uses a syntax very much used in computing and has a universal side. Its success is then required (Foster and Ford 2003).

There are many other examples of chance discoveries such as Archimedes' principle, Columbus' discovery of America, Isaac Newton's law of gravitation, smallpox vaccination, synthetic rubber, insulin, X-rays, nylon, polyethylene, Teflon, aspirin, the post-it note, the structure of DNA, Viagra and short message service (SMS) technology.

Serendipity is an essential element of creativity, which can be more or less important depending on the sector, the theme, as well as on the research method. Indeed, it can be limited in the case of electronic information research, for example, because of filters and other tools initially intended to facilitate any research.

Serendipity has been treated in many different fields. A link with creativity is moreover existing in the literature. Serendipity could have a more or less important weight in creativity, as in medical discoveries, technological innovations in companies or in moments of history. The serendipity of an event or an object could call for reflection and new ideas in order to develop moments of creativity (André et al. 2009). According to the authors, serendipity is a "discovery of unexpected information (relevant or not) in the course of an information activity" as well as "making an intellectual leap of understanding with that information to arrive at an insight". This is confirmed by Foster and Ford who identified this serendipity in interdisciplinary researchers. When a problem arises, avenues of solution are then sought in various fields and specialties, depending on the expertise of the researchers and the orientation in one direction as well as the location of the information sought, serendipity may be more likely to occur. It is the unexpected discovery of information in an unexpected environment, also with an unexpected value (André et al. 2009).

Serendipity then has its place and role to play in the generation of cross-sectional innovations. This serendipity can be managed by well-framed processes and tools. Kakko uses the term "serendipity management" in conjunction with innovative environments. The principle is to bring in talent from various fields in order to find unexpected, new and informal skills based on the management of trust. Finally, the role of chance management is to decrease the number of low value-added innovations and thus increase the number of so-called radical innovations.

1.2.3. *Creativity*

Innovation management has externalities on creativity which may or may not be favored depending on the working conditions and the environment

(Amabile et al. 2004). Creativity is a source of innovation for Robinson and Stern. In 2000, they defined the "creative company", emphasizing creativity as an indispensable key to business. Innovation can be unexpected, as described above with serendipity. Companies can thus create conditions in which this unexpectedness can occur, for example, by allowing employees to perform unfamiliar or everyday activities.

To be creative, that is, to be intrinsically motivated to work, to be absorbed in our work and to have pleasure in working, we must be in a state of "flow". The "flow theory" developed by the Hungarian psychologist Mihaly Csikszentmihalyi shows that being professionally challenged while having skills, know-how and knowledge allows us to reach a state of "flow". This state promotes the development of individual's creativity (Csikszentmihalyi and LeFevre 1989). Individuals who are motivated can thus be creative more easily. In a study, Amabile et al. (2004) identify the leader's behavior as an essential factor in the perception of the leader's support by employees. This support, combined with the criteria of competence, motivation and challenges, positively influences creativity.

This social aspect of innovation is substantial for innovation. Through employee support, progress management, a participatory approach through consultation of employees in making important business decisions and emotional support and recognition, a healthy and motivating work environment can be created, fostering creativity, and by extension innovation.

1.2.4. The absorption capacity of firms

Cohen and Levinthal (1990) observed that there are numerous objectives of Research and Development (R&D), such as the development of novelties at the internal level of companies and the creation of an absorption capacity in order to follow and evaluate developments outside the company's boundaries. They examined companies that invest heavily in R&D for their commercialization activities. These companies appear to be more likely to benefit from "spill-overs" (Cohen and Levinthal 1990; Dahlander and Gann 2010). What the authors call "absorptive capacity" is the firm's capacity to innovate, which is dependent on the company's level of prior knowledge, such as previous collaboration experiences. This capacity refers to the possibility of using the technology, depending on the firm's internal technical competence (Arora and Gambardella 2010).

The exploitation of technical knowledge can be done by generating knowledge, specific to the company, as well as by the capacity to recognize and integrate the external knowledge of the actors (Cohen and Levinthal 1990). According to Tripsas (1997), the presence or absence of key complementary assets strengthens the ability of incumbent firms to survive technological change (Teece 1986). Firms with "external integration capacity" are better prepared to respond to shocks such as the arrival of a radical innovation. This integration capacity includes investments in R&D which notably improve the company's absorption capacity to access knowledge from the external environment. In addition, investments in knowledge transfer in different departments of the firm such as R&D, manufacturing and marketing are crucial (Chesbrough 2008).

A nuance to this definition of absorption capacity is provided by Arora and Gambardella (1994). They distinguish between the "capacity to use" and the "capacity to evaluate". The first corresponds to the ability of a firm to extract the value that a technology possesses. This means that the firm must have in-house technical skills and downstream assets such as marketing. The second is the firm's ability to judge the value of the technology. This includes scientific and technical capabilities to recognize and identify technology value. This has an influence on the demands for external technologies. Indeed, with a high capacity of use, the firm will tend to have more frequent recourse to external technologies and will be able to grant licenses for their use. In the case of high evaluation capacity, the firm will use fewer external technologies, because of the identification of the potential value of these technologies.

R&D is necessary to make the transition from the traditional sector to the knowledge sector (Foray 2009). It generates information and knowledge that can increase the absorptive capacity of firms. The assimilation and exploitation of the generated data is easier to achieve (Cohen and Levinthal 1989). The R&D steps can be conducted internally in the firm, outsourced or in collaboration. If firms select outsourcing for R&D activities, the main motivations include access to new technologies for the firm, reducing the time between the start of research projects and the end with the delivery of the innovation, and filling skill gaps. For some tasks, the skills and know-how may be lacking in the company. Thus, it becomes necessary to resort to external agents to perform them, and remain competitive. In addition, the knowledge accumulated is crucial for innovation, whether technical, technological, organizational or social, and used at different stages of the innovation chain (Kline and Rosenberg 1986).

There is an endogenous absorptive capacity that depends, among other things, on the extent of the technological opportunity as measured by a survey conducted by Klevorick et al. (1995). Cohen and Levinthal (1989) and Adams (2006) consider that this latent technological opportunity is not equal for all firms, mainly because the evaluation, assimilation and exploitation of relevant knowledge is a fundamental capability to develop (Cohen and Wesley 2010).

The theme of territory as a place conducive to innovation has been widely discussed in the literature. Chapter 2 returns more precisely to this subject. Here, in this section, it is appropriate to see the territory as an environment where local knowledge and information are disseminated between economic agents, companies and any individual interested in the exploitation of these data. The regions and cities have become examples and subjects of study to investigate the propagation of information or knowledge between inventors and exploiters of the said researched. The information available to decision-makers varies from place to place and, in most cases, can be very costly to transfer. This "viscosity" of information can have several causes (von Hippel 1994). This viscosity can arise from the characteristics of the information itself, such as the way it is encoded (Nelson 1993). In addition, the stickiness of the information may be due to the holders or requesters of the information. A firm's lack of "absorptive capacity" could limit its ability to acquire information due to the absence of certain tools or additional information. Finally, the availability of specialized organizational structures such as transfer groups (Katz and Allen 1988) can significantly affect the costs of information transfer between and within organizations (Feldman and Kogler 2010).

1.2.5. *The various degrees of innovation*

Innovations, in addition to being classified by mode (product, organization, service, social, marketing, for example), can also be classified by the degree of novelty. Traditionally, four modes are distinguished:

i) incremental innovation, ii) radical innovation, iii) modular innovation and iv) architectural innovation.

Incremental innovation consists of a step-by-step improvement of the product or process to improve certain characteristics such as quality, productivity or diversity. This mode of innovation is very common and is very developed in companies. They have an importance in the gain of productivity, the effects of mode or the access to new markets. Moreover, the acceptance of this mode of innovation by end-users is generally important because there is no significant or sudden change at the time of adoption (e.g. a new goat's cheese, a new color of a piece of furniture, a smaller packaging for a household product) (Patris et al. 2001). Moreover, incremental innovation can help build skills and requires new knowledge (Kaine et al. 2008).

Radical innovation causes a real disruption by modifying the conditions of use, by provoking radical technological and organizational changes within the firm, by transforming production and marketing methods or by introducing a modification of the required skills, for example. This generates a high degree of change in the organization. The structural organization of the firm can be affected by this mode of innovation. Acceptance is generally lower, due to the requirement for reorganization within the firm (Patris et al. 2001; Kaine et al. 2008).

Radical innovation and incremental innovation are the types that are most often opposed in the literature and represent the innovations that are most often retained in firms' projects. Their opposition concerns the results and consequences generated, as well as the resources required for their implementation (Belz 2010). Moreover, the choice of innovation mode can be strategic depending on the final goal of the company. Companies that want to have a significant impact on consumer behavior may resort to radical innovations (Zainal Abidin 2011). However, two other modes of innovation have been described by Afuah and Bahram (1995): modular and architectural innovation.

Modular innovation does not change the appearance of the product but one of its components. An example from the agricultural sector is the HOLL (High Oleic Low Linolenic) rapeseed (meaning high oleic acid, low linolenic acid). This rapeseed variety has the same structure and architecture as a conventional rapeseed. Some components of this variety have been modified to obtain a certain oil quality. This oil aims to resist cooking at high temperatures, which standard rapeseed oil cannot, causing the formation of trans fatty acids, which are harmful to health (Aouinaït et al. 2014). This mode of innovation can strengthen skills in companies with the acquisition of new knowledge and know-how, for example. Modular innovation can also have impacts on the roles and responsibilities of personnel in firms (Kaine et al. 2008).

Finally, architectural innovation proposes a new architecture of a product or service while maintaining the same use. The basic scientific and technical concepts are not modified but can be arranged differently, thus changing the overall architecture of the product (Belz 2010). An example of this architectural innovation is the miniaturization of a piece of equipment to make it transportable, such as the compact disk as a replacement for the HiFi system and the cell phone as a replacement for the corded telephone. This mode of innovation is characterized by the potential obstacle to the adaptation of a company. This innovation is situated between radical and incremental innovation. It enables keeping skills as well as acquiring and destroying others, which can represent a barrier to its adoption.

As presented in Figure 1.5, the innovation hypercube (Afuah and Bahram 1995) allows us to differentiate the four innovations along two axes: the basic concepts and the links between the concepts and the components.

For radical innovation, the basic concepts and the links to the components are changed. In architectural innovation, the concepts are strengthened and the links are changed. Incremental innovation has also strengthened concepts but unchanged links. Modular innovation keeps the same links between concepts and components, but these concepts change. In addition to these two axes (concepts and links between concepts and components), an additional axis concerns the added value for the chain. All the actors of the value chain are impacted by the adoption and implementation of an innovation. The impacts can concern the capabilities, their knowledge and the positive externalities of the network among others (Afuah and Bahram 1995).

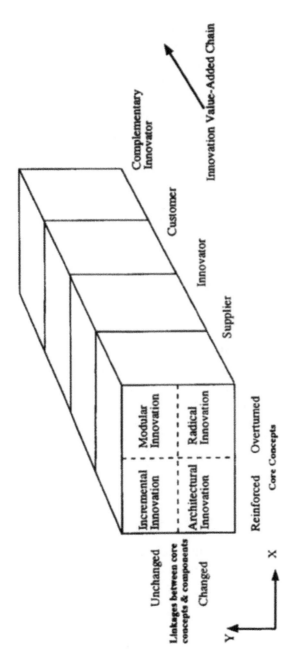

Figure 1.5. *Hypercube of innovation (Afuah and Bahram 1995)*

Finally, the perception of an innovation can be different from one user to another and it is the user's profile that will have an influence on the mode of innovation or its perception. Their position in the value chain can also have a role in this perception. In the case of the new variety of colza HOLL oil, the producer can have little repercussion on their daily work (the cultural practices can be similar or close to that with a variety of standard colza, the machines and useful knowledge for its cultivation are unchanged, for example). However, the industrialist who adopts this new variety and integrates it into their production lines may perceive this innovation in a more radical way, due to the properties of the new rapeseed (new production method, new packaging, etc.).

Finally, innovations can concern a part of a system or an entire system. In the agricultural sector, the introduction of a new technology, such as a tillage tool, represents an innovation of an incremental nature. The changes brought about by this new tool are not drastic for the operation of the farm. When the innovation concerns the entire production system (e.g. the transition to organic farming or the introduction of mechanization), it is more radical in nature, as it requires rethinking the entire functioning of the system already in place (Faure et al. 2018).

Afuah and Bahram (1995) used the example of the electric car. For the manufacturers of combustion engine cars, the electric car represents a radical innovation, as well as for the suppliers of the parts and materials necessary for its manufacture. For the authors, this product is, on the contrary, an incremental innovation for customers. These examples show that the position of actors in the value chain (suppliers, customers, service providers, etc.) is very important in categorizing the degree of novelty of an innovation, which impacts its diffusion and final adoption by users.

1.2.6. *Exploration versus exploitation in innovation processes*

In the innovation development process, companies can use two strategies that are well studied in the literature: exploration and exploitation. The acquisition of new knowledge is one of the main goals (Sarasvathy 2001; Bekkers and Bodas Freitas 2011).

Exploration is defined by March (1991) as "a learning mechanism whose purpose is to experiment with new alternatives". Exploration includes activities of research, discovery, innovation and thus risk-taking. This definition also includes exploration activities of new knowledge, exploration of new resources and experimentation with customer needs. Exploration is concerned with redefining what has been learned by mobilizing innovative ideas and remaining open to potentially implementable innovations. On the other hand, exploitation is interested in extending the capabilities and skills already present in the company. According to Auh and Menguc (2005), "it is possible to secure a comfortable position in the market by committing sufficient or massive resources to ensure the viability of the firm in the face of its competitors".

In general, companies choose a balance between these two strategies. An exploration strategy that is more important than an exploitation strategy could be costly because of the time scale for the realization of the exploration results. The higher uncertainty and the implementation of the solutions of this strategy possible in the medium and long-terms are therefore economically burdensome for the company. However, too much emphasis on exploitation can lead to a lack of visibility for the future due to the concentration on current opportunities and themes, leaving interesting investments for the company untapped. Thus, these two types of organizational learning strategies provide useful resources and organizational capabilities for firms seeking to maintain or develop a competitive advantage while adapting to a constantly changing environment (Auh and Menguc 2005).

The degree of openness of the OI model can be linked to the skills involved. Indeed, an OECD report (2008) states that open innovation projects to diversify into non-strategic technologies and markets, while projects using the core competencies, are developed within the boundaries of the companies. Openness is used to diversify, and rather use the exploration model (new opportunities, new markets, new customers) (Isckia and Lescop 2011).

Finally, Fagiolo and Dosi (2003) hypothesize that exploration, imitation and production activities may be costless and mutually exclusive. The mining industry was studied by both authors. They have shown that miners stop producing while carrying out imitation and exploration. This opportunity cost is borne by the agents to use resources initially dedicated to production but then diverted to R&D and imitation activities. A strategy of equilibrium between exploration of new technologies and exploitation of the firm's bases comes into play, for the use of the firm's resources.

1.3. The creation of innovation and associated partnerships

1.3.1. *Dynamics of collaborative innovation production*

Previous experiences are taken into account and are useful in the collaborations. Through the projects that companies carry out and develop, they accumulate knowledge. This knowledge is then useful for future projects, although not necessarily sufficient. Nieto and Santamaria (2007) apply this principle of reuse of knowledge accumulation through experiences in the field of alliances and collaborations. Through collaborations, companies learn to manage and work with partners with different profiles. The impacts on the performance of alliances are generally positive. One of the reasons for this is the development of routines, policies and procedures based on the experiences of the companies involved in these alliances.

Vertical collaboration, between suppliers and customers, leads to the acquisition of knowledge about markets, marketing opportunities and new technologies, for example (Whitley 2002). Faure et al. (2018) defined several stages of producing the results of research conducted in partnership between several actors. The creation of innovations can be divided into several stages depending on the progress in time. Stage 1 consists of the exploration and engagement of stakeholders. The problem(s) and solutions can be defined during this stage. Recruiting stakeholders and establishing a pattern of trust is also part of this first stage. The next stage focuses on the co-design of innovations with the development of actionable knowledge. The asymmetry and differences between the actors are reduced over time, the capacities of each are strengthened and the innovation process is set in motion. This is made possible by the use of a common language between the actors (same language, same epistemology and common references). The third and final stage is to assess the innovation process, to continue with the same partners on other projects or to select others.

In addition, companies may require coaching in their innovation process. Faure et al. (2018) have described the possible activities that actors can undertake to innovate, depending on their ability to innovate and the complexity of the innovation situation or changes required. The stronger the capacity of the actors to innovate, and the lower complexity of the innovation situation, the support ranges from the provision of tools to empower adaptation, the provision of references and the design of tools for informed decision-making. Indeed, if the capacity of actors to innovate is strong, their capacity to commit and learn can also be strong. When this capacity to innovate is weak, as well as the complexity of the innovation situation (little uncertainty about complexity), an incentive to apply technical or organizational know-how is required. In the case where this complexity is high, leading to uncertainties regarding the implementation of the innovation (e.g. moving from a conventional agricultural production mode to a production mode based on the principles of agroecology), and the capacity of the actors to innovate is low, the support can take the form of knowledge sharing and awareness raising. Finally, when the complexity of the innovation situation is high, as well as the capacity to innovate, the provision of tools to empower exploration, the application of methods for experimentation or monitoring of changes can be implemented.

The failures in these types of coaching processes are significant according to Faure et al. (2018). Many actors are involved in these processes. A unity and a common behavior of commitment, organization, reflection and exchanges cannot be guaranteed. The interests of each are to be taken into account to be weighed against each other to ensure that the collaboration is beneficial to all (Vall et al. 2016).

1.3.2. *Forms of partnerships and degree of openness of innovation*

The degree of openness of the innovation model has been much studied in the literature. The degree of openness of open innovation can be seen as restricted when the proprietary logic remains in place. In this case, a company can transfer its innovations via licenses (inside-out principle) or acquire them (outside-in principle) in exchange for financial compensation (Aouinaït 2021).

One of the purposes and benefits of using collaboration is to acquire resources and skills not produced internally, knowing that the risks of doing so in collaboration are not too significant. The profile of the partners could impact the degree of openness of the OI model. Companies would be more likely to collaborate with known and regular partners such as suppliers or customers, and more reluctant to engage with actors that are institutionally and cognitively distant (such as universities, research centers). The degree of openness is important to assess ex-ante in the development of certain types of innovation. Indeed, radical innovations can be developed through collaboration, especially for the initial research stages and then the production and marketing stages. The assets, resources and skills of several partners may be necessary for this type of disruptive innovation (Sachwald 2008). Moreover, disruptive innovations are also subject to collaborations with different types of partnerships. Indeed, the actors involved must remain so on a long-term scale due to the sudden changes brought about by these innovations. The knowledge required is also generally more numerous and more specific (Agogué et al. 2013).

The different modes of openness have been described by Dahlander and Gann (2010) in a table along two axes: inbound–outbound and pecuniary–non-pecuniary (see Table 1.2).

The authors present via a literature review the types of innovation openness in terms of the logic of the exchange of advantages and disadvantages. The authors found that in the 150 articles searched, the majority investigate one or two forms of innovation openness. Few studies examine the combination of several types of openness. However, as emphasized by Chesbrough and Rosenbloom (2002), a balance between these different types of openness should be sought and adopted for companies, depending on the company (its size, its economic model, its commercial objectives, for example).

The advantages and disadvantages of opening or closing the innovation process presented in Table 1.2 include access to resources, commercialization opportunities, partner support for new ideas, as well as issues related to IPRs, network density that can be a barrier to maintaining connections, or the use of sensitive knowledge by competitors.

	Outgoing innovation *Revelation*	Outgoing innovation *Sale*	Incoming innovation *Sources of supply*	Incoming innovation *Acquisition*
Logic of the exchange	Indirect non-monetary benefits	Money involved in the exchange	Indirect non-monetary benefits	Money involved in the exchange
Benefits leading to openness	Resources and support for disclosure to the external environment (Henkel 2006) Obtaining legitimacy from the external environment (Nuvolari 2004) Encouraging incremental action and cumulative innovation (Scotchmer 1991; Murray and O'Mahony 2007)	Market products that are on the shelf External partners may be better equipped to commercialize inventions for the mutual benefit of both organizations (Chesbrough and Rosenbloom 2002)	Access to a wide range of ideas and knowledge (Laursen and Salter 2006) Discovering radical new solutions to problems (Lakhani et al. 2006)	Access to resources and knowledge of partners (Powell et al. 1996) Leveraging complementarities with partners (Dyer and Singh 1998)
Disadvantages leading to closure	Difficult to understand the benefits Internal resources may leak to competitors (Laursen and Salter 2006)	Over-commitment to owning products and technologies makes licensing difficult (Lichtenthaler and Ernst 2007)	Many sources create an attention problem (Laursen and Salter 2006) Difficult to choose and combine between too many alternatives (Sapienza et al. 2004)	Difficulty in maintaining a large number of links with different partners (Ahuja 2000) Risk of outsourcing the critical dimension of the company

Table 1.2. *Four different types of innovation openness (adapted from Dahlander and Gann (2010))*

In the type of outbound innovation, with indirect non-pecuniary benefits, Henkel (2006) promotes the disclosure of information and innovations to the external environment. This strategy is also examined by Baldwin and von Hippel (2011) who write that innovators freely revealing their innovations reap benefits and also avoid underlying costs. The main reasons for this strategy include disincentives to the use of intellectual property rights. Depending on the financial resources of the inventor or the company, the possibilities of enforcing the sensitive and leaky trade secret (Mansfield 1985), and administrative impediments, free disclosure allows for the avoidance of IPRs. Moreover, the utility of patents for products from sectors other than pharmaceutical, medical or chemical is low (Mansfield 1985; Arundel 2001; Dosi et al. 2006). To avoid "protection myopia", companies combine several means of protecting their innovations (Laursen and Salter 2006).

The principle of open innovation, which deals with the use of external ideas, knowledge and technologies, reminds us that openness also works in the other direction. Chesbrough (2006a) argues that unused ideas can be used by other firms. Thus, this outward innovation makes it possible to exploit potential patents or innovations that are dormant in firms. The notable advantages are the increase in the visibility of innovations that then find a market, new or not, through intermediaries and partners interested via the collaborations created in OI. However, in this framework, relational contracts such as R&D agreements, joint ventures or licenses are necessary for a firm's R&D results to be usable externally. On the other hand, outward innovation does not necessarily require contracts for the exploitation of the resources sought in the innovation process. Procter & Gamble, with its "Connect and Develop" program, is looking for solutions to print images on Pringles chips, data and information on potential innovations in order to develop them internally and commercialize them on markets that the company traditionally uses.

In addition to the degree of openness of the innovation and the associated partnerships, the collaborations are different depending on the stage of the innovation process. In Figure 1.6, the modes of innovation are presented in a matrix with two axes: the technology and the company's markets. This matrix demonstrates the multiplicity and possibilities of the types of partnerships possible according to market positioning (unfamiliar, non-strategic or strategic market positioning) and technology (unfamiliar, non-strategic or strategic). In a strategic market and with a technology that is also strategic, in-house acquisition and development are recommended. In order to be able to position ourselves competitively using specific resources, restricting the openness of the innovation process allows for maintaining a comparative advantage. On the contrary, for an unfamiliar technology and an innovation dedicated to an unfamiliar market, external sale or spin-off is indicated. The use of partnerships such as joint ventures, equity investments or joint development is more appropriate in the case of unfamiliar or non-strategic markets. The use of know-how and knowledge that is missing internally becomes crucial for the development of innovation.

State of the market	Unfamiliar	Joint venture	Venture capital	External sale or distribution
	Non-strategic	Acquisition	Transfer of licenses	Venture capital
	Strategic	Acquisition	Transfer of licenses, internal development, acquisition	Joint venture, contractual R&D
		Strategic	Non-strategic	Unfamiliar
		Technological axis		

Figure 1.6. *Forms of partnerships for innovation development by market and technology (based on Khedher (2010))*

According to Sakkab (2002), the types of partnerships vary depending on the stage of the innovation process (see Figure 1.7). Internally, communities of practice, corporate innovation funds, technology-oriented entrepreneurs or internal "smart learning" relationships are preferred. Additionally, externally, university research grant programs, partnerships with technology providers or contracts with laboratories at the national level can be developed. Venture capital and licensing, which companies prefer because they have identified IPRs such as patents that may be relevant to their needs, are also one strategy.

Finally, the number of partners varies throughout the innovation cycle. Indeed, depending on the type of partnership established, the number of actors involved is greater or lesser and the number of links to establish varies. In the R&D stage, the creation of the ideas that will lead to future innovation may involve several different actors. Building a network is all the more important during this stage to optimize the emergence of new ideas and to identify the useful knowledge to be mobilized.

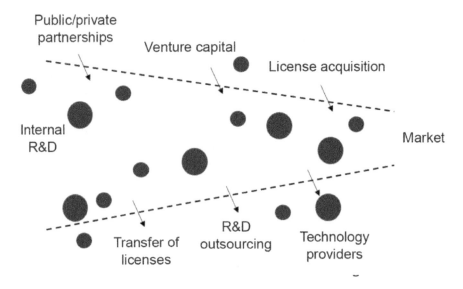

Figure 1.7. *Open innovation instruments used by Procter and Gamble (Steiner 2014; based on Sakkab (2002)). For a color version of this figure, see www.iste.co.uk/aouinait/innovation.zip*

1.3.3. *Collaborative models: from the triple helix to mode 2, via the NSI*

In this type of model, knowledge is transferred via a structured network in which actors with varied profiles are brought together (such as universities, industries, government). New approaches to the analysis of innovation processes appeared at the end of the 1980s. Mode 2, the national innovation system (NIS) or the triple helix (TH) are well-known examples.

Mode 2 is presented by Gibbons et al. (1994). This model promotes the production of new knowledge that is context-dependent, interactive and transdisciplinary. The linear model of scientific production transferred to practice is no longer appropriate. The interaction between actors and partners in collaborative projects is one of the driving forces of these new models. In mode 2, knowledge is produced in a specific technological context, where the academic and industrial environments are combined in interdisciplinary teams to produce directly applicable innovations, such as applied research projects. The triple helix differs from mode 2 in terms of the role of partners. The university plays a leading role in relation to companies, which is the opposite of the national innovation system model. However, a dynamic and balance between the implications and importance of the actors must be found. In the "triple helix III" model, there is evidence of cooperation and balance between the three types of infrastructures that generate knowledge. Hybrid organizations can then emerge in this collaborative environment (Etzkowitz and Leydesdorff 2000; Leydesdorff and Etzkowtiz 2000).

The state can play a financial support role by granting direct or indirect aid or by changing the rules of management of operations. The nonlinear and recursive nature of these innovative models allows for the optimization of contacts between stakeholders while giving them a certain independence.

In the national innovation system, the concomitant use of resources and assets of companies, governments and universities for the production of knowledge, its dissemination and use is anchored in a broad territory. The orientation of technological learning is defined, as well as the political framework in which the innovation process is impacted. This concept emerged with Christopher Freeman (1987) and Bengt-Åke Lundvall in the late 1980s. Freeman defines the NIS as "a network of institutions in public and private sectors, whose activities and interactions initiate, import, modify and diffuse new technologies". Lundvall's definition comes close: "the elements and relationships which interact in the production, diffusion and use of new, and economically useful knowledge and are either located within or rooted inside the borders of a nation state". Nelson (1993), Patel and Pavitt (1994) and Metcalfe (1995) have also developed their own definitions.

The territorial disparities that can exist within nations can hinder the efficiency of the national innovation system. Therefore, a regional approach has been developed with the main theme of the relationship between industry, innovation and technology in well-defined territories. The geographical factor plays an important role for collaborations, enabling frequent exchanges of a different nature than exchanges using ICT (Önday 2016). This aspect is described later in the book in Part 2, with the concept of clusters.

This first chapter has presented innovation, through its official definition in the Oslo Manual, its different characteristics (degree of novelty, type). Moreover, the difficulty of understanding this notion of innovation due to its multidimensional aspect is also part of its characteristics. Serendipity and creativity are also notions often associated with innovation. A combination of serendipity and creativity has proven to be successful in the development of innovations. Moreover, many actors are often involved in the innovation process, from the upstream stages with its emergence and formalization, to the downstream stages with its commercialization and implementation. This mosaic of different profiles (different sectors, different disciplines) generates a multiplicity of points of view and therefore of exchanges to be ensured in order to collaborate in the most efficient way possible. Several partnerships are possible throughout the innovation process, to be selected according to the companies' existing strategies and resources.

2

History of the Evolution of Collaboration Between Actors, and Creation of Innovation Networks

2.1. Genesis of collaboration and its evolution through different innovation models

2.1.1. *History of collaboration*

Collaboration as a work tool or as a way of organizing actors in a given environment is not new. Through an analysis of the socio-economic foundations of collaboration within the framework of organization theory, Barondeau (2015) suggests a synthesis of the evolution of collaboration in companies. From the end of the 19th century, collaboration was established in a divided manner by targeting simplified tasks that collaborators could take on. Different activities are coordinated with each other, according to the Taylorism of the 1880s. In this model, production techniques are standardized to optimize the pace of work and achieve the best possible output, through the one best way or the best way to produce (Sandulache 2019). In the 1930s, Chester Irving Barnard proposed the concept of cooperation based on collective efficiency. He defined the formal organization as "a system of conscious coordination of activities and forces of two or more persons". In this definition, individuals are considered as full-fledged agents who have their own interests, on the one hand, and who voluntarily cooperate, on the other hand (Bourguignon and Novicevic 2012). Furthermore, Barnard notes the essential function of cooperation in hierarchical systems by noting that "the weakest link in the chain of cooperative effort is the willingness to cooperate". This underscores the power and importance of voluntariness in collaborative relationships. Actors who are reluctant to engage in collaboration may distort the links that are created and this would likely result in a failure of the collaboration.

It was in the middle of the 20th century that Likert (1961) introduced a theory of human management with a central role, hierarchy and vertical collaboration. The employees intervene in a voluntary way while submitting to the constraints and requirements of an organization managed by leaders or managers, who impose rules and tasks to them. The principle of integrated relations developed by Rensis Likert focuses on the relations between workers and their hierarchy, taking into account each individual's personal values. The interactions between the hierarchy and the members of the organization are based on motivation to perform tasks, recognition of the usefulness of each individual and multilateral dialogues. Moreover, participation in decisions, in the definition of objectives for the company or in the resolution of problems, would have a positive impact on the effectiveness of employees in their work. Likert (1974) deduced four types of management: i) the authoritarian exploitative style, ii) the authoritarian paternalistic style, iii) the consultative style and iv) the participative style. It is in this last style that the human dimension is strongest. Thus, the effectiveness of the collaborators is the strongest and this brings us back to the voluntariness that is crucial for collaboration.

The terms cooperation and collaboration have been studied extensively by Benali et al. (2002), Polenske (2004) and Capdevila (2015), among others. These two terms can be distinguished by their purposes. For Albert-Cromarias and Asselineau (2013), collaboration can be seen as, on the one hand, cooperation, and, on the other hand, coordination. The first refers to the permanent adjustment of agents' actions in a common work environment. The second represents the project management processes for the organization of activities. Polenske (2004), in his analysis of the uneasy triangle of the 3Cs (collaboration, cooperation, competition) takes a position on the hierarchical structure in which cooperation or collaboration takes place. Cooperative relationships take place at the horizontal level between actors who do not work together to design a product, for example. The relationships can be established through formal or informal agreements with the aim of sharing information, knowledge or support in the financial or managerial aspect. Collaboration is seen as a mode of inclusion of actors in the different phases of an innovation process, upstream with design or downstream with marketing. The relationships are mainly internal and in a vertical logic. For Capdevila (2015), collaboration is an activity that enables the achievement of objectives commonly defined by the actors involved in the activity. Cooperation, on the contrary, is an activity to achieve different goals belonging to the agents involved in the activity. Furthermore, three types of collaboration can be differentiated according to their managerial involvement. Collaboration linked to costs, collaboration linked to resources and their complementarity, and collaboration linked to the creation of relationships. The links developed in these collaborations diverge and imply a varied depth. In the collaboration linked to the creation of relationships, the exploration of knowledge and the collective identity is strong.

Through the analysis of the differences between the two terms collaboration and cooperation, it is important to note that these concepts are used together in organizations. Cooperation is seen as the achievement of goals by a group, and defined by that group. Collaboration involves more social ties between individuals, between departments of firms and takes more time to establish.

2.1.2. Evolution of the innovation models used

Innovation developed in a linear way, which passes through the stages of Research and Development before market study and feasibility, then marketing and adoption, was the dominant model during the 20th century until the 1980s. This model is referred to as the "hierarchical linear innovation model" (HLIM) by Micaëlli et al. (2014). This model is intended to be hierarchical, using a transfer of ideas, orders and other assets from higher to lower levels. The transition to a non-linear format of the innovation process has been studied and discussed in numerous works (Kline and Rosenberg 1986; Chouteau and Viévard 2007; Micaëlli et al. 2014). The interactive model is gradually replacing the linearity initially proposed. What the open innovation paradigm promotes translates into interactions between research, the market and existing technologies (Crépon and Duguet 1994). Feedback loops and feedback are fundamental, as well as the circulation and availability of information and knowledge. Kline and Rosenberg's model (1986) entitled "the chain linked model" (CLM) sums it up in every respect.

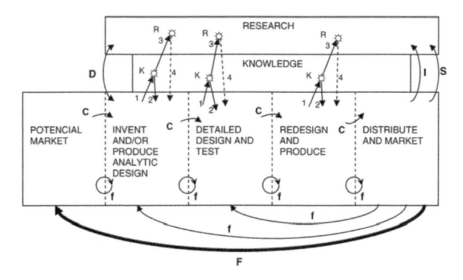

Chain-linked model showing flow paths of information and cooperation.
Symbols on arrows: **C** = central-chain-of-innovation; **f** = feedback loops; **F** = particularly important feedback.

K-R: Links through knowledge to research and return paths. If problems solved at node K, link 3 to R not activated. Return from research (link 4) is problematic - therefore dashed line.

D: Direct link to and from research from problems in invention and design.

I: Support of scientific research by instruments, machines, tools, and procedures of technology.

S: Support of research in sciences underlying product area to gain information directly and by monitoring outside work. The information obtained may apply anywhere along the chain.

Figure 2.1. *The "chain-linked model" (Kline and Rosenberg 1986)*

Figure 2.1 highlights the different types of feedback that take place during the innovation process. The authors break down what was considered the "black box" of innovation. These loops are present at each step of the process, from the distribution of the innovation on the market to the initial potential market through invention, analytical design, detailed design and testing, final design, production and intermediate adjustments. It is important to note that these feedback loops appear to be horizontal, along the phases of innovation. Nevertheless, exchanges with research are constantly taking place, with the aim of providing scientific support in the design and development phases of innovative products and services. Links between research and knowledge are also part of this model proposed by Kline and Rosenberg. The intervention of science can take two forms: i) a lack of knowledge at one stage of the innovation process suggests drawing on available knowledge bases (link K in Figure 2.1); ii) updating knowledge when that which is needed is not available (link R). Moreover, the knowledge used differs according to the stages of the innovation process. The results of fundamental research will be used more upstream in the chain, while technical knowledge and the results of experiments will be used more during the design and development of the innovation (Forest 2014).

However, Micaëlli et al. (2014) suggest considering innovation as a system, an entity in which three elements are assembled to create the full system: innovation actors (with their capabilities and willingness to innovate), interactions with institutional nodes and indicators of innovation capacity. These elements are not constitutive of Kline and Rosenberg's model. Thus, critiques of the CLM emerged in the late 1990s. Firstly, the external environment of the innovation system is not taken into account in the CLM model, such as the institutions that can facilitate the implementation of the innovation (e.g. the legal system, the political system, the educational system). The end product of the innovation process in the CLM is not emphasized. This demonstrates Kline and Rosenberg's emphasis on the dynamics of the system and not on the end product.

Another criticism of the CLM model concerns the interactions between different innovation systems and the way these interactions are structured. The environment and the ecosystem in which these innovations are developed is important, which is not an apparent element in the CLM. The actors who develop and participate in this process also have a significant role to play in terms of their contributions (notably financial, resources and knowledge). Finally, the notion of the limit of innovation does not appear in the Kline and Rosenberg model, which assumes that any innovation can always be produced whatever the conditions in which the system finds itself (research funding and investment vs. profitability). In contrast, the HLMI model is stationary (Godin 2005).

2.1.3. *Top-down and bottom-up approaches*

Collaborative innovation is a process that responds to several dynamics or logics, such as top-down dynamics or bottom-up dynamics. These creative logics have often been contrasted and are much discussed in works from the fields of social sciences, management, business management and economics, such as transition economics (Seyfang et al. 2013; Muller 2021). Each approach is determined by the profile of the actors behind the initiatives.

The main purpose of the top-down approach is to disseminate innovations that have been created by public or private institutions at a high hierarchical level, or further upstream in the sectors and industries concerned. The top-down approach is a "process that is facilitated or directed by actors at the top level of a hierarchical structure and that leads to the progressive involvement of lower levels". The most cited disadvantage of this approach is the lack of confrontation and integration of the points of view of the practice community and the actors working in it. In addition, the dissemination of innovations is intended to be broad and the innovations to be adopted by many actors in different socio-economic systems and sectors. The competitiveness clusters in France are an example of the implementation of a top-down logic. They are political initiatives and benefit from the preponderance of public authorities in their operation (Chabault 2010; Thiaw 2013, 2021).

The bottom-up approach or grass-roots approach involves starting from the practitioners and needs of the actors in the field, and bringing about the innovations potentially created. This approach focuses on initiatives and proposals coming from lower levels in the hierarchy, or even from actors outside the organizations. This logic is based on the co-construction of solutions targeting the needs and shortcomings identified through surveys and experiments in local structures (Younes et al. 2019), with a gradual integration of solutions and proposals into the higher hierarchical levels (Capdevila 2015). The main actors present in this bottom-up logic are industries, universities, research laboratories among others. They can be concentrated geographically and form clusters, industrial districts or business ecosystems. The Silicon Valley cluster in the United States is an example. The alliance between Stanford University in California and entrepreneurs William Hewlett and David Packard is at the origin of this cluster. This implies the implementation of specific strategies, which can result in the decontextualization or even standardization of initial solutions.

Each approach has its advantages and disadvantages. For the first approach, it is interesting to note the general, even universal, nature of the proposed solutions. The homogenization of solutions to certain problems can be beneficial (e.g. ease of "replicability", transferability to different contexts or territories, the possibility of wider dissemination). However, in order to solve difficulties or provide answers at a local level, there will be shortcomings, such as taking into account territorial specificities and the specific needs of their populations The benefit of the bottom-up approach is the particular and individual character of the innovations, responding to local needs, because they are created by the populations that benefit from the innovations. This will facilitate their adoption and their use will be adapted to the production context. Nevertheless, the main disadvantage of this approach lies in the difficulty of appropriating innovations at collective levels that diverge from the context of their emergence (Muller 2021). A translation of the innovations and their characteristics should be necessary for their adoption on a larger scale. Akrich et al. (1988) define this translation according to four stages: problematization, interest by other actors, enrolment (acceptance of the solution and creation of a network of interests) and the mobilization of the new network to implement the innovative solution. In this actor–network theory, the fate of the innovation and its success are conditioned not only by its intrinsic characteristics but depend mostly on its environment and the actors or "actants" and "non-actants" capable of creating a network (Krupicka and Coussi 2017).

A "decontextualization" may prove necessary in order to make the solutions generated by the bottom-up dynamic more general, leading to other barriers such as its distortion from the point of view of innovators. The potential weakness of resources (manpower, financial, material or social) can hinder the diffusion of innovations developed in this framework to a higher level. For this reason, a hybridization of these two approaches is often carried out by the actors. In the case of social innovations, the French mobility sector is an example of this hybridization of the two approaches. On the one hand, a development of state platforms supports private and public initiatives. On the other hand, the population involved develops local solutions (Szostak et al. 2018; Muller 2021). However, the governance and actual implementation of these two logics simultaneously may raise concerns in terms of the satisfaction of the targeted populations and the use of adequate resources. An asymmetry of collaborative roles between stakeholders can occur if the role of each is not well defined beforehand. This is the case in the energy sector, and more specifically in the energy transition of a territory, a study proposed by Krauz (2016). Moreover, succeeding in jointly defining objectives and sharing a common vision of the problems of the projects developed in collaboration is an assurance of seeing the adoption and dissemination of the innovations work (Thiaw 2021).

In recent years, the participatory approach to research has been increasingly used. This approach consists of starting from the needs and expectations of the actors present in the field and coming from the practice and to "bring up" these elements to find solutions adapted to the localized contexts. Participative action research emphasizes the participation of different actors in a project and activities and their actions. The emphasis is on collective experimentation around issues related to the participants' interests (Reason and Bradbury 2008). The advantage of involving stakeholders in collaborative projects as early as possible is to avoid or minimize the gaps that can be created between the expected responses and needs, on the one hand, and the selected solutions, on the other hand (Aouinaït 2019). Traditionally, practitioners, industries, firms or individuals fall into the category of solution seekers. Academics and scientists belong to the second category, the one proposing the solutions. Early involvement of stakeholders in the innovation process can lead to more effective and relevant innovations (Kemmis and McTaggart 2007; Buur and Matthews 2008; Paus and Réviron 2010). A holistic view can be derived from a participatory approach, bringing several important benefits to stakeholders. Consumers, citizens and other stakeholders for whom needs are expressed are actively involved in these definitions, in the research process and in building social relationships with many people they would not normally collaborate with. In addition, this active consideration of clients' needs by the clients themselves makes them feel valued. On the contrary, the researchers involved in these participatory approaches learn from the method used and the concrete demands and expectations of the actors.

Other approaches, complementary, broader or more targeted to participatory action research, exist. One of them, well used all over the world, is citizen science, named by Joël Primack and Franck von Hippel (1971). In this approach, a larger community of citizens is included in the processes of finding solutions, improving knowledge, for example. The participants are scientists or not scientists, forming a network around a common theme and subject, in relation to research in various fields. In addition, the "lead-user" approach focuses on the consumer. It was developed by von Hippel (1988, 2005). The author based this approach on the understanding that companies that base their innovation creation process on market trends or research results do not see guaranteed success in their developments. Some customers or consumers at the forefront can define what the future needs of other consumers will be. These lead-users or users can therefore provide companies with crucial information on consumer behavior, their future expectations and thus guide the direction of R&D projects.

These aspects of collaboration for innovation in conjunction with end-users is developed in Chapter 4 of this book.

In addition, there is no consensus among researchers on traditional technology-push versus market-pull models (Gibbons et al. 1994; Lundvall 2005). National and international research centers, farmers, extension services and non-governmental organizations represent important sources of innovation that collaborate for the generation and transfer of knowledge through formal and informal research activities. These types of research are conducted through the network, through the interactions that are established between the actors anchored in this network.

Indeed, the three major innovation strategies cited by Buisine et al. (2017), which are the technology driver strategy, the market reader strategy and the need seeker strategy, contain the main approaches related to innovation development. The technology driver strategy is reminiscent of the technology-push strategy, which consists of creating products oriented towards a strong technological axis, and which is intensive in Research and Development. The market reader strategy is similar to the market-pull strategy, which consists of creating innovation, generally incremental, with product customization. The need seeker strategy is based on anticipating needs and expectations of users and customers. This strategy, like the technology driver strategy, is conducive to the generation of radical innovations. User-centered approaches are developed in Chapter 3.

2.1.4. Location of actors for collaboration and impact on the type of innovation

The emergence of incremental and radical innovations may be partly related to the level at which collaborations take place. Collaborations established at an international level in global networks are more likely to produce radical innovations, due to the greater opportunities to access new knowledge to escape path dependency. The synthetic or symbolic knowledge is notably path- and context-dependent, influencing future innovations (Asheim et al. 2011). Furthermore, Le Roy et al. (2013) confirm these results via their study on a sample of French firms from the 2004 community innovation survey (CIS) database. The authors studied the potential correlation between product innovation and the competitor's location (in a coopetition strategy) with which the innovation is produced. Thus, the authors find that coopetition strategies significantly increase radical innovation performance, if and only if the competitors are located in America or Europe. A result that may seem surprising is the negative impact of collaboration with a competitor located in the same region on radical innovation. This is why coopetition strategies are more likely to succeed and produce radical innovations when these strategies are not based on geographical proximity, with competitors collaborating located in distant areas.

2.2. Business ecosystems

The concept of the business ecosystem (BE) emerged in the 1990s in the work of James Moore (1993). The author defines the BE as a framework for analyzing changes in the business environment, particularly in terms of cooperation. Its aim is to study innovation as a tool for competitiveness through the structural modification of industries. The latter are organized in networks where the collaboration fluctuates between actors to mobilize skills and knowledge which are complementary in order to offer innovative and marketable products and services. A focal firm is at the heart of this arrangement.

BEs can be defined as frameworks for analyzing open innovation. Innovation and its diffusion as well as the central role of firms in a BE are crucial drivers for innovation dynamics, with value creation being an important goal (Isckia and Lescpo 2011). "Integralogy" as cited by Hafsi and

Martinet (2007) represents an integration and reconciliation between science and broader explanations to undertake industrial strategies. James Moore focuses on the importance of managing of the innovation process while adopting an open and broad view of the business world. The BE takes its name from a comparison to the biological domain, where interactions (or interdependencies) between firms contribute to the innovation process. Properties (or co-evolution) emerge in the environment of firms through collaboration between agents, based on open innovation (Isckia 2011).

Moreover, this specific environment is characterized by relationships of collaboration and also of competition, attesting to a BE dynamic. "Coopetition" is a behavior combining cooperation and competition between several companies operating on the same market, offering similar products and targeting the same customer segments (Le Roy et al. 2013). The advantage of this practice lies in the willingness to cooperate with competitors while not negatively impacting the competition between actors. "Coopetition" promotes the emergence of projects, opportunities and ideas for companies. A firm has a leadership role, being a focal firm that will serve as a point of attraction for potential new partners (Iansiti and Levien 2004). This leader firm can identify the collaboration modalities that are most in line with the different partners. The collective skills generated in a BE allow it to evolve. However, the interdependence of this coopetitive environment can create tensions, especially on the value creation and value capture that the interconnected firms pursue. Explanatory factors for the emergence of coopetitive strategies include the "race to global size" and the "race to technology". The race for technology means businesses exploring the tools needed to develop innovations. While R&D budgets may be increasing in some companies or sectors, it is increasingly common to pool resources to develop research activities. As a result, many companies have to apply coopetition strategies. The information and communication technologies sector is particularly affected by this strategy, both in very large companies such as Microsoft and in smaller companies (Le Roy et al. 2013).

Teece (2007) defined in turn the BE, close to the definition of Moore. Teece adds a notion of dynamic capabilities necessary for companies to adapt to changes and evolutions of the environment (markets, consumer demands, regulations, policies, for example). The integration framework (of knowledge and the environment), construction (of the ecosystem) and reconfiguration (of internal and external competencies, resources) described in the work of Moore and Teece respectively allow us to understand the processes used in the framework of open innovation defined by Henry Chesbrough.

Information and communication technologies (ICT) play an important role here. Platforms are proving to be an indispensable support tool for collaborative work, particularly in a globalized and crisis context (Iansiti and Levien 2004). Platforms can have an impact on the value potentially created by collaborations in BEs. Access to data, information, exchange opportunities and resource sharing are conditioned by the characteristics of the platforms (open or closed) (Schmalensee and Evans 2007). Indeed, with the use of a closed platform, firms will not be able to create as much value as with an open platform. Access to resources and skills is a key issue in this context. For Iansiti and Levien (2004), the BE is more than a collaborative environment to supporting innovation, which is what Moore promotes. For both authors, the platform becomes part of the collaborative space and allows actors to reach resources for innovation. Thus, the platforms can exploit indirect network externalities helping to develop the innovation initiated by the focal firm and its partners. This type of environment echoes the concept of open innovation, with collective innovation based on collaborations between actors pooling their skills and knowledge.

In the development stage of an innovation, platforms can be used by actors wanting to innovate at several points in the process. Indeed, companies such as Dell with its "IdeaStorm" concept, or Procter & Gamble with "Connect & Develop by P&G", or IBM with "IBM IdeaJam" use platforms in the upstream phases of the innovation process, during the development of the innovation idea. However, some companies may prefer to involve platforms downstream of the innovation process, for example, to promote the innovation (co-innovation) or to shape it (co-design). A typology of open innovation practices related to platforms has been drawn up by Isckia (2011).

The exclusivity (closing or opening) of the platforms is crossed with the instructions on the questions asked for the partners and users of the platform. Depending on the company's strategy (i.e. valorization of its internal knowledge, creation of intellectual property via a tool such as a patent, or broader exploration of a new market, new knowledge), these companies will not open their innovation process at the same time and the type of actors solicited may also vary (specialists or novices). Because of the multiplicity of actors involved, the BE must balance the satisfaction of common and individual interests, with a common final goal: innovation.

2.3. Partnership experience

2.3.1. *Creation of innovation networks*

The use of repeated collaborations in the development of projects has a beneficial effect on companies (Nieto and Santamaria 2007). They accumulate knowledge and learn from past experiences (Levitt and March, 1988). Firms also learn about partnership management, as in the case of alliances. Routines can be developed and procedures put in place on the basis of the experiences of the different partners in the alliance. The performance of these alliances can then be increased, particularly when common working methods and an adapted language are established (Hoang and Rothaermel 2005; Laursen and Salter 2006). Furthermore, the reputation that firms build by engaging in collaborative projects is important for future projects (Powell et al. 1996).

There are various sources of information that can help in the innovation process. For radical innovations, the links established with suppliers and customers in the different phases of innovation development are strong. The earlier these links are established, the earlier the results will come (Meyers and Athaide 1991). In addition, pooling resources between partners allows for results that vary according to the type of partner. An analysis of risks versus expected outcomes can provide insight into the ultimate benefits (Nieto et al. 2011; Powell et al. 1996). Relationships with suppliers can reduce product development risks and delays, as well as improve product quality (Tether 2002; Chung and Kim 2003).

Similar to the history of collaboration presented above, the formation of networks has been studied in works since the early 2000s. The fields of industrial economics, industrial organization and technological cooperation have been areas where the notion of networks has emerged (Cohendet et al. 2003). In the 1980s, the field of engineering was a springboard for the development of networks through the industrial economy. The network infrastructure, computer or telecommunication networks represented a gateway. The network is taken as an object of study at the technical and economic system level (Shapiro and Varían 1998). The network becomes a tool for creating coordination dynamics between different actors, which can act on the markets (Curien 1999). Subsequently, in the 1990s, the network as it is now studied was introduced. Schelling (1978), in the line of work that will focus on the economics of interactions, examines the network as a structure of interactions between economic agents. The network is deeply rooted in the economic analysis of agents in a given territory or structure. In parallel, Granovetter (1973) published works on the sociology of social networks. Swedberg (1990), White (1992), Uzzi (1996) and Callón (1999) also analyze social networks with an economic approach. The contribution of their theories concerns the object of analysis which passes from the individual and their behavior to the relation as a unit of analysis. This one is then characterized by its strength (weak or strong link), its direction (direct or indirect) and its content (types of exchanges in the relationship between agents).

The link represents a connection between two individuals. The so-called "weak links" are infrequent connections between agents, but which can provide access to resources or other entry points to more diverse networks than strong links. The latter refer to frequent connections between agents, with exchanges of resources (information, material or financial resources) requiring more commitment, or even professional intimacy (Granovetter 1973).

At the end of the 1990s, the economics of interactions and the sociology of networks came together to study the formation and evolution of networks in an interdisciplinary manner. Economics, physics, sociology and biology shed light on the genesis of interactions between agents by taking into account their environment and in particular the institutional context which can have an influence on the interaction processes.

Different analytical frameworks are added to the studies already provided by the literature. Dynamic or static, local or global interactions are observed by Kirman (1998). The size of the network is important in static interactions. The number of agents sharing a common characteristic is thus essential. The adoption of technologies or other innovations by an agent in the network is dependent on the other agents present. An agent's satisfaction in adopting the innovation increases with the number of agents that adopt compatible technologies (positive network externalities) (Cohendet and Schenk 1999). In the case of dynamic interactions, Barnejee (1992), Kirman (1993) and Orléan (1998) write about the imitation behavior or mimetic contagion of agents in the same network (herd model or epidemic behavior model). The behavior and choices of individuals can condition the choices of other individuals in the network. In dynamic and local interactions, these are the Markov, Gibbs and Ising field models (Schelling 1978; Kinderman and Snell 1980), as well as the lattice network structures (Berninghaus 1980). Blume (1995) and Berninghaus and Schwalbe (1996) have been the most studied in recent years. Moreover, the open model of the innovation process as defined by Chesbrough in 2003 emphasizes the diversity of sources of information and innovative proposals from actors inside and outside the company. Bénézech (2012) asserts that the more the porosity of the boundaries of firms is, and therefore the greater the openness to the external environment, then the greater the probability that the innovations developed will be adopted.

Finally, any social network is imprinted with a history of links established between agents embedded in interpersonal relationships and organizations, through which relationships evolve over time. The experience of collaborations that are generated with these links becomes interactions through repetition, energizing the network (Doreian and Stoneman 1997). Watts and Strogatz (1998) introduced the notion of small worlds. According to the authors, the shortest possible links between agents in a network can be representative of the entire structure of the network and are a sign of good network connectivity.

Furthermore, the openness of the innovation process is impacted by several factors, which can be categorized into factors external to the company (the environment in which companies evolve) and internal to the company. The openness of the process has been studied by Bageac (2013) by specifying three types of factors: (i) factors related to the environment such as technological and economic factors and the perception of the environment (ii) factors related to the firm (e.g. increasing the opportunity to collaborate by making itself known, identifying the added value of using an open innovation model or targeting the markets that the firm wants to conquer); and (iii) catalytic factors (Figure 2.2). The author identifies two types of catalysts, namely generation Y and information and communication technologies (ICT). The latter two elements can go hand in hand by including a young workforce, generation Y, which is increasingly using ICT. Their experience, knowledge and know-how in digital technology, as well as in certain fields, can be an asset for the positioning of firms in the open innovation model.

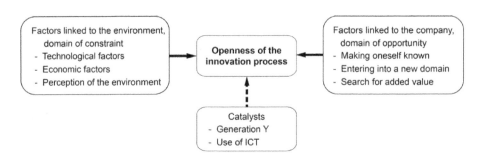

Figure 2.2. *Determinants of the openness of the innovation process (Bageac 2013)*

2.3.2. Profiles of the partners involved in the collaboration

Actors can be categorized according to their position and role in innovation. Bageac (2013) cites peers, that is, companies of the same size that work in the same sector of activity and generally competing with each other, suppliers, customers, as well as universities and academic organizations, research laboratories and start-ups. All these actors can be involved in innovation collaborations. However, they do not all intervene at the same time in the innovation process and also not in all projects. Indeed, depending on the strategy that companies choose, certain actors will be advantageous to intervene in the collaboration. For example, in the energy sector, the company EDF collaborates a lot with start-ups and emphasizes collaboration with academic research. These actors are preferred to private or public sector companies or competitors. EDF promotes this collaboration with research and small companies on its website. One of the reasons why the company prefers to collaborate with this kind of partner is that research can propose innovative, up-to-date solutions that are adapted to the conditions of the companies. The studies cited by Bageac are in line with this and state that academic collaborations with research institutes and universities are one of the most common sources of motivation in open innovation. The possibilities of developing cutting-edge products or products that are very specific to the field of activity or market segment are great. However, the necessary knowledge and know-how can be provided by such partners. Thus, the upstream phases of the innovation process are targeted by academic partnerships and/or entrepreneurs. When the development phase of the innovation has begun, the partners are different. They are mostly start-ups, suppliers and sometimes competitors. Start-ups are therefore partners of choice because they are in a prime position to acquire specific technologies, already developed or under development, which can be used by other companies. The example of the Air Liquide company reveals the importance of the role of start-ups in the open innovation process. The company has developed a program called "Scouting and Partnering" within the Research and Development department, which aims to detect the start-ups that are best situated in terms of resources and skills, in order to be able to initiate collaborations. In the same vein, EDF has created two areas of start-up identification: one via the creation of an investment fund dedicated to start-ups and the other by establishing an "open innovation team", with one of its main activities being to identify new small companies and integrate them into the open innovation process. Partner intelligence or "sourcing" is now part of the open innovation process, which was not the case for closed innovation, where all the resources necessary for the development of the innovation were found within the company itself.

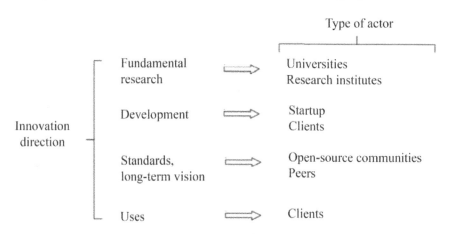

Figure 2.3. *Types of actors and partnerships according to the goals of the innovation (Bageac 2013)*

The theme of intellectual property rights is also addressed in Chapter 4, through the advantages and limitations of collaborative innovation.

This chapter concludes with the possible uses of the different collaboration mechanisms according to their scope, content and the stage of the process at which the innovation is taking place. Upstream of the project, in the idea and concept generation stages, virtual communities that call on a large number of users or clients, advisory panels (e.g. Hallmark Idea

Exchange from the company Hallmark to collect customer opinions on specific themes) can provide a wealth of content. The suggestion box is another example. Ben & Jerry's offers consumers the opportunity to suggest ideas for new products or services such as packaging or distribution through a project called "Suggest-a-Flavor" accessible online. The online patent markets, open source, will tend to be used in a product testing stage (see Table 2.1).

		Chapter 1: Upstream (invention and design)	Chapter 2: Downstream (product design and testing)
Nature of the collaboration	**Great richness (depth)**	Idea box	Toolkits for user innovation
		Advisory panels	Open access mechanisms
		Virtual communities	Internet patent market
		Online marketplace of ideas	
	Large scope (extended)	Online survey	Mass customization of the product
		Market intelligence service	Online prototyping
		Joint online analysis	Virtual product test
		Listening techniques	Virtual market test

Table 2.1. *Internet collaboration mechanisms by nature of collaboration and stage in the new product development process (Sawhney et al. 2005)*

There are multiple partnerships that can be established during the innovation process. They involve actors from different sectors, with varying levels of expertise, as well as different resources available. Open innovation has enabled the creation and development of a fully fledged step in the innovation process, namely "sourcing" or the identification of key players for collaboration. Large companies have created services dedicated to this identification because it is a key element of the success of the collaboration and, by extension, of the success of the innovation that will be commercialized in the future. In addition to this strategy of monitoring or identifying important actors such as start-ups that are at the cutting edge of technology and up to date in the development of products and services best suited to customer demand, this Chapter 2 has focused on the use of intellectual property rights. These IPRs provide legal and financial protection to their owners. We have seen that the use of patents can be useful for companies in highly competitive and mainly technology-intensive sectors such as and mainly being technology intensive such as the pharmaceutical, chemical or medical sectors. The sectors of aerospace, robotics, nanotechnology, biotechnology and also information and communication technologies are high-tech users. However, most of the patents that have been created and registered in an intellectual property institute are dormant and not used. Trademarks are widespread and represent a very powerful commercial tool to attract customers and increase the market share of companies. Secrecy is also used by some companies for key products, which are sensitive and may embody specific knowledge.

The degree of openness is also a strategic element that partners aiming for collaboration need to identify and clarify. A low degree of openness implies a greater possibility of managing the innovation process as well as a restricted access to interesting resources that are outside the company's boundaries. However, this strategy can be judicious for some companies that have sufficient resources and that have identified few weak points that collaboration can improve (a lack of visibility, access to a market that is a little different from the traditional market, know-how or very specific knowledge). On the contrary, a large-scale opening, such as the use of open source software, Creative Commons or online platforms, can bring a lot to innovation, by making a whole community of enthusiasts and experts work and stimulating them. Thus, many levers and success factors of innovation must be studied by the actors. The appropriation of the innovation and its rents, the number of partners and their role, the delegation of tasks are all potential sources of conflict, which should be clarified before any collaborative innovation project. Chapter 3 presents the classic models of innovation to the new models of third places, coworking spaces, Living Labs and FabLabs.

Finally, we have seen that the concept of collaborative innovation has evolved over the last few decades, notably through the type of actors involved as partners in the collaboration, and also through the tools used to implement this collaboration. Indeed, many platforms have flourished on the Internet, to connect actors asking for solutions to problems, and "innovators" who propose innovative solutions. Intellectual property rights have been introduced through the process of exchanging licenses. Finally, the aspect of proximity at the territorial level takes its importance in collaborative processes and has been highlighted.

2.3.3. Importance of the territorial level for the governance of innovation

The notion of territory is frequently highlighted when talking about open innovation. The collaborations that are established between actors can be based on several types of proximity. Geographical proximity is weighed against institutional, organizational, social and cognitive proximity. This is the case of the five types of proximity: institutional, organizational, social and cognitive. Table 2.2 presents these five proximities that Ron Boschma was the first to describe in 2005. A balance in terms of proximity must be established so as not to create disadvantages and put obstacles in the innovation process. In this way, when too little proximity is established, it can lead to misunderstanding between actors, opportunism or a lack of positive externalities for the network. On the contrary, too much proximity could lead to a lack of openness, of novelties and a risk of missing out on interesting opportunities by dependence on a plan drawn up in advance.

	Key dimensions	Too little proximity	Too much proximity	Possible solutions
Cognitive proximity	Lack of knowledge	Misunderstanding	Lack of novelty sources	Common knowledge base with diverse but complementary capabilities
Organizational proximity	Control	Opportunism	Bureaucracy	Loose coupled system
Social proximity	Trust (based on social relationships)	Opportunism	No economic justification	Mix of integrated and market relationships
Institutional proximity	Trust (based on common institutions)	Opportunism	Locking and inertia	Institutional obstacles and counterweights
Geographical proximity	Distance	No spatial externalities	Lack of geographical openness	Mix of local buzz and extra-local links

Table 2.2. *Proximities and their implications (Boschma 2005)*

Geographical proximity is not a "given" element. On the contrary, this proximity comes from a combination of human organization and constitutional contexts (Rallet 2002). Thus, the author emphasizes that proximity is not a "permissive condition" that encourages interactions but is a product of institutions, hence the fact that geographic proximity is dominated by organized proximity. The latter is constituted by a sharing of similarities, referring to an organizational proximity and of belonging to the same subset, referring to an institutional proximity. Institutional proximity guarantees a dynamic within a territory, when agents can share their experiences, frames of reference and representations. This proximity may not be homogeneous at all times during an innovation process. The governance that results from this allows the drawing of clear territorial strategies for the actors, who are embedded in social relationships (Gilly and Grossetti, 1993).

The contextualization of actors is an integral part of the structure of the interactions that are established between them. Thus, the concentration of agents in a given geographic space is a "result of the projection of social or institutional networks located on the space of economic relations". In addition to this local scale at which actors develop interactions, the global scale is added because these actors also connect with partners on a larger scale. Institutional proximity is therefore very important because of the possibility of creating links at the local level with actors present in the same territory and beyond, with actors present in other territories. These elements are all the more important in the current period, with crises of all kinds (environmental, health, economic, social), where increasingly different publics such as institutions, companies and civil society are becoming a force for proposals for innovative solutions.

Economic actors such as companies and business associations, institutional actors such as local authorities, chambers of commerce and the State, and social actors interact and form territorial governance. The interests of each actor are pooled to work on projects with a local or territorial scope. Thus, different proximities may come into play for the proper functioning of this governance (Mendez and Mercier 2006).

The example of Grasse and its perfumers suffering from a loss of territorial competitiveness underlines the importance of the social relationships that are built and give rise to the weaving of a network that can support the development initiatives of companies. The territorial specificities that can lead to competitiveness are partly based on relationships and proximities within the territory, social, cognitive and geographical. The knowledge and know-how of perfumers who learned with informal (oral and interpersonal) methods of knowledge transmission have helped to build the specificity of a rare resource historically linked to Grasse. Despite attempts to remain competitive, by positioning themselves on niche markets, by promoting a traditional image of perfumers linked to the region, Grasse companies are in direct competition with the knowledge and skills developed by specialized schools training future perfumers, not based in Grasse. The resources and technological resources used by the companies are becoming strategic and a competition of territories is created.

2.3.4. Emergence and use of collaborative platforms

Platforms, as described in the section on the business ecosystem in Chapter 1, appear to be a solution to these obstacles. Indeed, platforms allow companies facing specific challenges or with specific needs, for example, in technology, to be connected with various audiences (experts, novices, private sector, public sector, etc.), on a large scale.

The innovative aspect of the appearance of these platforms lies in the organization of exchanges and the possible relationships between different actors, who would not have had the opportunity to collaborate without these digital tools. On the one hand, the consumer or customer can innovate together with the companies, as is the case for the Lego company, where the consumer is called to provide ideas for high-tech bricks. On the other hand, Internet users can collaborate jointly to propose solutions. The collective work of Internet users is a co-design tool, beneficial to companies that require innovative solutions (Pelissier 2008).

On the contrary, the not-invented-here (NIH) syndrome is the tendency for organizations or individuals to avoid or reject what has not been invented by them. Companies can avoid this syndrome by going outside-in and adopting outside technologies into their own development processes. Chesbrough adds to this NIH, not sold here (NSH). This syndrome leads the rights holder to refuse to allow third parties to exploit the innovation. It is in this context that platforms such as Innocentive have developed, with the aim of acting as an intermediary in a technology market (Ayerbe and Chanal 2011).

Another possible form of collaboration by platforms is the outsourcing of innovation to external actors who will act individually. An example studied by Liotard (2010) is the Innocentive platform. She defines it as an innovative way of innovating because it represents a tool for outsourcing to a community of anonymous people, whether they are informed or not. This site is an intermediary between companies (seekers) with needs for new ideas and problems to solve, and Internet users (solvers) with solutions to propose. These solvers can be academics, consultants or private sector actors. For Innocentive, challenges are presented to the solvers. They are then rewarded with prizes ranging from 5,000 to 100,000 dollars. Thanks to the success of Innocentive, initially created by the Eli Lilly company in 2000, other sectors are now using the platform's services. The chemical and biochemical sectors, consumer goods, plastics, genetics and high tech are now among the users of this innovative tool. To increase the participation of firms in this new process, the Rockefeller Foundation collaborated with the Innocentive platform between 2006 and 2008 by taking into account the costs of revealing the challenges and a part of the bonus paid to the solver who will have brought the solution to the challenge. In 2016, more than 2,000 external and 3,000 internal challenges were posted, with contributions from more than 375,000 people in 200 countries around the world[1]. Approximately 33–50% of the challenges were solved (Liotard 2010; Liotard and Revest 2015).

The advantages for companies entering this system include time savings (divided by 10 between the post of the challenge and the delivery of the solution), a minimum of financial and human resources involved. The risk of failure is also minimized for the company. However, large companies have an advantage in using this collaborative innovation process. Indeed, the codification of knowledge and the resources necessary to implement this method of challenge can limit the scope of the innovations found. Few studies have been conducted on the real contribution of solutions by solvers to seekers and to companies in general (Liotard and Revest 2015).

Other models similar to Innocentive's flourished in the 2000s, with specialties such as video (Mofilm, Poptent, Userfarm, Zoopa), engineering design and industrial projects (NineSigma, Innocentive, YourEncore), or design and photography (Jovoto, Shicon, Springleap) among others (Arfaoui 2015; Pelisser 2015). YourEncore is used by companies to hire retired scientists (Howe 2006).

---

1 Press release from Innocentive: https://www.innocentive.com/open-innovation-pioneer-innocentive-celebrates-15-years/.

This subcontracting of innovation, as in the case of the Innocentive platform, can be done through individual contracts in various phases of the innovation's development. Finally, Pélissier (2008) proposes a last category of intermediation, the "democracy of consumer opinion". Consumers propose solutions and then vote for the one that will be proposed to firms, with a view to its adoption and diffusion.

An increasingly common example of a platform that aims at innovation is crowdsourcing. This system allows Internet users to participate, most often financially, in a project. The innovation potential of networks of Internet users is put to good use for a common goal. Lebraty (2007) defines it as "outsourcing by an organization, via a website, of an activity to a large number of individuals whose identity is most often anonymous". Outsourcing can concern different departments such as marketing, commercialization and innovation design (Cardon 2006). This innovation process is similar to a bottom-up process, which goes from the Internet user to the firm, in which individualized forms take place (Guilhon 2008).

Collaborative platforms can be non-profit as they do not commercialize any goods or services like Wikipedia. Within this platform, Internet users can write articles on all types of subjects, without financial compensation. The advantage of virtual platforms and environments is the possibility of accessing a much larger potential user and customer base than by using traditional corporate channels for co-design, marketing or innovation design. Interactions remain rich, even if they become numerous, frequent and can be extended over the long-term by future projects, for example. However, the confidentiality issues inherent to any collaboration can hinder the willingness of users or customers to interact with companies requesting solutions. The information and proposals submitted by customers may be limited, constraining the opportunities to move forward effectively in the project (Sawhney et al. 2005).

The open innovation paradigm allows for inside-out and outside-in of knowledge, material and immaterial goods and resources not held by the firms that use openness in their innovation process. Liotard then asserts that platforms have the advantage of opening up the boundaries of the firm more intensively by allowing them to reach communities or networks that they do not have in their direct environment and which is solicited more frequently. Furthermore, companies have flexibility in the way they partner, not favoring contractual forms with virtual partners. Another advantage of virtual environments lies in the nature of the exchanges between firms and users or customers. Thanks to the platforms, exchanges tend to take the form of a conversation, where any informal information not initially targeted by the theme of the exchange can be heard and captured by both parties. Interpersonal relationships are created through these exchanges, which is not the case through codified knowledge exchanges (Sawhney et al. 2005; Ayerbe and Azzam 2015).

2.3.5. Intellectual property rights: license exchange and other notable examples of collaboration

The subject of intellectual property and the underlying rights is an integral part of the concept of open and collaborative innovation. Various means can be used to protect innovations. The most studied tool and the one that represents the indicator of identification of the differences in progress in the acquisition of knowledge between firms is the patent (Pakes and Griliches 1980). The patent is used as a "proxy" for innovation activity. However, this indicator contains significant flaws. Some intellectual property rights, such as patents, are very expensive, which represents a significant barrier for small- and medium-sized enterprises. In addition, analyzing innovation through patents greatly limits the results and reality of innovation activities, since non-patented innovations are very widespread and in the majority (Pakes and Griliches 1980). This is confirmed by the results of the community innovation survey (CIS), which revealed that, by half of the innovative firms, patents are considered ineffective as a protection mechanism against firms or individuals who might imitate. The practice of secrecy and the use of highly qualified personnel tend to be effective, with differences between sectors (e.g. patents are mainly used in high-tech firms or in the medical, pharmaceutical and chemical fields) (Hall et al. 2014). Secrecy, on the contrary, is widespread in industrial sectors such as agriculture and food, particularly in the internal innovation practices of companies, in order to maintain a competitive edge (Biggs and Clay 1981). Nevertheless, the development and disclosure of patents tend to encourage the flow of knowledge between the firms that develop them and those that use them, whereas secrecy tends instead to impede them (Hall et al. 2014).

As far as licenses are concerned, their use can be used to appropriate of knowledge (Liotard 2010). However, the asymmetry of information (of the licensed knowledge) between the two partners can lead to risk-taking on the part of the license buyer and a competitive advantage on the other. This asymmetry is found at different moments of the transaction and for both parties. The uncertainty linked to the nature of the licensed product can be an obstacle for the buyer. Liotard (2010) describes this problem as "adverse selection", where the quality of the innovation is unknown to the buyer. Conversely, the seller does not know ex-ante the quality of the buyer and their real capacities to make the most of the innovation that will be licensed. This asymmetry arises even before the purchase and transfer of the license, before the contract is signed. Finally, after the sale, the seller may find themselves once again in an asymmetry of information as to how the licensed product will be used. Moreover, Ayerbe and Chanal (2011) attest to the difficulty of defining a price in this framework of asymmetric information. The buyer could not take the price as a criterion of product quality. These concerns inherent to intellectual property tools are linked to their transfer.

Moreover, despite the codification of the licensed asset, a part of the knowledge linked to it is tacit and anchored in the environment and the personnel linked to its creation. Licensed innovation is therefore subject to improvement and adaptation through testing, training or industrial secrecy (Liotard 2010).

Licenses have different purposes such as preventing the patent holder from implementing their innovation, receiving financial rewards with the royalty system, controlling the market through the selection of licensees and obtaining expertise if licenses are offered bilaterally (Gallini and Winter 1985; Katz and Shapiro 1985; Liotard 2010).

In the transfer of technologies subject to intellectual property rights, such as licenses, Chesbrough (2006b) has studied intermediaries whose role is to facilitate transactions that enable the supply of technologies to meet demand. Innovation thus benefits from an intermediary where new actors can intervene, completing the network of actors already collaborating in an open innovation perspective (Ayerbe and Chanal 2011). An example of technology transfer in open innovation is the use of so-called free software. The source code is free to use, as is the case with copyleft or General Public Licenses. In this framework, any user is free to use the source code, as well as modify it, copy it or distribute it elsewhere in their network, under the condition of specifying the copyleft, with possible access to the improvements. These must also be modifiable for any other user interested in doing so (Pénin 2008).

Rayna and Striukova (2010) introduce the concept of patent pools, adding it to open innovation in the landscape of large-scale open innovation. For both authors, patent holders can share and license their patents. The goal of this type of organization is to avoid bilateral agreements by making the maximum number of potential users benefit. In this patent pool notion, Rayna and Striukova put forward the principle of coopetition. Indeed, both collaborative and competitive practices are jointly integrated in open innovation (Ayerbe and Azzam 2015).

The principles of inside-out and outside-in emerge from Chesbrough's (2003) definition of open innovation. The inside-out approach allows companies to use external resources to commercialize their innovations, not only in the markets they traditionally use, but also in new markets. Thus, licensing-out and spin-off can come into play. When a new independent company is created by another company through the sale or distribution of new shares in the original company, a spin-off is created. A spin-off is a type of divestiture. A company creates a spin-off in the hope that it will be more valuable as an independent entity. A spin-off is also known as a spin-out or starbust. Licensing-out is a practice of granting licenses, focusing on opening the distribution channel and finding commercial partners to bring the product to market..

In parallel to this search for sources to integrate them and go outside the firm, the outside-in process makes it possible to complete a firm's internal resources such as knowledge. This process includes licensing-in and crowdsourcing-type communities (Ayerbe and Azzam 2015). The principle of licensing-in makes it possible to acquire intellectual property rights on externally developed products. New practices are being added in this environment, such as crowdsourcing and community management. Crowdsourcing is a term of debate due to the difficulty of its definition, resulting in semantic confusion. Some authors define platforms as examples of crowdsourcing; others do not categorize them as such. Crowdsourcing is formed from *-crowd*, people participating in initiatives, and *-sourcing*, meaning the process of finding and evaluating solutions, products or suppliers (Estellés-Arolas et al. 2012).

The coupled process lies between the two processes mentioned above and the patent pool. Companies join forces on the basis of their complementarity. This is referred to as co-creation, as in the case of joint ventures, alliances and other cooperations in research and development. Finally, the patent pool acts as an organization managing the patents of several holders and thus adds a notion of multi-party plurality to a traditionally bilateral environment where the seller and the buyer of licenses are linked (Rayna and Striukova 2010).

Ayerbe and Azzam (2015) have highlighted several themes. The appropriation of the rents of innovation that takes place in the open innovation process via collaborations between different partners is taken up by Dahlander and Gann (2010); Rayna and Striukova (2010) and Huizingh (2011). The authors specify the forms of patent pool, open source (Rayna and Striukova 2011), private open innovation, public innovation and open innovation models dealing with the degree of innovation openness and accessibility of data by users internal to firms or external, the general public (Huizingh 2011). Dahlander and Gann (2010) focus on the acquisition of inputs (such as licenses, patents or expertise) on the market, the transfer of firms' technologies through sales or licenses, and sourcing, which consists of scanning the environment of firms to launch new innovation projects. The authors conclude by revealing internal resources to the external without financial expectation and looking for externalities that will fall back following these projects involving innovations.

Accessibility is also an important point of any innovation model, specifying then the distinction between accessibility and authorization of the different parties (Lessig 2004) according to the strength of the openness (Pénin 2008). Moreover, the type and number of partners to be selected in open innovation can vary according to the degree of openness desired (e.g. as many partners as possible, specific selection of partners based on their skills and expertise) (Gandia et al. 2011). And Mention (2011) focuses on the provenance of the information that will be used, highlighting the diversity of partners (universities, customers, suppliers, competitors). Finally, the balance of importance between internal and external knowledge, which responds to a strategy of the firm regarding its position in terms of competitiveness, is discussed by Barge-Gil (2010).

Ayerbe and Azzam (2015) classify intellectual property tools according to the criteria of resource accessibility, the possibility of appropriation and the variety of partners. Thus, licensing in and licensing out as described earlier in this section is found in the environment of low openness, with few partners and close profiles, low accessibility to resources and a high possibility of appropriation. On the contrary, open source, the Creative Commons and patent platforms are characterized in a very large-scale openness by a great accessibility to resources, as well as a notable diversity of partners, but without a marked appropriation. Companies can thus make strategic choices such as preferring the wealth of information to create new ideas or, on the contrary, their scope to validate hypotheses previously elaborated with a consequent number of users or experiments (Sawhney et al. 2005).

Lelong and Gayoso (2010) argues that the importance of resources and information, and knowledge exchanged through collaborative projects, has become a key to the functioning of open innovation. A reorganization of the management of these resources can be done through homogeneous and stable structures with partnerships, clusters or heterogeneous structures with horizontal relationships, which do not require the intervention of the managerial organization of firms.

Creative Commons (CC) are licenses that indicate that works that are protected by intellectual property rights such as copyright can be shared and distributed for free, under certain conditions. Thus, the reuse of intellectual works promotes their visibility and promotion, instead of the author. A notorious example is Professor Lessig's "Free Culture". The conditions of the CC license specified that "derivative works may be made and distributed" only for non-commercial purposes and with a citation of the source included. As a result, many different formats of the book have appeared on the Internet as an audio version. This form of licensing allows individuals to use their creativity, based on works already produced. This can only encourage innovation and be a source of ideas and motivation for many users or novices who just need a basis to start the creative process (Weitzman 2004). CC licenses can be used anywhere in the world. It is possible to use them as long as copyright lasts, because they are linked to it. In addition to these fundamentals for using the CC license, authors can grant additional rights, including how they want their work to be used, copied or distributed.

There are six types of CC licenses that differ on the criteria of whether or not they can be shared, modified or not, and used commercially or not. In addition to these, a new license has appeared in the scientific field, the CC0, which allows the authors of the data to diffuse them in the public domain without any restriction of diffusion, use, sharing, improvement or modification, for possible commercial purposes. This license facilitates the compilation of data without cumulating licenses (Fily 2015). Finally, this type of license enables an interesting dissemination of works and innovations, as much for the authors and rights holders as for the users. The indirect collaboration generated by the use of Creative Commons represents another strategy that authors of innovations can consider to bring value to their product.

PART 2

Dynamic and Causal Innovation

3

The Reasons Behind Open Innovation and its Evolution

3.1. Evolution of the use of collaborative innovation: from classical to new models

Collaborative innovation has evolved over the last few decades and is now used on a large scale, in many different sectors. We can cite new models using open innovation and collaborative processes to generate innovation, such as coworking spaces, FabLabs, incubators or collaborative platforms among others.

As seen in Chapter 1, the processes of knowledge exploitation and exploration of capabilities on the part of companies are crucial and are part of open innovation strategies. These two approaches are complementary and help maintain competitiveness in increasingly complex and competitive markets (Andriopoulos and Lewis 2009). The right balance is needed to avoid causing lock-in or competency traps for the operation (Gupta et al. 2006). These two terms used by Gupta underline the influence of the routines established by companies and the limitations that this creates. On the other hand, exploration is important in these different collaborative spaces. The two approaches of exploitation and exploration are related to the types of governance (i.e. top-down and bottom-up) of the collaborative projects that take place in the mentioned spaces.

3.1.1. FabLabs

Capdevila (2015) differentiates collaborative spaces according to the actors' strategy (exploration or exploitation) and the type of governance (top-down or bottom-up) (Table 3.1). FabLabs are thus identified as spaces that promote an exploration approach in a top-down governance system. This is in contrast to the internal laboratories of companies or Living Labs, in which the focus is on exploitation. Indeed, the purpose of the organizations remains the commercialization of the products resulting from the experiments and different test phases, in order to be present on the markets traditionally used and also on new markets. For the bottom-up approach, hacker spaces and coworking spaces opt for different strategies in the sense that hacker spaces focus on exploring new possibilities and not on exploiting the results of the projects carried out in the space.

		Actors' strategies	
		Exploration	Operation
Types of governance of collaborative projects	Top-down	FabLabs	Living Labs Internal company labs
	Bottom-up	Hacker spaces	Coworking spaces

Table 3.1. *Collaborative spaces according to the strategies and types of governance in place (based on Ignasi Capdevila (2015), p.91)*

Collaborative innovation involves bringing together actors from different backgrounds, sectors and value chains. The relationships that are established can be based on several types of proximity, as seen in Chapter 2. Geographical or spatial proximity as well as cognitive proximity (Boutillier et al. 2020) have led to the creation of spaces where collaborations have been structured for several years in a community, in which individuals, all motivated by their own projects, come together to increase the possibilities of interaction. These spaces are FabLabs, Hacker spaces, Living Labs, creative labs, design labs, open labs, maker spaces and coworking spaces. The synergies that are created in such spaces lead to innovations. The autonomy of the individuals participating, coupled with their experience, knowledge, know-how and a strong community spirit, leads to ambitious collaborative and innovative projects (Fabbri and Charue-Duboc 2016; Garrett et al. 2017). Collaborative spaces such as FabLabs, Living labs, coworking spaces and hacker spaces allow their members to pool their resources in order to reduce costs, share common material or immaterial resources, and to maintain and extend social relationships based on trust and reciprocity (Auboin and Capdevila 2019). Business clubs as described by Marinos (2018) operate on the same principle of resource sharing. The added value of these clubs is that they can be used as a means of sharing resources, mobilizing peers and providing advice and decision-making support. In addition, the added value of such spaces allows entrepreneurial actors to come out of isolation and create a network that will be mobilized in the future through innovative collaborative projects (Marinos 2018).

These spaces are either autonomous or managed by a public institution (Capdevila 2015). They involve a multitude of sectors, ranging from industry and services to health or art, for example. However, the social relationships that emerge in these settings can be damaged in the medium term due to the hidden goals inherent in the true motivations of individuals involved in these collaborative projects. The need for visibility and to expand one's network is an underlying reason for individuals to join collaborative spaces. Another reason relates to the financial aspect. Individuals may have a need to reduce costs by pooling resources and infrastructure, access to geographically well placed spaces (e.g. in the heart of a city where renting is expensive), fairly large spaces, or access to assets that would not be accessible by being on their own. These reasons mentioned by Capdevila (2015) and King (2017) explain the downside of individuals' motivations, which are generally not studied by authors of research on the management of relationships in innovation and the structuring of experience and knowledge transfer in innovative ecosystems.

All of these spaces have the similarity of promoting knowledge sharing and fostering collaboration through the implementation of iterative and open processes. In addition, the connection between innovators and users, as well as the construction of a knowledge community, are encouraged in these environments. The open innovation approach takes on its full meaning. The boundaries of companies are erased in favor of collaborations and exchanges between actors present in the collaborative spaces. These exchanges are partly informal and allow for increased interdisciplinarity represented by the collaboration between actors with varied profiles, such as entrepreneurs, engineers, citizens and designers (Auboin and Capdevila 2019).

Nevertheless, the approaches used by each of them differ. In FabLabs (or manufacturing laboratories), "makers" or "tinkerers" value access to knowledge as well as to the means of production. This is based on open design, for which several examples from the digital world demonstrate their success. Wikipedia, Linux or open source and the free use of software are all examples where common use resources have led to the creation of digital innovations that everyone can benefit from, enjoy and contribute to. Moreover, 3D printers have been generated in this type of space, where digital technologies are put to work to allow a greater number of users to use them in non-industrial and professional settings. It was at the Massachusetts Institute of Technology (MIT) that the idea of FabLabs was born, with Professor Neil Gershenfeld in his course discussing "how to 'make (almost) anything' (Gershenfeld 2005) that allows anyone to develop, prototype, and try their own designs" (Mikhak et al. 2002; Gershenfeld 2012).

3.1.2. *The Artlab*

In the art sector, Artlabs emerged in 2011 in the form of autonomous laboratories specialized in their field (Auboin and Capdevila 2019). The startup Digitalarti was at the origin of this space dedicated to collaborative projects related to art. The firm promotes digital art through services to various actors such as companies, local authorities or agencies; and a community site. The Artlab has completed the offer of these services with a production, research and development approach with a desire to integrate digital artists within it. The valorization of the networks linked to the artistic production and the production of new works is possible in the Artlab. Artists who have the opportunity to create artistic products in this environment can benefit from the experience and expertise of professionals specialized in communication and economic development, as well as in artistic and digital skills such as engineers. One of the outstanding results of this innovative space is measured in the number of patents filed. Since the creation of the Artlab, three patents have been created and registered. In addition, advanced technologies are used to participate in the creation of innovative products, such as a 3D printer, a digital milling machine, a wood and metal lathe, or an engraver and laser cutter. The artist enters the space and can create works via the available network. This business model is similar to a club, where access is restricted to invited users (artists and engineers). The public can access on demand.

Finally, all works created in collaboration with actors with complementary expertise, using common specific resources (human, material and technical resources) will be commercialized while ensuring a sharing of the intellectual property rights inherent to these artistic works between the stakeholders.

3.1.3. Coworking spaces

There is no consensus on the definition of the term coworking and many works have addressed it (Jones et al. 2009; DeGuzman and Tang 2011; Kwiatkowski and Buczynski 2011; Davies and Tollervey 2013; Jones 2013; Capdevila 2015). Coworking spaces have been defined by the author, taken from the literature, as "open office spaces in which unaffiliated professionals work for a fee" (Capdevila 2015). This definition does not reflect the dynamic nature at work in such shared spaces. The interpersonal relationships that develop between individuals coming into these environments are important and are the basis of the collaborative dynamics that drive individuals to innovate. Any commercial success of a project developed within such spaces can only be based on physical colocation (Boutillier et al. 2020). The sharing of tangible and intangible resources, as well as knowledge and know-how is essential and should be included in the definition of coworking. Thus, coworking spaces facilitate informal exchanges and reduce transaction and operational costs due to the collaboration and the costs of searching for information necessary for the development of projects, innovations and new initiatives. Coworkers are co-located on a small scale and face-to-face interpersonal interactions are favored.

Coworking spaces are flourishing around the world, growing very rapidly since 2005 (Capdevila 2015; Bouncken et al. 2018). The first space emerged in San Francisco to meet a demand in terms of sparse social interaction and the unproductiveness of telecommuting. By 2007, there were 75 coworking spaces around the world. Rapidly, they grew, with 310 two years later, 1,130 in 2011, 3,400 in 2013, and nearly 7,800 coworking spaces have been counted, with approximately 510,000 people collaborating in them (Deskmag 2015; Spinuzzi et al. 2019). The distribution of these spaces is heterogeneous across the world, and the growth is mostly in cities. Many of these types of spaces are located in the heart of cities. This factor is paramount for individuals becoming coworkers, as access to clients, suppliers and any potential partners is encouraged due to this advantageous location (Capdevila 2015). The cognitive and cultural dynamics of such cities allow for an abundance and concentration of individuals wanting to generate innovation and profit for their marketable products down the road. Technological innovations, the digital context and entrepreneurial models are all factors that favor the insertion of coworking spaces in these ever-changing areas (Bouncken and Reuschl 2018).

Examples of coworking spaces include Impact Hub, NextSpace and Urban Station. An example of an agribusiness coworking space is Agropole in Molondin, Switzerland. In the country, it is the first space entirely dedicated to the agri-food sector, hosting a center of industrial skills and innovations located within a production complex in a rural area. Agropole focuses on the entire value chain, "from farm to fork" or "from field to fork", by connecting the stakeholders in the food chain: producers, processors, manufacturers, service providers and consumers. Agropole's ambition is to shape the sustainable and healthy agriculture of the future, using new technologies. Several start-ups are working in the space. Despite numerous and diverse buildings (greenhouses, offices, packaging halls, land for production trials), the site will be completed with new infrastructure in the coming years. In the meantime, important innovations have been developed in this space, such as automatic optical sorting systems for vegetables (carrots and potatoes), based on artificial intelligence, new crop technologies such as the "Aero41" drone used to treat vines in particular, the Internet of Things, online food sales, a container-grocery for automatic distribution of drinks, sandwiches, local food, to be ordered by application on the phone, called "Kiosque 724", or their traceability via QR codes or blockchain methods.

In general, this type of space is generated on an individual and private level. However, spaces can join together to provide their members with a multiplicity of services and possible connections between members. For example, some spaces have been formed at universities or companies. The manager of the space thus has a leading role in the success of the collaborations (Boutillier et al. 2020). Furthermore, Spinuzzi et al. (2019) distinguish between the terms coworking and community. For the authors, all coworking spaces can be categorized as communities. However, different communities can include a variety of activities that are not performed only in coworking spaces. This research is still recent and should be explored further.

Events are regularly organized with the aim of bringing together members of coworking spaces in the same place, facilitating their networking. The added value of such networking lies in the additional possibility for members to offer a range of services and to develop innovative services and products by benefiting from interdisciplinary knowledge and experience (Lave and Wenger 1991). Boutillier et al. (2020) have taken up the work of Diane-Gabrielle Tremblay and Arnaud Scaillerez to explain the main driving forces of the emergence of collaborations within coworking spaces, between their members and with external firms. These factors are located at three levels: human resources, financial resources and the infrastructure available to the spaces.

3.1.4. Hacker spaces and maker spaces

The terminologies hacker spaces and maker spaces are used with little differentiation in articles and works studying them. Nevertheless, it is often accepted that hacker spaces are about software development and maker spaces focus on machines and the production of physical items (Capdevila 2015). As with coworking spaces, the ideas created and products produced can be more innovative when multiple disciplines collaborate with each other[1]. Both maker spaces and hacker spaces advocate openness and sharing as incentives for all collaboration, with a peer-to-peer relationship that develops between the members of these spaces. The passion of various disciplines and fields allows for fruitful sharing leading to innovation. According to Capdevila (2015), "members of these communities share the same ethical principles and interests", with a notable difference between members of hacker spaces and maker spaces. The former are interested in the playful and educational dimension of the projects, while the latter are more interested in a "counter-culture" ethic. The economic returns of the results disseminated in these spaces are not their priority, unlike the improvement of society as a whole. Similar to coworking spaces, maker spaces are located in urban areas, to foster potential collaborations with a diversity of actors such as universities, politicians and companies[2].

---

1 Retrieved from: https://www.interregeurope.eu/fileadmin/user_upload/tx_tevprojects/library/file_1556879611.pdf.
2 Retrieved from: https://www.interregeurope.eu/fileadmin/user_upload/tx_tevprojects/library/file_1556879611.pdf.

3.1.5. *Living Labs*

Living Labs are laboratories for observing agents with technologies in real environments or conditions that are as close as possible to the reality of using these technologies (Bergvall-Kåreborn and Ståhlbröst 2009; Béjean et al. 2021). Access to new technologies is one of the priorities of Living Labs, as is putting actors in real-life situations, who take an active part in the innovation process. The concept of Living Labs appeared in the early 1990s, but it was not until the 2000s that it gained traction, at least in Europe. For the researchers who initially described these living laboratories, it was a question of implementing a pedagogical model of learning-through-doing. Students are confronted with a real-life situation in a residential shopping area in a US city in a course organized by Drexel University in Philadelphia. Being able to study the behavior and reactions of "ordinary" people in situations involving new technologies, as close to reality as possible, was innovative at the time (Béjean et al. 2021).

At the European level, the European Network of Living Labs (ENoLL), founded in 2006, has seen the number of these laboratories increase significantly since then. More than 440 of these spaces have been created in the last 15 years, of which more than 150 are still active throughout the world[3]. Various sectors are concerned by the experimentation of these Living Labs, such as energy, mobility, agri-food, health or even the media. The exchange of information, best practices and collaborative processes are particularly supported and strengthened in these environments.

There is no consensus on the definition of Living Labs because they may, despite their goals of testing and understanding people's behavior towards technologies in near-real-world settings, use several approaches (Leminen 2013). One criticism reported in works is the top-down approach of these environments. Indeed, Living Labs are usually created by large public or private organizations or institutions. Moreover, the results of the activities are intended to be commercialized, in order to ensure an economic value for the actors involved in the related projects (Capdevila 2015).

---

3 https://enoll.org/.

3.1.6. *Creative Labs*

Creative Labs are open innovation spaces such as Living Labs, hacker spaces, maker spaces or coworking spaces with the aim of creating new products that will be put on the market and can bring an added value to its inventors. These environments are also present within companies, as is the case in the automotive sector with Renault, which has created a space (Renault Creative People) where new technologies such as 3D printers and a vinyl cutter are available for testing and prototyping. The space is open to all employees, so as to include as many people as possible who can contribute new ideas and integrate them into the early stages of the innovation process. The interdisciplinarity that characterizes this environment is therefore a key element of its success. The incentives to create innovations through a bottom-up approach is also its strength (Lo 2014).

Nevertheless, the scale at which these types of spaces are built is important. The larger these spaces are (over 1,000 square meters), the more innovative they are considered to be and the more diverse the activities that are carried out are diversified, combining different open innovation spaces (e.g. a maker space in one location and a coworking space in another location, still in the same large-scale space) (Capdevila 2015). The advantage of this kind of space is the possibility of creating formal and informal relationships through the arrangement of workplaces and breaks (open spaces, cafeterias, meeting rooms). Thus, exploration and exploitation as defined in Chapter 1 are easily implemented.

Marinos (2018) studies collaborative spaces and entrepreneurial clubs. The author empirically demonstrates that coworking spaces and other similar spaces are close to entrepreneurial clubs in the mechanisms that drive collaborations, namely, the emergence of social capital and the facilitated circulation of tacit knowledge. Social capital is defined by Bourdieu (1980) as the "sum of current and future resources resulting from the networks of relations of an individual or a social group". These third places have a convivial dimension that promotes exchanges between the actors present at the same time in these spaces, which characterizes them as environments of sociability and solidarity (Marinos 2018). Third places are historically spaces created to get to know each other and where services can be exchanged. The combination of physical, ergonomic and aesthetic space with a friendly atmosphere makes them an effective environment to develop and maintain collaborations. The atmosphere is very important to develop strong links between actors. Thus, more and more clubs are developing. They offer morning coffees, relaxation moments for company employees, sports meetings or company visits, for example. All these events aim to bring people together in a relaxed atmosphere that will foster interpersonal relations and thus relationships and therefore collaborations. The Business Network International has 211,000 members spread throughout the world in 7,800 local clubs. In France, the "500 pour 100" club located in four cities in Brittany, France, organizes frequent meetings between members to build links between them. The Wework platform has more than 80,000 members worldwide, including 150 offices in 35 cities. Thus, at local levels, many third places can depend on geographically larger entities.

3.2. Diversity of collaborative forms: an organized space of actors based on geographical, social and organizational proximity

3.2.1. *The spatial organization of actors in the form of clusters*

Proximity is defined along different dimensions, of which there are five, as described in Chapter 2: geographical, institutional, cognitive, cultural and organizational (Boschma 2005). Geographical proximity between actors collaborating in local ecosystems has been studied and classified as being able to improve innovation efficiency and knowledge transfer. In addition, the transaction costs of information, materials and knowledge are lower (Schartinger et al. 2002). However, this geographical proximity must be weighed against other proximities, as several studies have shown that cognitive proximity can surpass geographical proximity and be stronger for knowledge transfer, technology transfer and diffusion of innovation (Rallet and Torre 1998; Lissoni 2001; Breschi and Lissoni 2006).

A categorization was made by Boschma (2005) in his article "Proximity and Innovation: A Critical Assessment" to be able to differentiate the impacts of each factor and thus identify effective strategies for coordinating innovation processes. Mahdad et al. (2020) studied the influence of geographic proximity to university and industry on other types of proximity, which they illustrated as in Figure 3.1. The proximities defined by Ron Boschma (2005) were introduced in Chapter 1 of this book. Here, we focus on their implication for innovation and collaboration.

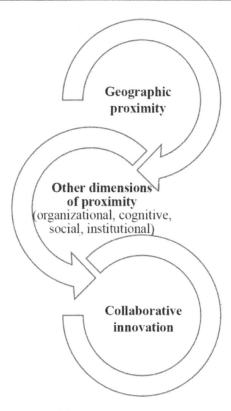

Figure 3.1. *The different dimensions of proximity and their influence on collaborative innovation (based on Mahdad et al. 2020)*

In Figure 3.1, geographical proximity is highlighted by its influence on other proximities. Indeed, being located close physically does not guarantee an ease of collaboration and innovation creation in the context of open innovation. Even though the transfer of knowledge is considered easier in such an environment, the territorialization of economic activities does not guarantee the success of interactions between actors. Cognitive, social, institutional and organizational proximities are also important. Cognitive proximity is based on a close knowledge base between actors. The actors draw on and share this knowledge to pursue research, develop technologies and create innovation (Boschma 2005; Aouinaït 2021). Cognitive proximity is influenced by the capacity to absorb new knowledge. The more firms are able to digest and use knowledge and information received from other firms, the more effective the innovation process will be. Institutional proximity reflects the common characteristics of institutions, representations, rules and thought patterns (Gallaud et al. 2012). This proximity is important for an understanding of the environment of the companies, the administrative or political strategies put in place. Any process implemented by companies with close institutional proximity has a better chance of being accepted and successful. Social proximity refers to actors belonging to the same network, with common relationships. These relationships established over a period of time are marked by trust and even friendship. These factors allow for deeper exchanges and interactions between actors (Mahdad et al. 2020). The university–industry interactions studied by the authors are characterized as successful by increased social proximity. Geographical proximity intervenes here by positively influencing social proximity. Interpersonal relationships are favored in a delimited territory. Finally, organizational proximity includes the internal coordination rules of firms (Gallaud et al. 2012). All of these types of proximities improve and increase the exchanges and organization of actors, to foster innovation (Boschma 2005).

Balas and Palpacuer (2008) define the cluster as a strategic network in which companies participate in order to organize their innovation activities in the most efficient way possible. For Michael E. Porter (2007), clusters are formed by "dense networks of interdependent firms" located in specific territories due to spillover effects or externalities. They are represented by a geographic concentration of interdependent firms or "clusters" with activities in the same sector (Porter 1990).

In addition, the cluster form enables, like the open innovation spaces described above, reducing transaction costs and access to information, to have greater flexibility, to share resources more easily, such as technologies and knowledge. The pooling of resources and access to a diversity of skills are other advantages that promote innovation activities. The innovation process is also facilitated and stimulated in such an environment. Indeed, in an environment that is more and more greedy for intangible resources intangible resources such as knowledge and information and the increasing complexity of production processes, a vertical specialization of companies is at work. In such an environment, the geographical proximity of economic actors through co-location is justified in order to reduce transaction costs, transport costs, uncertainty linked to innovation activities, supply economies such as energy, or access to competitive markets (Rallet and Torre 2004; Torre 2016).

Physical proximity also explains the regional level of clusters (Porter 2007). Tacit or informal knowledge circulates and is favored in a defined geographical space, notably thanks to the face-to-face contacts of individuals (Pecqueur and Zimmermann 2004). The usefulness for one actor depends on the presence of other actors in the network. These network externalities are one of the advantages of structuring companies in this way. Like the open innovation process, clusters allow for exchanges with the outside, leading to firms anchored in the cluster local spin-offs generated by external actors (Rallet and Torre 2004).

The transdisciplinary nature of the skills present in a cluster allows the various co-located actors to access them in order to strengthen their own internal skills and to acquire others. The same is true for resources, which can be specific and typical of a territory. Hence, the combination of skills and resources is a major asset for clusters and integrated economic agents, in an increasingly competitive environment where differentiation is a source of added value. Bréchet and Saives (2001) speak of "territorially based competitiveness", where firms can use resources and skills specific to a given territory. Companies have an incentive to become locally involved by soliciting the actors present in the territory. Moreover, firms anchored in clusters have the possibility to access public goods such as specialized skilled workers, certain types of infrastructure that are also specialized or technologies that are not easily accessible outside the cluster.

The clusters can be represented as in Figure 3.2.

In this figure, three distinct dimensions refer to the characteristics – or dimensions – of the territorial anchoring of innovation networks. First of all, spatial embedding integrates the characteristics of the territory and the nature of the relations of proximity. Secondly, inter-organizational embedding is concerned with the strategies of firms and the nature of inter-organizational relations. Finally, social embedding takes into account the history of the actors and the nature of their social relations. All these dimensions overlap, so as to combine the fields of economic geography, strategic management and economic sociology and structural analysis of the markets. The latter is therefore interested in the different aspects of the business environment. The latter is thus interested in multiple aspects of the anchoring of firms collaborating in networks on organizational, social and geographical levels (Balas and Palpacuer 2008). The intersection of these three dimensions can be found in the organization of clusters. The hypothesis of locality or spatial proximity as a factor in strengthening the social and inter-organizational embedding of firms within the cluster is widely established in the literature. Many authors (Jaffe 1989; Audretsch and Feldman 1996; Bottazzi and Peri 2003; Santamaría et al. 2021) have studied this proximity or locality thesis in the dynamics of innovation and creation of collaborative projects by firms (Uzunidis 2010; Aouinaït 2021).

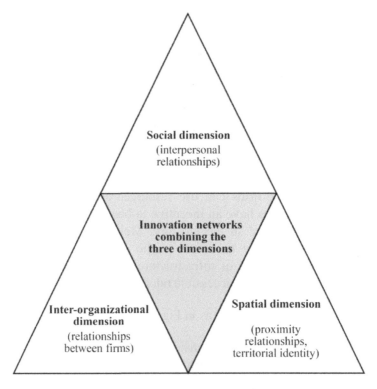

Figure 3.2. *A model of territorial anchoring of innovation networks*

Actors co-located in a cluster can share knowledge, which will be all the more useful since their activities are part of the same industrial specialization. The values and norms they share in addition to this knowledge are important and play a role in the formation of the epistemic community. This notion comes from the work of Cowan et al. (2000), who found that it is easier to "unite these actors in a more sustainable way and strengthen their potential for innovative convergence" (Aliouat and Thiaw 2018). The generation of consensual knowledge, relevance judgments and "cultural epidemiology phenomena" such as scientific and technical are at the basis of the formation of epistemic communities. Within these communities, actors, as co-located in clusters or other forms of organizational and geographical grouping, create activities and generate elements for common projects. Moreover, these epistemic communities influence the technological choices and the use made of them by the partners and promote knowledge spillovers (Balas and Palpacuer 2008; Aliouat and Thiaw 2018). Their importance is such that they can influence market requirements and structure the territory.

In addition, cognitive distance can be reduced in such a configuration, facilitating collaborative approaches around common goals and projects. However, the homogeneity and stability of the interpersonal relationships created by the generation of epistemic communities is a pre-existing condition for the success of collaborations. Indeed, the routines established between individuals, as well as the information exchanged through informal communication, are dependent on this. The fact of being anchored in multidisciplinary dimensions, the tacit knowledge becomes more easily transferable. Its informal nature, transmitted by individuals through regular contact, is a fundamental advantage in structured and organized spaces such as clusters; on the contrary, codified and transferable knowledge in a more systematic way but independent of the context (Balas and Palpacuer 2008). The importance of informal channels in collaboration is no longer in doubt. In low-tech industries, these interactions are widespread and are based on tacit connections (Aouinaït 2019). Social structures, information inherent to the use of a method, process or technology are mainly transmitted through tacit interactions. Contextualization becomes essential to understand and integrate all the information that will be useful to all actors engaging in the collaboration.

The cluster as a network can be identified as a "neighborhood structure" for Cohendet et al. The authors define this neighborhood structure by the distances between the actors in the network, which fall into several categories: geographical distance as traditionally defined in the cluster, and also technical or technological distance and social distance. All the actors (network nodes) are connected to each other by these distances or proximities (links) and form a network that is activated during collaborations for innovation purposes.

Finally, the notion of temporality comes into play when it comes to the needs of companies in collaboration and partnerships. Not all territories are suitable for creating an innovation dynamic resulting from geographical proximity and inter-organizational, spatial and social embedding. The direction of the innovation and the inherent stakes (such as the desire to produce a radical innovation rather than an incremental one according to a strategy of conquering new markets) partly define the types of partners and their geographical position. Balas and Palpacuer (2008) specify that for incremental innovations, firms tend to collaborate with actors that are spatially close; whereas these same firms may internalize innovation for the creation of radical innovations or resort to partners that are geographically distant, with the aim of accessing skills that are not present locally.

Competitiveness clusters, industrial districts and geographical groupings of activities in a given territory are seeing the arrival of a wide variety of players. These actors can be part of the public or private sector. Their identity is also diverse. They are companies of all sizes, laboratories and research centers, associations, consulting or training organizations, among others.

Territorialized public policies are designed to emphasize the particularities of the territories and group together several themes. A well-known example is Silicon Valley in the United States. Companies are co-located in a defined geographical area and specialize in the high-tech and electronics sectors. In Europe, these policies have also been widely used since the 1980s. France is no exception with its Local Production Systems and competitiveness clusters. National public policies have supported their implementation. These clusters promote innovation and development of the territories in which they are anchored. In Spain, the regions of Catalonia and the Basque Country are often studied in the literature. In the Spanish Basque Country, the automotive, port industries, electronics and energy sectors have been targeted by various cluster policies (Institut d'aménagement et d'urbanisme de la région Ile-de-France 2008). Denmark has established a cluster for biotechnology and pharmaceutical-related products in the cross-border region of Öresund with Medicon Valley. In Italy, the Turin region has promoted the wireless technology sector. Veneto has specialized in nanotechnology, while Lombardy is characterized by its biotechnology industries and Bologna by mechanics (Rallet and Torre 2004; Institut d'aménagement et d'urbanisme de la région Ile-de-France 2008).

Collaborative innovation is a key factor in these environments to optimize innovation capabilities on a collective level (Leroux et al. 2014). The temporal scale of innovation is also interesting because the time lag between when the innovation is created and when it is brought to market can be reduced. Firms involved in collective collaborative actions can benefit from this, having added value and financial return of the product earlier.

External factors such as market developments and competition between companies influence the strength of clusters and their ability to sustain themselves in an increasingly competitive environment is being challenged (Porter 2007). The development of information and communication technologies drastically reduces the costs of access to tangible and intangible resources. Access to qualified and cheap labor is thus simplified, and technologies that are not available locally are also more easily accessible. Globalization has a positive effect on clusters, despite their regional nature.

3.2.2. Industrial districts

Industrial districts were described at the end of the 19th century by Alfred Marshall. These industrial districts are an "aggregation of a large number of small workshops, like the creation of a few large factories". They have the particularity of being able to achieve the advantages of large-scale production. The different stages of production are divided in such a way as to achieve economies at each stage "thus forming a district composed of a large number of similar small establishments specialized to carry out a particular stage of the production process" (Daumas 2007).

In addition to these territorial systems of innovation (national, regional or local), there are other types of aggregation of firms at the geographical, technological or organizational level. Indeed, the literature describes through numerous works carried out in recent years, Local Productive Systems (Aydalot 1986; Grossetti 2004), "Local Industrial Systems" (Raveyre and Saglio 1984), "Broader Systems of Innovation" (Edquist 1997), the "Regional Learning Economy" (Cooke et al. 1998) and industrial spaces (Saxenian 1994).

3.2.3. *National Innovation Systems and Local Innovation Systems*

The National Innovation System (NIS) is a set of institutions collaborating to create, disseminate and use new technologies. The interactions between several actors such as universities, private sector companies, public sector companies and government agencies facilitate the production and diffusion of knowledge and technologies (Casadella and Benlahcen-Tlemcani 2006). Within this framework, there are also public policies that focus on technological progress and are implemented in the NIS (Wang et al. 2011). This forms an innovation ecosystem (Laperche et al. 2019). In this ecosystem, institutional, political, research, economic and other actors are connected to each other, as well as the activities and institutions. This network evolves over time according to the relationships that are established between the actors. The innovative performance of the actors, individually or jointly, is subject to the complementarity and substitution of the relationships that bring the ecosystem to life. Several innovation dynamics are then implemented (Laperche and Uzunidis 2007). The National Innovation System evolves in a knowledge and learning economy. This learning concerns the appropriation of technical organizational capabilities through different tools, including education, training, learning-through-doing and imitation. All of these elements are fundamental to the success of companies at the national level. Casadella and Benlahcen-Tlemcani (2006) argue that the speed and form of learning are very important factors for the creativity of countries.

On another scale, the NIS takes shape at the regional level with the Local Innovation System. This system includes regional innovation systems, innovative environments and industrial districts. The relationships that companies create with the other actors present in the system are essential for the system's dynamics. The business, financial and scientific relationships and transfers that are at work are part of the identity and place of companies in the local innovation system, often referred to as the "innovative environment" (Uzunidis 2008). Just as in the National Innovation System and in the paradigm of open innovation paradigm, exchanges and interpersonal relationships are facilitated within a Regional Innovation System. The tacit nature of knowledge is a driving force. Moreover, a common culture and language play a role in this facilitation. The dimensions of proximity are highlighted in such systems (NIS, RIS, clusters and any other territorialized ecosystem), whether it is social proximity, with increasing trust on the part of the actors collaborating within these systems, geographical proximity, institutional proximity, organizational proximity and cognitive proximity (Levy and Woessner 2006). Finally, competitiveness at the regional level is impacted by the capacity of the actors in the regional innovation system (Doloreux and Bitard 2005).

The openness of companies in terms of innovation processes leads them to collaborate with local and international players. The internationalization of open innovation, with companies collaborating with local and also international actors, allows all actors to strengthen their skills. Some skills may be lacking at the local level and are available at a wider geographical level. This is the case for research laboratories that create partnerships with other actors at the international level (Sachwald 2008). Network externalities also come into play in this context, with various types of spillover effects at the territorial level.

3.3. The intermediaries of innovation

Experiences from previous collaborations positively influence future collaborations with both traditional and recurring partners (e.g. suppliers or clients) as well as with partners who collaborate less frequently. Actors who are used to managing collaborations develop certain routines, become familiar with the processes implemented and are therefore more efficient as they use them (Nieto and Santamaría 2007). Laursen and Salter (2006) state that firms "need to maintain a pattern of interaction over time, developing a shared understanding and common ways of working". In addition, collaborations with suppliers enable products to be brought to market more quickly. These types of partners have a significant impact on the generation of marketable innovations, as these innovations benefit from a high degree of novelty (Nieto and Santamaría 2007). The next section presents the role of so-called innovation intermediary actors who form the interface or transition between other actors.

Innovation intermediaries are crucial to the creation and dynamism of "an effective innovation ecosystem" (De Silva et al. 2018). In innovation networks where actors collaborate and interact with each other in projects of innovation generation, transfer and diffusion, specific of innovation, specific actors can play relay and facilitator roles. These actors are innovation intermediaries, which emerged in the 2000s (Capdevila 2015). Howells (2006) defines innovation intermediaries as "an organization or agency that acts as an agent or broker in any aspect of the innovation process between two or more parties". Dalziel (2010) adds that innovation intermediaries are organizations or groups within organizations that facilitate innovation by promoting the innovation capacity of firms, or by improving the innovation capacity at the regional, national or sectoral level. The innovative capacity, according to the author, includes the competitiveness, growth and survival of firms in their environment. Intermediaries search for information, process it, "digest" knowledge and disseminate it with the aim of facilitating its use by the actors of the innovation system. Their other activities are the marketing of products, the evaluation of results, legal support and assistance in the search for financing in particular (Howells 2006). In addition, these intermediaries connect actors to each other, actively involve them and mobilize them. These innovation intermediaries network various actors in the ecosystem in order to improve, fluidify and promote technology development, knowledge transfer, materials and collaborations in a more general way. In addition to these activities, some innovation intermediaries provide services through physical spaces, offer training and consulting workshops for sales and marketing activities (Dalziel 2010). Their role also includes resolving conflicts of interest and stimulating the innovation process and its outcomes (Agogué et al. 2013; Capdevila 2015). Dalziel (2010) adds other roles of innovation intermediaries including "providing access to expertise and equipment, developing standards and supporting systems development, testing and validating new technologies and equipment, adapting technologies to other applications, and managing intellectual property and other activities associated with the commercial exploitation of inventions by university and other public sector researchers". These activities may be funded only by intermediaries and undertaken by the firms themselves. Two American examples are the government's Technology Innovation Program or the Small Business Innovation Research Program. In Europe, the ESPRIT and EUREKA programs are also examples.

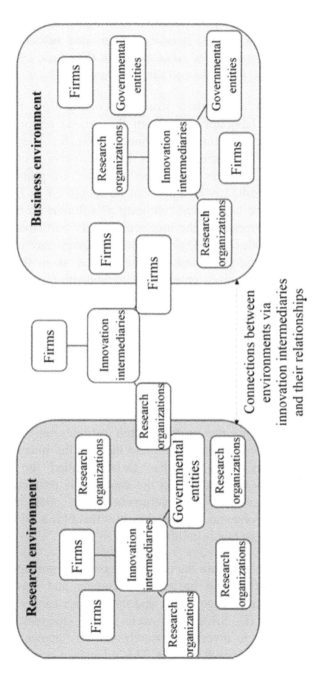

Figure 3.3. *Innovation system (based on Dalziel 2010)*

Clients have the opportunity to actively engage with intermediaries by specifying their needs. Thus, the specialization of intermediaries is redefined according to these specific needs. It is the clients and actors using the intermediaries' activities who know what expertise they lack and need to achieve the desired results (Pecqueur and Zimmermann 2004).

Intermediaries are diverse in their structure, coming from the public sector such as research laboratories or from the private sector, such as companies specialized in consulting and technology transfer. They can also take the form of digital platforms such as Innocentive or Yet2.com or localized spaces where companies come together to solve a problem in an innovative way. As a result, Living Labs can be identified as innovation intermediaries. Indeed, the companies "requesting" solutions contribute to the financing of these spaces, and the local community participates in the search for solutions (Capdevila 2015). The intermediaries may offer local policy support and specific local and specific advice, as in the case of German small- and medium-sized enterprises implementing eco-efficiency innovations (Klewitz et al. 2012).

Commercialization gap or "valley of death" are terms describing the innovation gap that exists between the world of research and the world of commercial activities commercial world (Dalziel 2010). Figure 3.3 presents this gap that is created between the research environment (on the left of the figure) and the business environment commercial environment (on the right of the figure). There is little collaboration between companies, public or private research organizations, non-profit research institutes, universities and government agencies. These actors collaborate through the intervention of innovation intermediaries. This is what Dalziel called the research community. The business community, on the contrary, is characterized by collaboration between companies, government actors and innovation intermediaries. Both environments thus need entities that play a bridging role to reduce the innovation gap that is building.

The innovation gap results from the divergent goals and strategies of the two communities (scientific and business) (Dasgupta and David 1994; Dalziel 2010). Gaps in knowledge, skills and capabilities can be filled by innovation intermediaries (De Silva and Howells 2018). One reason for this is the reluctance of firms to invest in research and development activities that the research community could provide. This reluctance is supplemented by a lack of financial means and also a pressure to create measurable commercial results. Companies that can deliver commercially and financially attractive results are favored for investments and collaborations. Research is shifted away from these economic actors. In Figure 3.3, innovation intermediaries carry out networking activities between actors from both the research and commercial communities. Some of these intermediaries are specialized in networking with one of the two communities and not the other, as with research intermediaries who will not interfere with business support. Figure 3.3 shows the innovation intermediaries that conduct or support technology development activities and operate in the development activities and operate in the innovation gap (Dalziel 2010).

De Silva and Howells (2018) focus on the mechanism of value generation for innovation intermediaries and not only for the actors with whom they collaborate. For both authors, the values generated are pecuniary, on the one hand, with the revenues coming directly from the services rendered to the actors of the ecosystem in which they intervene, and the funding obtained through research grants. On the other hand, non-pecuniary values such as benefits related to the market and network can be identified. Indeed, in view of their active involvement in collaborative projects, co-creation and co-development of innovative projects and products, knowledge, skills and capacities to implement them are created. It is this non-financial aspect that has been identified as the most important for intermediaries. They participate in the reconstruction of innovation systems, in the construction of bridges in these systems. All their activities can strengthen them internally, by increasing their own capacities in helping clients, and externally, by increasing their attractiveness to different actors.

In the agricultural sector, innovation intermediaries are very important for assisting small- and medium-sized agricultural enterprises in the innovation process, to support the Knowledge Intensive Business Service (KIBS) system and to connect demand with supply. Innovation intermediaries can thus articulate this supply-demand correspondence by clarifying them respectively, to create links and social interactions between R&D producers and users. This demand is essential to orient the actors of the customer-oriented knowledge system. Figure 3.4 presents the modalities.

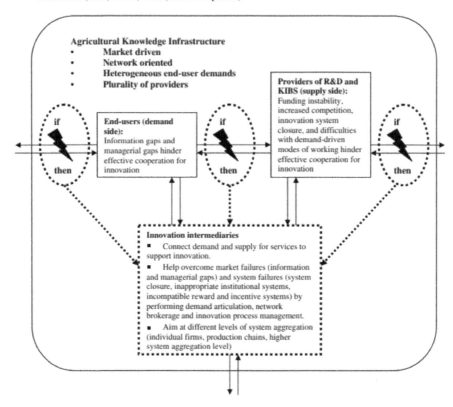

Figure 3.4. *Functions of innovation intermediaries in the agricultural knowledge system (Klerkx and Leeuwis 2008)*

In this agricultural sector, the knowledge structure is built around an agricultural knowledge and information system (AKIS) (Leeuwis 2004; EU SCAR 2012; Barjolle et al. 2014;). This model is effective for knowledge transfer. The goal of AKIS is to consolidate communication and knowledge flow of knowledge between rural communities (Spielman and Birner 2008; EU SCAR 2012). In this system, farmers, processors, associations, and all value chain actors interact with entities outside of agriculture such as public extension services, the policy sector, and government, universities and national public research organizations to disseminate and strengthen the adoption of technological and non-technological innovations in agriculture (Aouinaït 2019).

In addition, innovation intermediaries are present to facilitate the innovation process by identifying the real needs of the actors in order to use an efficient creative process and achieve optimal results. This articulation of the demand is done via informal methods using tacit knowledge, the associated resources and formal methods.

Another function of innovation intermediaries in this agricultural knowledge system cited by Klerkx and Leeuwis (2008) consists of network brokerage. The aim is to overcome market and system failures. The information deficit that may exist between the actors of the system, those present in the market and those wanting to participate in it, can be diminished by the intervention of innovation intermediaries, by a transparency of the market offer of R&D and KIBS. The networks in which innovation intermediaries operate are made available to small- and medium-sized agricultural enterprises. This solution increases the visibility of the firms and the possibilities for future collaborations.

In the case of the Netherlands, the generation of innovation intermediaries emerged as part of a rationalization and centralization of the privatized knowledge infrastructure. The intermediaries then acted as innovation catalysts to maintain a regional innovation capacity. In addition, the provision of advice from independent actors and the formation of a critical mindset for actors embedded in KIBS was paramount. Finally, institutional barriers (standards, legislation) represent barriers for some actors. Innovation intermediaries come into play to reduce these structural barriers.

3.4. Innovation jointly created with users

The product innovation process is described in the literature as a multi-stage process: ideation, concept development, product design, product testing and product market introduction. These stages are reflected in theories of new product development (NPD). These five stages are carried out by companies in collaboration with external actors, as the open innovation process defines it. Among these actors, the customers for whom the products are intended can be among the individuals helping companies to develop innovative products. Thus, firms can use customers at the ideation and concept development stage. By using market research such as focus groups or customer surveys, important information can be collected (Sawhney et al. 2005).

This use of clients and employees in the ideation and development stages of products and projects was introduced by Michelin in the 1920s. It created the idea box, in which employees could submit proposals for improvement on different themes. As employees are closest to the production lines, they are at the heart of the creation process and are therefore an important source of improvement proposals. The success of this strategy prompted other manufacturers such as SNCF to implement this system a few years later. This type of mechanism has been developed in several sectors (industries, banking, telecommunications, for example), advocating a bottom-up strategy where actors or practitioners bring back needs and information from the field. This "idea box" was renamed "participatory platform", "collaborative tool" and "idea management system" (Denervaud et al. 2010).

Thus, users are an important source of innovation. Nearly 40% of consumers in a population have already innovated and are considered innovators themselves (Brem et al. 2019). These users can help increase the innovative capacity of an industry as a whole (Baldwin et al. 2006). Users also contribute to major innovations in consumer goods (Brem et al. 2019). Furthermore, according to von Hippel et al. (2012), the economic power of users can outpace the industry's national R&D spending in value (von Hippel et al. 2012). Innovators who are users may be motivated to create products that they really need and that do not yet exist in the market. These users expect to gain benefits from using the innovation. This primary motivation, as well as the satisfaction of realizing the innovation by themselves, drives them to develop the innovation themselves. According to Füller (2010), factors such as "the fun task, curiosity, self-efficacy, skill development, information seeking, recognition (visibility), community support, making friends, dissatisfaction with existing products, and monetary benefits" are the main underlying motivations why users push to innovate. The financial investment and time spent developing these innovations are done within the communities of innovative users. Peer support and access to a variety of skills make this an innovative creative space (Brem et al. 2019).

Buisine et al. (2017), on the contrary, developed the extraordinary user method. In this method, the principle is to use a user-centered design, taking as a base a population of "extraordinary" users, so-called because they have cognitive, motor and sensory abilities that diverge from the norm. Moreover, they are generally not targeted by advertising campaigns and marketing developed by companies to encourage customers to consume. These extraordinary users may therefore be children, non-users of the targeted products, seniors, or people with disabilities. In Figure 3.1, the needs of these users are studied because they are considered to stimulate radical innovation. This also serves to avoid the innovator's dilemma. This phenomenon was described by Clayton Christensen (1997), explaining that companies that are already well established in the market may fail in the face of radical innovation (e.g. creation of a whole new market), maintaining their leadership position by performing rather incremental innovations. This dilemma is therefore to be avoided as much as possible by companies. Therefore, after having identified the new needs of extraordinary users, solutions are sought and evaluated. Finally, the attention is turned back to the classic users, in the traditional cycle of innovation development, to perfect the development cycle, to perfect the innovative solutions to be brought to the initially studied needs.

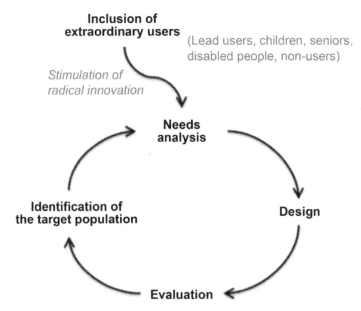

Figure 3.5. *Extraordinary user method (Buisine et al. 2017)*

This method induces involuntary user collaboration in the innovation strategy. With increasingly heterogeneous needs from users and consumers, this method could be used more and more in the future by companies with the necessary resources. The method will help them to be able to develop innovations, whether radical or not, that are most suitable for customers.

Previous research has shown that innovative users are likely to have specific personal characteristics that make them more likely to be actively involved in new product development. In analyzing who is most likely to innovate, research has identified some personal characteristics that innovative users may have in common, for example: domain-specific skills, adoption and capacity innovation, novelty seeking (Lüthje 2002; Füller 2010). Interestingly, different people with an innovative user character and mindset may behave differently in the long run. Some continue to innovate by themselves and for themselves, while others evolve into new roles and eventually become entrepreneurial users.

Rosenberg (1976) described the involvement of users in the development of new products in the American machine tool industry. Lathes and milling machines were thus developed by customers with a defined need. Machine tools were developed by textile manufacturing companies, firearms manufacturers and sewing machine manufacturers. The oil refining industry also saw users create, develop and market innovations (Enos 1962), as did the chemical industry (Freeman 1968). Von Hippel (1976) has, in this way, studied the importance of user involvement in the innovation process. As a result, about 80% of the most important innovations in scientific instruments and semiconductor processing were developed by the users of these products. The same is true for Shah (2000) with regard to the sports equipment sector. These studies demonstrate the great importance of the role of users in the innovation process, for which they have been at the origin of many initiatives and developments in many sectors.

These users are also starting to sell their innovations to other users, the Internet being a very powerful tool for putting all these actors together, in networks. The ease of communicating and collaborating facilitates the diffusion process of innovations. Resources and skills are pooled. However, the financial resources needed to stimulate innovation are limited for innovative users. They can then develop innovations using inferior products, and play on variable cost structures. The new crowdfunding-type platforms have made it possible to reduce these situations and to be financially supported. These platforms are intermediaries for the acquisition of funds that reveal greater potential for innovation for innovative users. The advantage of using crowdfunding platforms lies in the possibility of accessing larger markets and reaching a larger sample of users for the innovation generated (von Hippel 2005). Moreover, in the field of open source software, user communities have become very important over the years and are now indispensable in user-driven innovation processes (Brem et al. 2019). In addition to the accessibility of resources, skills and knowledge from the presence of users and peers within these communities, the temporal aspect becomes non-negligible. All these elements are available over a long period of time. The phenomenon of "free revelation" described by von Hippel (2005) takes place between innovative users sharing similar ideas. These innovators are led to share their results in an environment of exchange and support. This phenomenon is considered crucial in user innovation theory (von Hippel 2005; Brem et al. 2019).

Not all innovative users can bring to market the innovations they have created. Indeed, financial resources are required to bring a product to market. For radically new products, users with limited financial resources can rely on a structure of high variable costs and low investments. When the economic limits are too strong, it is the large companies that can manufacture the innovation that take over and commercialize it, due to their superior resources and capacities, especially for development and marketing activities (Shah and Tripsas 2012).

Like user communities that facilitate the collaborative creative process leading to a user solution, pools of consumers serve as catalysts, but support the scaling and commercialization of user solutions. They are the "fuel" that allows truly new ideas to come to life and thrive, as they provide significant financial resources by tapping into "markets before the market" that bring together users with a need for a certain situation beyond the boundaries of a user community.

Examples of major innovations developed by user companies were presented by von Hippel (2005) in his literature review. Thus, in the oil refining sector, major innovations have been developed by user firms, as well as in the chemical production sector, scientific instruments or semiconductor processing. In his work, von Hippel (2005) establishes that innovative products developed by individual users or user firms of consumer goods are bound to be disseminated and used by many users and not only internally. This is the case for 24.3% of the respondents who use design software for printed circuit boards, or 19.2% of the cyclists located in a region that stimulates innovation in mountain sports. The use of user communities, online, via platforms and other digital tools that are easily accessible with the development of new information and communication technologies is essential at this stage. Dissemination of these innovations takes an important part in the innovation process, because unlike large companies and organizations with financial resources to be able to communicate on their innovations, if users do not disseminate their innovations, future users who would need to be aware of the novelty. They could in turn decide to develop the same innovation. The collaborations implemented to jointly develop innovations must be implemented efficiently for the optimal use of resources and the creation of value *in fine*.

Motivations to participate in a creative process were classified by Bonnemaizon et al. (2013). Motivations to participate in a creative process can be extrinsic or intrinsic. For extrinsic motivations, the consumer expects to receive a benefit that will be independent of the activity in which they will participate (e.g. receiving a reward or gaining approval). For intrinsic motivations, on the contrary, the consumer acts according to the interests, curiosity and potential pleasure generated by the activity (e.g. a feeling of success, a feeling of prestige, simple pleasure, the playful nature of the activity or the expression of their creative potential). These motivations, crossed with the type of resources mobilized (ordinary – financial, communication resources; extraordinary – logistical resources, specific capacities to carry out a specific task), leads the authors to present four classes. Through this classification, they show that consumer intervention can take various forms and importance in innovation. Four types of customers are identified through this categorization: the executing customer (ordinary mobilized resources and extrinsic motivations), the relay or subcontracting customer (extraordinary mobilized resources and extrinsic motivations), the solution-providing customer (extraordinary mobilized resources and intrinsic motivations) and the marketing and operational assistant customer (ordinary mobilized resources and intrinsic motivations). Their tasks are different, subject to divergent motivations and resources, but all have the same goal to innovate.

Similarly, Cova (2008) identifies four types of processes along two axes. The first differentiates between the co-creation of the offer and the co-creation of the experience. Consumers are involved in the definition of products in the first case (upstream of the production process), while consumers are involved in their experience of the product in the second (downstream of the production process). The second axis defines the expertise of consumers. These can be ordinary or creative.

Co-innovation takes place by creative consumers who are involved in the production of products and services. Platforms have been created in this context such as "MyStarbucksIdea" and "share your ideas Nokia". Co-promotion concerns the production of advertisements by the consumer and the firm. Ordinary consumers are consulted by firms in the form of a competition for the production of advertising visuals. Word-of-mouth is also part of this co-promotion phase. For the co-production, the firm proposes to the consumers to realize its experience. This was the case with the music group Radiohead, which invited consumers to remix one of its tracks. A vote was then carried out publicly to select the best remixed track. Finally, co-determination allows the firm to promote the correspondence between the needs of the company and creative consumers. The latter can share their desire for innovation, without acting on the offer as is the case for co-innovation.

Moreover, collaboration exists between companies, between universities and companies, between the public and private sectors, and also between students and teachers. A new educational approach consists of collaborative learning that aims to emphasize the group effect, to find solutions to defined problems. This is the educational paradigm in which students themselves manage their learning using the group as a working tool (Delgado et al. 2020). The social and cognitive dimensions are emphasized in this paradigm, to increase the success of collaborative learning, on which mutual help is one of the bases.

Finally, "collective intelligence" was studied in particular by Pierre Lévy in his 1994 book. Bageac (2013) studies this concept and outlines principles that can be found in open innovation drawing some interesting characteristics. The author defines collective intelligence as "an intelligence that is distributed everywhere, constantly enhanced, coordinated in real-time, and that leads to an effective mobilization of skills". Already at that time, Lévy discussed the digital development that promotes remote connections via facilitated communications and can encourage collaborative work. Indeed, in the above definition, open innovation takes up the principle of universal distribution ("distributed everywhere"), in which knowledge is possessed by many individuals, fragmented on a geographical scale, and who, put together, can reconstitute a more complete knowledge. Second, constant valorization ("a constantly valorized intelligence") resonates with the locality where the actors are located. The valorization is done at the local level, where each individual or organization involved in the process of open innovation, contributes. "Real-time" coordination takes place via information and communication technologies. Finally, the "effective mobilization of skills" implies that a social organization of individuals anchored in the collaborative networks is based on a diversified knowledge base. Thanks to this collective intelligence decentralization of knowledge is possible. The actors complement each other, each bringing their expertise and specialties to a collaborative project. All actors are thus valued, regardless of their size and location. Thus, Lévy stipulates that companies involved in open innovation "must be open to a continuous and ever-renewed circulation of scientific, technical, social or even aesthetic know-how" (Lévy 1994).

New physical spaces where collaboration and/or the concentration of innovators is the main asset have developed a lot in the last few years. Numerous FabLab, maker spaces, Living Labs, hacker spaces, coworking spaces and all these third places outside the premises belonging to companies have flourished around the world. We have seen that the mode of governance (top-down vs. bottom-up) of these environments and the strategy of the actors (exploration vs. exploitation) vary. Within these spaces, the innovation ambitions of the actors are concretized by the exchange of experience, knowledge and know-how of each other. Geographical proximity facilitates the creation of collaborative projects. It can be joined by social proximity with an increased possibility of sustained social relationships in an incubator environment such as these third places. The other proximities (i.e. institutional, organizational and cognitive) can also support the innovation project and thus promote the interesting development of collaborative innovations.

In addition, the structuring of actors in a geographically limited space has also been studied with many examples of clusters or industrial districts. These are determined by spatial, inter-organizational and social forms of embedding in which the history of the actors and their interpersonal and inter-organizational relationships and the strategies that the companies adopt in order to develop new innovation processes are inscribed. The actors in the innovation ecosystem have varied profiles and are present at several levels of the sector (e.g. suppliers, customers, industrialists), in several sectors (e.g. public or private) and fields. Entities that have proven their ability to facilitate the innovation process, for example through scientific popularization, knowledge transfer or technology transfer, for example, are said to be "intermediaries" of innovation. This role is becoming increasingly important in general. Companies are dedicating more and more resources to open innovation, a key mechanism for ensuring that innovative products or services are adapted to market demand.

Finally, this chapter presented the development of innovations by and with the users of these innovations. The idea box, the use of notices to improve products or working conditions or the solicitation on a larger scale of an informed or novice public via participative platforms are increasingly part of firms' strategies to innovate, whether internally or externally and collaboratively.

4

Advantages, Disadvantages and Issues Related to Collaborative Innovation

Open innovation and collaborative innovation come from the field of innovation management and technology management. This model of innovation has been used and studied in Research and Development (R&D) activities in various sectors. The fields of business strategy and organizational behavior are interested in open innovation and the possible strategies to implement. Indeed, it appears that this approach to innovation is growing in a plurality of ways, in social sciences in particular. Moreover, open innovation is not confined to large companies with greater resources and possibilities than small and medium-sized enterprises. The same is true for the sectors using it. Whether they are focused on new technologies, traditional manufacturing of mainstream products or niche production, collaborative innovation has a great future and many opportunities (Gassman et al. 2010).

4.1. Benefits of collaborative innovation for the actors involved

The benefits of open innovation are numerous. They include the results of the innovation, the innovation process itself, access to markets (e.g. new markets or a strengthened competitive position in existing markets) or the reputation of the actors involved in the collaboration (Isckia and Lescop 2011). Moreover, an improvement in the innovation process can be achieved thanks to the knowledge acquired through the collaboration with actors contributing this knowledge. Cross-licensing can avoid patent infringement, feared by companies (Mention and Torkkeli 2014).

One of the most obvious advantages of collaborative innovation is the creation of innovative projects, materialized by different kinds of collaborations between agents (Loilier and Tellier 2001). The fact that these agents have common interests enables the creation of co-development logics (Isckia and Lescop 2011). This collaborative development can take place through the implementation of activities carried out in the research and development departments that many companies (especially the larger ones) have integrated. This department is crucial for generating innovation. It is also an economic and technological position where the implementation of collaborations is strategic.

Another of the direct benefits of establishing collaborations in order to generate innovation is the externalities and impacts, which can be spread within and outside the boundaries of the company. The process of opening up innovation is crucial for companies, which can then integrate knowledge and materials within their borders that will be useful to them and that can be part of the R&D in subsequent projects. Moreover, the inside-out and outside-in processes enable "dormant" or little-used ideas that reside inside firms to go outside these boundaries and be valued by other actors first, and to internalize inputs and assets in firms second (Chesbrough 2011; Isckia and Lescop 2011). The combination of these two processes allows for an aggregation of "sourcing" possibilities, in other words, finding new sources useful for innovation, whether inside or outside the firms, in the network created by the collaborations developed. The knowledge base can be expanded and the accumulation of this knowledge brings new ideas and potentialities. The various partners involved in innovative projects are fundamental entry and dissemination points for producing usable and interesting elements for all stakeholders. Through these components, the use of several information and knowledge research mechanisms to be able to innovate is a strategic axis.

The benefits of open innovation have been studied and highlighted in many works. Diversity of partners is often cited as a key to innovation Burger-Helmcehn et al. 2013). The more heterogeneous the collaboration networks are, the greater the access to sources of information. This engenders a greater likelihood of innovating differently, developing less expected or even more original innovations. Selecting ideas from different disciplines, as well as actors with different views of the world, or at least of the sectors in which they operate, can become a great strength of the collaboration. However, this strength needs to be at least minimally framed in order to be able to control the direction in which the ideas are formalized and not diverge too much. Moreover, the value capture possible with open innovation adds to the advantages that the open innovation model brings. The ecosystem in which companies are included changes with the collaboration with actors from different environments. This ecosystem can thus act as a point of attraction for new customers and markets (West 2006). Firms open up to their external environment and position themselves as entities with which collaboration becomes attractive to various types of partners. The gain in knowledge and specialized skills necessary for the innovation process acts as an attraction factor for new partners (Loilier and Tellier 2001). This attractiveness of firms and the increase in visibility is a definite advantage of collaborative innovation (Mention and Torekkli 2014). The positive spillover effects created by such partnerships spill over to all actors, and the presence of one actor in the network can benefit others.

The environment in which actors operate is equally important for the implementation of collaborative innovation strategies. The flows of knowledge and material and immaterial goods that circulate between the actors of the network, and within companies themselves, between their departments, do so in a specific environment. The actors must analyze this environment to make the most of it. Mintzberg (1982) writes that the environment is defined by (i) stability or dynamics, (ii) complexity, (iii) diversity of markets and (iv) hostility. Stability and dynamics refer to the changes that occur in the environment, allowing it to become dynamic through the innovations developed and put in place. An example of this characteristic is the sector of new information and communication technologies, which wants to be active and can accelerate the transition of certain sectors in view of the societal and environmental transformations at work. The complexity of an environment takes into account the level of skills required to acquire new knowledge and to use it efficiently and frequently. The aeronautics sector is a good example in which the knowledge and skills inherent in the activities to be carried out are complex. Once this knowledge and these skills are acquired, they can be implemented and integrated into innovations on a daily basis. This brings us back to the capacity of companies, which must be at a minimum threshold to be able to use the knowledge collected. The diversity of markets reflects the needs of the customers, as well as the distribution methods and the capacity of players to diversify and adapt to market fluctuations (including constantly changing customer and consumer demand). Finally, hostility, according to Mintzberg, includes the socio-political environment in which the firm operates. This hostility criterion is defined by the modes of governance of the markets, the regulations associated with these markets and the changes that they undergo. The oil industry sector is characterized by a hostile environment due to strong competition and a strong tension at the level of the prices and the actors who evolve there. As a result, the environment in which any firm is embedded, conducts its business and creates partnerships is a key element that can be beneficial in driving innovation strategies (Steiner 2014).

Open innovation is a well of possible and available ideas and technologies that companies can tap into to extract opportunities and strengthen internal innovation and growth (Khedher 2010). Docherty (2006) sees open innovation as leveraging R&D to the outside of the firm. It is possible to focus on certain internal resources selected upstream on the process of discovery, selection and management of the implementation of the innovation. These resources are initially present in the firms and are also acquired through collaborations. Consequently, other resources can be dedicated to the management of ideas and technologies drawn from collaborative networks.

Khedher (2010) further explores the benefits that Vanhaverbeke et al. (2008) report. They argue that any involvement of firms in the innovation process, technology development and business opportunity is a benefit of open innovation. In addition, the possibility of delaying any financial commitment, due to the flexibility of the time frame for bringing the innovation to light, represents a consequent advantage. In this sense, spin-off activities that consist of entrepreneurs creating their own company such as the spin-off allow companies to manage the development of entities founded outside the company itself. In addition, companies also have the possibility to leave the market promptly to avoid any loss that would occur following the marketing of the innovation concerned. The capacity to valorize internal projects that stagnate and do not find a dynamic to develop them is also superior in collaborative innovation projects.

In addition to the positive impact of collaborative innovation on companies, it is to the actors that this collaboration process brings a positive effect. The change of attitude on the part of the actors involved in the collaborations can bring positive effects. St. Pierre and Hanel (2005) use the example of collaborations between universities and private sector industries.

Conflicts based on institutional and cultural dissension can hinder established collaborations. However, even though the motivations and interests of each party may diverge, their engagement in such collaborative strategies leads them to find common ground. Cohen et al. (1994) take this university–firm collaboration and cite as benefits to firms the acquisition of scientific and technological knowledge that can be used to create economic value, and the improvement of employee skills and knowledge, which is confirmed by Guillemot et al. (2016). Conversely, the university derives other benefits such as additional revenue, increasing attractiveness to new "star" researchers and students, facilitating placement of graduates in companies and the potential to acquire new research contracts.

In addition to the benefits for actors such as university and company in bilateral collaborations, Guillemot et al. (2016) identify benefits based on the type of project. The economies of scale that are achieved by sharing knowledge, or even technologies and infrastructures, are one of the motivations, even if indirect, for actors to join these projects (Mention and Torekkli 2014). The budgetary synergy and the pooling of equipment allow companies to use infrastructures that would not have been accessible without collaboration and opening up the innovation process. In addition, the reduction of risks represents a crucial advantage for all actors involved in an innovation process. By definition, innovating includes some of the risks that the actors accept to incur. The costs are shared by the stakeholders of the projects, and then the risks and the negative repercussions are also shared. Guillemot et al. (2016) cite projects created between suppliers and principals that facilitate a long-term and common vision, as well as the acquisition of commercial contracts. The benefits may outweigh the risks in cases such as this.

In terms of small and medium-sized enterprises, the scope of vision that they can have can be broadened in addition to the advantages mentioned above (possibility of using infrastructures and equipment present in large companies, universities or research laboratories for example, reduction of risks and costs related to innovation, and broadening of skills and knowledge bases). The use of information and communication tools and technologies can lead to sustainable habits that can help SMEs in their future management. Opening up to projects with partners of various profiles such as suppliers, customers or public institutions allows for integration into the ecosystem and a more secure place (Guillemot et al. 2016). The fact of entering a collaborative network can be beneficial for companies in the long-term, as their visibility is increased.

Trust is a factor that is sought after by the actors entering into collaboration. It can be a lever for development at several levels, whether it is between companies, between collaborators within companies, between partners in collaborative projects and between hierarchical levels in organizations. In addition to trust at the institutional level, interpersonal trust is also established. Actors collaborating in projects over the long-term interact frequently, with multiple means of communication (e.g. face-to-face, virtual conference, telephone, email exchanges), through formal meetings, project-related events such as field visits, conferences, seminars, meetings, discussions, annual, bi-monthly, or other initially decided frequency updates (Teece 1986; Goffin et al. 2011). All of these opportunities for interaction create interpersonal bonds of varying strength, which may extend beyond the project and lead to informal meetings. This aspect of collaboration is important, as a sense of trust also allows for creativity and flexibility in projects (Dupont et al. 2019). Trust also relates to the methodologies and tools used in projects.

Dupont et al. (2019) identifies a scale of trust that ranges from limited trust to collaborative trust. Trust is composed of the benevolence "of the other to which we submit" and the ability "of the other to have the skills, knowledge, know-how in a given field" and integrity or "adherence to a group of values such as respect for our commitments". Indeed, the authors take up the work of Pirola-Merlo (2010) on agile innovation and speak of a positive correlation between the speed to complete an R&D project and the climate of a team. As described above, the trust established between collaborators and actors of a project not belonging to the same organization can positively influence the project. Thus, Pirola-Merlo describes the climate according to four characteristics: "(1) the sharing of clear and appreciated objectives; (2) a non-threatening environment where members can influence discussions and decisions; (3) the concern to achieve excellence through quality work and critical evaluation; (4) valuing innovation and supporting work practices that achieve innovation". These characteristics are typically found in projects conducted collaboratively by actors from different backgrounds, as well as those that may have a history of collaborating as well. Mignon and Laperche (2018) refer to relational capital and cognitive capital as vectors of knowledge transfer in the network between different actors, organizations, companies, associations, industries and within these entities. The trust characteristic of this relational capital and a defined common vision reflecting the cognitive capital prove to be strengths of collaborative projects.

The structuring of actors in Living Labs is another example where mutual trust between actors guarantees the progress of projects (Dupont et al. 2019). The Living Labs environment allows for exchanges between actors, in an ecosystem or community logic. The openness of these spaces is often high, so sharing of intellectual property can be facilitated. Moreover, stakeholders can participate to several degrees, depending on their willingness to be involved. Finally, Béjean et al. (2021) indicate that Living Labs can serve as intermediaries in open innovation processes within the community and the territory under consideration. Research is still underdeveloped on the theme of community innovation ecosystems, where Living Labs can be integrated. Koenig (2012) emphasizes the aspect of decentralization of resource control in this type of ecosystem. One of the goals of the actors is to operate on a global scale based on the resources of the community and the strength of the network. Authors who have studied examples of Living Labs also see an interesting trust established in these spaces, and several forms of sharing for innovation are possible.

Measuring the performance of innovation can be a method for identifying the added value of it. Indicators based on the inputs and outputs of innovation projects are generally used (Le Bas and Torre 1993). Research and development activities are frequently measured, such as investments and expenditures on human resources. The number and level of education of researchers, for projects involving universities and/or research laboratories, is another indicator measuring input. As far as outputs are concerned, the rate of adoption of innovations and the rate of user satisfaction are often measured. This is also the case for the number of publications to measure knowledge transfer, the number of patents filed and the share of sales generated by commercialized innovations over a medium-term period (Daane et al. 2009). All these measures shed light on the success of innovations, but are limited because crucial information is missing from the analysis. The scope of the R&D involved is not measured, the skills used and the knowledge mobilized, and the many innovations that are not patented or not protected by another intellectual property right are other examples (Le Bas and Torre 1993).

4.1.1. *The modes of knowledge transfer and their implications on collaborative innovation*

In established university–business collaborations, D'Este and Patel (2005) identified interactions as "creation of new physical facilities, consulting and contract research, joint research, training, meetings and conferences". In general, the interactions that are established are a long-term construct that allow for the exchange of knowledge (Wood et al. 2014). Collaborative innovation involves the co-creation of knowledge and a transfer of that knowledge to multiple recipients. This knowledge transfer occurs in a tacit/uncoded or formalized/coded manner. However, the exchange or transfer of knowledge and information involves significant costs and is dependent on the type of knowledge (i.e. codified or tacit knowledge), as well as the integration of technology (Schartinger et al. 2002). The advantage of using tacit knowledge transfer lies in its nature, that is, embedded in individuals because it is acquired through accumulated experiences. Tacit knowledge is a non-rival good; it can be transmitted to other firms (Gilbert et al. 2004) and is "a powerful means of exclusion" (Foray 2004). These characteristics induce the need for profound relationships between actors, so as to be able to transmit this knowledge, which is dependent on the context in which it was generated and known as sticky (von Hippel 1994). The term stickiness is used to define information that has the potential to be transferred in different environments, taking into account its quantity, its nature and the characteristics of the future user. On the other hand, tacit knowledge is important for the use of new technologies (Dosi and Nelson 2010). It is embedded in organizational routines and transmitted via social processes (Ingram 1985), hindering the transfer of this knowledge in different environments (Ruttan 2002) and reinforcing daily collaborations with different partners (Lawson and Lorenz 1999). Knowledge produced in a local context is transferred through social processes, because it is embedded in a social setting (Ingram 1985). As a result, informal interactions represent an effective channel for knowledge diffusion (Dahl and Pedersen 2004).

On the other hand, opportunities for innovation can be increased by the effective distribution of knowledge (Foray and Lundvall 1994). The flow of knowledge between actors involved in collaborative projects is fundamental to the success of the project, hence the importance of relationships created over the long-term.

In contrast, codified knowledge found in documented information (e.g. patents, certificates, archives, databases) is more easily transferable. Some authors have noted, however, that experience and know-how are not exclusive to informal interactions and can be part of formalized collaborations between partners (Almeida and Kogut 1999; Russell et al. 2004). They also require sustained collaboration, which requires trust through the disclosure of potentially sensitive data (Howells 1996; Cowan et al. 2000). It has been shown that formal relationships are preceded by informal relationships (Bercovitz and Feldmann 2006), such as the sharing of experiences, or the transfer of know-how between partners in local and specific contexts (Teece 1986; Goffin et al. 2011). The evolution of the sociotechnical network initially anchored in interpersonal relationships can be formalized and expand, arriving at a formal network of diverse stakeholders localized in an extended space (Mignon and Laperche 2018). As a result, the new network created on the basis of initially informal interactions solidifies and can make way for the establishment of potentially successful collaborations in the future.

Another angle of analysis of the tacit and codified knowledge flows that take place in innovation ecosystems composed of actors seeking to create innovation focuses on the difference between the STI (Science Technology and Innovation) and DUI (Doing Using and Interacting) modes (Parilli and Alcade Heras 2016). The exchange of both types of knowledge is the basis of the first model, while the second model encourages the use of both types of knowledge in parallel, coming from experiments performed and creating a knowledge base for future projects. In sum, whether the collaborations use informal and/or formal interactions to create contextual knowledge and information flows of contextual, scientific or economic knowledge and information, both types of knowledge and interactions are fundamental and used in collaborative innovation strategies.

Thus, tacit and codified interactions are used in a multitude of sectors (Grimpe and Hussinger 2013). Their combined use ensures effective knowledge transfer and innovation adoption (Morgan and Murdoch 2000). Mignon and Laperche (2018) also note the influence of sharing of a common language and the frequency of these formal and informal contacts in facilitating knowledge transfer (Burger-Helmcehn et al. 2013), as does the connection and frequency of contact (Argote et al. 2003). Sharing a common language facilitates knowledge transfer, as companies in different sectors may not use the same vocabularies (Aouinaït 2021). A similar language is then the basis for agreement and understanding between partners and facilitates their communication (Burger-Helmcehn et al. 2013).

One notable effect of university–industry collaborations through informal research and development is the contribution to technological change (Biggs and Clay 1981). The processes at work in informal R&D make direct use of the users of the technology to solve problems inherent in a local environment using knowledge embedded in that environment. Therefore, collaborative innovation can use informal interactions to create and maintain relationships between partners, traditionally studied between universities and industries (Kongsted et al. 2017).

4.1.2. The role of collaborative innovation at the economic, social, societal and environmental levels

Collaborative innovation has the advantage of being able to push actors in directions that are socially, economically and environmentally on the agenda. Indeed, the movements generated by civil society, taken up by the private sector and public institutions that support the initiatives of actors advocating a more eco-responsible, sustainable and healthy world, have been important for several decades (and increasingly so). Developing short food supply chains (i.e. finding a social link between producers and consumers, to reduce the number of intermediaries and ownership of our food choices), developing well-being at work and supporting the local economy are all examples of movements and sectors that can be supported and improved with open and collaborative innovation processes (Dupont et al. 2019).

4.1.2.1. Importance of information and communication technologies

The advent of new information and communication technologies (ICT) has had an impact on the economy and the environment in particular. ICTs have enabled many advances and facilitation of processes in companies. They are considered as vectors of transformation of organizations (Lethiais 2015). The use of ICT is frequent in the innovative activities of companies (Cainelli et al. 2006; Deltour and Lethiais 2014). In addition, their development and mass diffusion have influenced people's lifestyles such as in the world of work, communication modes, travel and also leisure activities. Changes have occurred at both the individual and organizational levels.

From an environmental point of view, significant impacts can be identified, due to the manufacturing of the electronic components of all the devices needed in the use of ICT. Liénart and Castiaux (2012) take the example of an electronic chip that needs mostly non-renewable resources, which uses 160 times more of these resources than for a computer and almost 300 times more than for a car. However, these electronic chips are found in a very large number of products that we use every day. Moreover, the disposal of these electronic components is very significant. The obsolescence of devices increases this rotation of electronic devices, pushing production to continue to intensify and innovate. In 2014, 75 billion kilos of electrical and electronic equipment waste were counted worldwide. The environment, which is an increasingly important aspect in the strategy of firms and which integrates it in innovation projects, is thus subject to very strong negative externalities. ICTs are therefore ambivalent, representing part of the problem as well as the solution thanks to their capacity to reduce the amount of greenhouse gases or the carbon footprint of the users of all these technologies. The "greening" of ICT equipment and their support functions, as well as their potential to green other sectors, make them a crucial source of innovative solutions.

Moreover, the improvement of digital tools enables exponential gains in their material and socio-economic performance. ICTs are used to store, process and transmit data. The capacities of the machines used to perform these activities can be increased, as well as their functionalities and the costs inherent to their commissioning and maintenance. ICT allows for efficient and less expensive information transfer through reductions in travel by collaborators to discuss and work together on a common project (Steiner 2014; Lethiais et al. 2015). Nambisan (2013) classifies ICT as a "means of activating key resources internally or mobilizing resources externally". The possibilities of communication between partners collaborating in innovation projects are multiple and facilitated through the deployment of these digital tools on a large scale. The barriers of space and time are thus diminished, if not completely reduced. The sharing of files and the possibility of modifying documents in real-time thanks to digital tools greatly facilitate these collaborations (Gangloff-Ziegler 2009). In addition, studies have shown the positive externalities in terms of innovation that ICT can create (Cainelli et al. 2006; Martin and Nguyen-Thi 2015). Information and communication technologies are used as project and resource management systems, knowledge management systems, work knowledge management systems and collaborative work systems. These four uses give impetus to collaborations and can foster the development of innovations. Banker et al. (2006) support this theory by mentioning the development cycle and the related costs that would be reduced by the use of ICT. The quality of the innovation would be positively impacted, as well as the potential reuse in other contexts. Collaborative methods, tools and software used by project stakeholders support collaboration between these people. Certain types of ICT are able to refine the understanding of the market that stakeholders must achieve before launching and commercializing an innovation. It is through fruitful exchanges with customers via easy-to-access digital spaces (such as discussion forums, social networks or even just e-mails exchanged between customers and suppliers) that we can improve the quality of our services, social networks or even just e-mails that the innovations produced can best correspond to the expectations of customers and consumers (Cainelli et al. 2006).

Many examples of uses of the new digital tools that comprise ICT exist on the market and have also been studied in the literature. A growing example of the use of ICT in collaborative innovation practices is crowdsourcing, as presented in Chapter 2. In the early 2000s, Internet platforms were created and were becoming more and more widespread. They bring together actors, those who propose problems to be solved, those (experts or amateur novices) who invest themselves in providing solutions, those who ask for financial support to develop a project and those who commit to helping them. Steiner (2014) evokes Lebraty's (2007) terms to define crowdsourcing. The author describes it as "outsourcing by an organization, via a website, of an activity to a large number of individuals whose identities are most often anonymous". Since their development two decades ago, these communities have sprouted like plants in full vegetative season to concern an abundance of issues and sectors. Crowdsourcing platforms and other participatory funding models are becoming increasingly diverse. In a period marked by a very significant increase of virtual relationships and more and more restricted physical displacements, especially against the backdrop of the global health crisis, the future of these platforms and of digital innovations in this sense is practically assured.

ICTs are therefore capable of increasing the innovation capacity of actors, provided that these actors collaborate efficiently (Lethiais 2015). The author considers that this situation holds for a variety of types of innovations (product or process) with generic or innovation-specific technologies. Compared to firms that use four or fewer different types of ICT, the probability of innovating would be multiplied by 1.8 when firms use five to seven different types of ICT. This probability is multiplied by 2.2 when firms use eight or more different types of ICT. It is clear with these data that multiple forms of ICT contribute to innovation (Cainelli et al. 2006; Martin and Nguyen-Thi 2015). These results are conditional on the availability of a skilled workforce experienced in the use of these new technologies. The IT departments or services of companies are thus increasingly developed and have their importance in the firm, in the same way as the Research and Development department, which is at the heart of the innovation process.

In addition, the development of manufacturing technologies and the digitalization of organizations encourage the development of collaboration between actors in innovation projects. A digital transition has begun in recent years, which is changing the business through the use of new information and communication technologies, such as applications, the use of the cloud for storage and sharing of data (Zacklad 2020). The development of digital technology has enabled the multiplication of innovations, especially those that are easily accessible to innovators or leaders. One of the drawbacks cited by the author lies in the nature of the digital technologies that are developed. These can be classified as substitutive, "rationalizing" or "enabling". For the first category, the major negative impact is the elimination of jobs in sectors where technology replaces humans to do fairly basic tasks and where productivity is of great interest to the firms that implement these technologies. For the second category, even if humans are not replaced by technology, the latter imposes strict and normative "coordination mechanisms". The so-called "enabling" technologies are used in symbiosis with human beings, such as applications that are integrated into the work environment and are not intended to replace or manage employees.

4.1.2.2. *Innovation and corporate social responsibility*

Responsible innovation is part of innovation and research policies, notably with the development of seminars or conferences, or in programs developed in the European Union such as the H2020 program with an interdisciplinary approach dedicated to it (science with and for society). This theme aims at a better connection between science and all stakeholders of society, with a particular focus on responsible research and innovation (e.g. open science, access to data, ethics, gender, science education). In the OECD, projects take it into account, such as the Responsible Innovation for

Personalised Health project, dedicated to emerging technologies (Debref et al. 2019).

Many studies have focused on corporate social responsibility (CSR) and its link with innovation. There is no consensus on the definition of CSR, especially since managerial culture is an important contextual factor. The vision of CSR in Europe and the United States is thus divergent, where in Europe the social aspect is very important with interactions aimed at being implemented in different departments of companies. The delimitation of the concept of CSR and the weighting of criteria for its implementation are debated (Rodié 2007). However, CSR has been defined by the European Commission as "the voluntary integration by companies of social and environmental concerns into their business activities and their relations with their stakeholders" (Commission de la Communauté Européenne 2001). Even if this definition is not unanimous among the actors interested in it, the link between CSR and innovation is increasingly highlighted. Berger-Douce (2015) emphasizes the importance of CSR as a "catalyst for innovation" and no longer as a peripheral factor used to lower business costs in several niches. One of the key elements is the active involvement of stakeholders in the innovation process.

The entrepreneur enters into a process of continuous innovation based on "humanistic values constituting the foundation of a new economic model based on CSR" (Berger-Douce 2015). CSR can address several different issues: economic, social and environmental (Boutillier and Fournier 2009). It concretizes at the firm level the environmental ambitions of the sustainable development project of the Brundtland report.

Introductory text of the Brundtland report

"In the middle of the 20th century, we saw our planet from space for the first time. Historians may eventually find this vision had a great impact on thought than did the Copernican revolution did of the 16th century, which upset the human's self-image by revealing that the Earth is not the center of the universe. From space, we see a small and fragile ball dominated not by human activity and edifice but by a pattern of clouds, oceans, greenery and soils. Humanity's inability to fit its activities into that pattern is changing planetary systems, fundamentally. Many such changes are accompanied by life-threatening hazards. This new reality, from which there is no escape, must be recognized – and managed."

Box 4.1. *Excerpt from the Brundtland report*

This introduction refers to the need for awareness of the fragility of our planet. In 1987, the report Our Common Future by the United Nations World Commission on Environment and Development was the result of several years of hearings with stakeholders from both developed and developing countries. Environmental issues are at the heart of this report, which also highlights the gaps and shortcomings in infrastructure, institutional tools and resources at both the national and international levels. The term "sustainable development" emerged from this report (see Box 4.2 for definition).

> "Sustainable development is development that meets the needs of the present without compromising the ability of future generations to meet their own needs. It contains within it two key concepts: the concept of 'needs', in particular the essential needs of the world's poor, to which overriding priority should be given, and the idea of limitations imposed by the state of technology and social organization on the environment's ability to meet present and future needs" (World Commission on Environment and Development 1987).

Box 4.2. *Definition of sustainable development included in the Brundtland report*

This definition emphasizes the link between generations, which is the Earth and the resources it has given us in the past, with a repercussion of human activities on the future. The means to be implemented with the target of restoring the order of things, to mend our ways as much as possible, is what humanity has already undertaken over the last few decades, including cooperation and collaboration between actors. Activities and institutional and regulatory frameworks must be put in place at the international level as a red line to be followed by States. They must be adapted at the national and regional levels according to the specific and local contexts in which they will be implemented. Thus, since the end of the 1980s, several key acts have been carried out, such as the creation of the Intergovernmental Panel on Climate Change (IPCC). It brings together 195 countries to study the state of the art of scientific, social, economic and technical knowledge on climate change, its causes, effects and policy options to slow it down. As a result, the United Nations Framework Convention on Climate Change (UNFCCC) was drafted in 1992 with 197 countries having ratified it. It provides a framework for intergovernmental efforts to find strategies to address climate change.

Since human activities are widely identified as being responsible for this warming, international collaboration is necessary to remedy or at least mitigate it. The Kyoto Protocol (1992) and the Paris Agreement (2016) follow all these activities trying to put in place a legal and regulatory framework for all. The Climate and Resilience Bill was validated on May 4, 2021, in France. It is a good example of the involvement of various actors in the design of a law to reduce global warming by the activities produced by France. A total of 150 citizens have thus written ideas to be part of this law; they were drawn at random during the Citizens' Climate Convention. In addition, the French government proposed most of the measures. Examples of these measures include targets to halve the rate of land concreting by banning the construction of shopping malls on rural areas and a halt to all domestic flights when an alternative exists with lower CO_2 emissions in less than 2.5 hours. Furthermore, a measure concerning food and the reduction of the consumption of animal products with a compulsory vegetarian option in the canteens and catering facilities of administrations from 2023. On the subject of fossil fuels, a ban on the marketing of heavy goods vehicles using them will be put into effect.

Responsible innovation developed in the 2000s, with a clear acceleration of research dealing with it starting in 2011 (Gay et al. 2019). The authors relate it to competitions as a political instrument for creating responsible innovation. Because of the characteristics of competitions (possible partnerships, intellectual property clauses, profile of participants, selection of proposed solutions, etc.), responsible innovation can emerge for and by society. Stakeholders are varied, including private sector companies, non-profit organizations and citizens, on a variable scale (i.e. from local to international). These actors can collaborate to find innovative solutions to significant current problems in areas such as education, health or the environment. Many of these competitions provide financial rewards to those who find the solutions that will be selected, but some do not provide monetary incentives. As Gay et al. (2019) state: "the objective is to change behaviors or to raise awareness of major issues (environment, education). Thus, competitions can combine technological and societal objectives". The openness conferred by competitions allows for collaborative processes that bring together many different actors, in order to maximize the positive effects that networking and the transfer of ideas and information can generate.

Responsible innovation is becoming a theme increasingly used by actors in the face of current societal changes. However, distinguishing between the collective responsibility of collaborating stakeholders and individual responsibility is becoming difficult. Indeed, responsibility has undergone adaptations in the last five decades. Companies are at the heart of these changes. Corporate social responsibility, or CSR, in the United States first, has prompted the initiation of changes to address the growing problems of globalization of American companies. The profiles of the actors and stakeholders who became involved diversified, starting with religious charities, employees, unions, as well as customers and suppliers of companies and citizens on a larger scale. This responsibility has thus become a significant and growing issue for society and science. The innovation process is becoming the repository of the bubbling of responsible innovation by considering social well-being as a crucial factor of any innovation. Moreover, social and environmental issues are also taken into account upstream of the innovation process, fully integrating the principle of responsibility in its development (Debref et al. 2019).

Responsible innovations can occur between companies and universities and require collaborations. However, they are not the exclusive domain of university–business links. Indeed, each actor can undertake the creation of responsible innovations. In light of the implications that responsible innovation generates, we can clearly see its multiform and transdisciplinary nature. The resources necessary to produce it are varied, as are the inherent implications.

Lacoste and Pardo (2016) add to the use of CSR as a collaborative tool, joint practices of CSR, where actors usually in a so-called vertical or commercial relationship (a company and its suppliers) collaborate. Actors who are usually in competition can thus collaborate and create social links through these joint practices. The two types of relationships (commercial and social) coexist within different collaboration and competition projects.

Ouellet (2013) listed factors that slow down innovation in a collaborative context. The Oslo Manual lists the obstacles to the smooth running of innovation activities. Firms can then refer to it to analyze the reasons for the problems incurred. These barriers include: economic factors such as high costs; lack of appropriate sources of funding and excessive length of time to achieve return on investment in innovation. There are inherent factors such as: insufficient innovation capacity; lack of qualified personnel; lack of information on available technologies and markets; innovation expenses that are difficult to control; resistance to internal changes; insufficient availability of external services and lack of cooperation. The lack of technological possibilities, lack of infrastructure, norms, regulations and standards that are not adapted; and finally the lack of interest of customers for new products and processes can also be found.

Blandin et al. (2016) insist on the opposition that can emerge from the terms organizations and innovation. Indeed, organization allows for the reduction of uncertainty in activities, by structuring them and anticipating, while innovation induces uncertainty and risk-taking. Therefore, collaborative innovation combines these two aspects by taking charge of the resolution of paradoxes related to innovation.

4.1.2.3. Research trends on responsible innovation

On the topic of responsible research and innovation, I did a brief search on the Web of Science and Scopus websites using the keywords "responsible research innovation", "responsible innovation", "collaborative innovation" and "open innovation". It turns out that, as presented in Table 4.1 and Figures 4.1 and 4.2, the topic of responsible research and responsible innovation are recent. The search that was done via the two bibliometric tools did not specify a time period. The first occurrence on the subject of responsible research and responsible innovation appeared in 1972 according to Scopus.

Key words	Number of WoS results	Number of Scopus results
"responsible research innovation"	1,701	2,757
"responsible innovation"	3,505	6,353
"collaborative innovation"	6,356	12,650
"open innovation"	13,786	22,439

Table 4.1. *Results of the bibliometric search on keywords related to the theme of responsible research and innovation, and collaborative innovation*

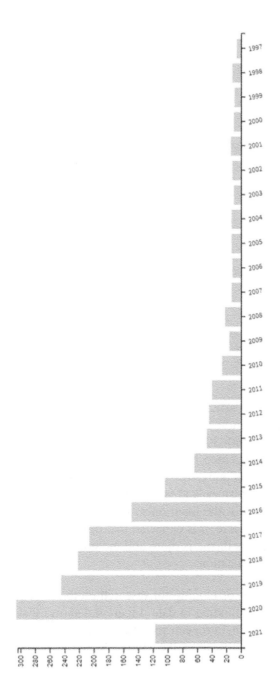

Figure 4.1. *Number of articles published on the theme "responsible research innovation" on the Web of Science, between 1997 and 2021. For a color version of this figure, see www.iste.co.uk/aouinait/innovation.zip*

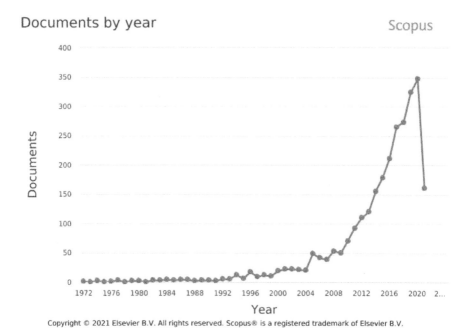

Figure 4.2. *Number of articles published on the theme "responsible research innovation" on Scopus, between 1972 and 2021. For a color version of this figure, see www.iste.co.uk/aouinait/innovation.zip*

From the 2000s, more articles were counted: between 15 and 20 until 2004, then a clear acceleration of interest in this subject began in 2007–2008 to reach a peak in 2020, with 304 publications counted on the WoS and 347 on Scopus. The areas concerned by the publication of work on responsible research and innovation (Figure 4.3) include economics, social sciences, environmental sciences, history and philosophy of science, technological sciences and engineering for the main ones. It can be seen from this figure that the fields are quite diverse. It is expected that this diversity will increase in the coming years, as this theme is more and more at the heart of research, financed by different organizations.

In terms of the sources of funding for research on this topic, Europe has been the largest source of funding to date. Figure 4.4 shows that about 25% of the funding comes from European programs and/or organizations, with the remainder coming mainly from the United States, Canada, Japan and China.

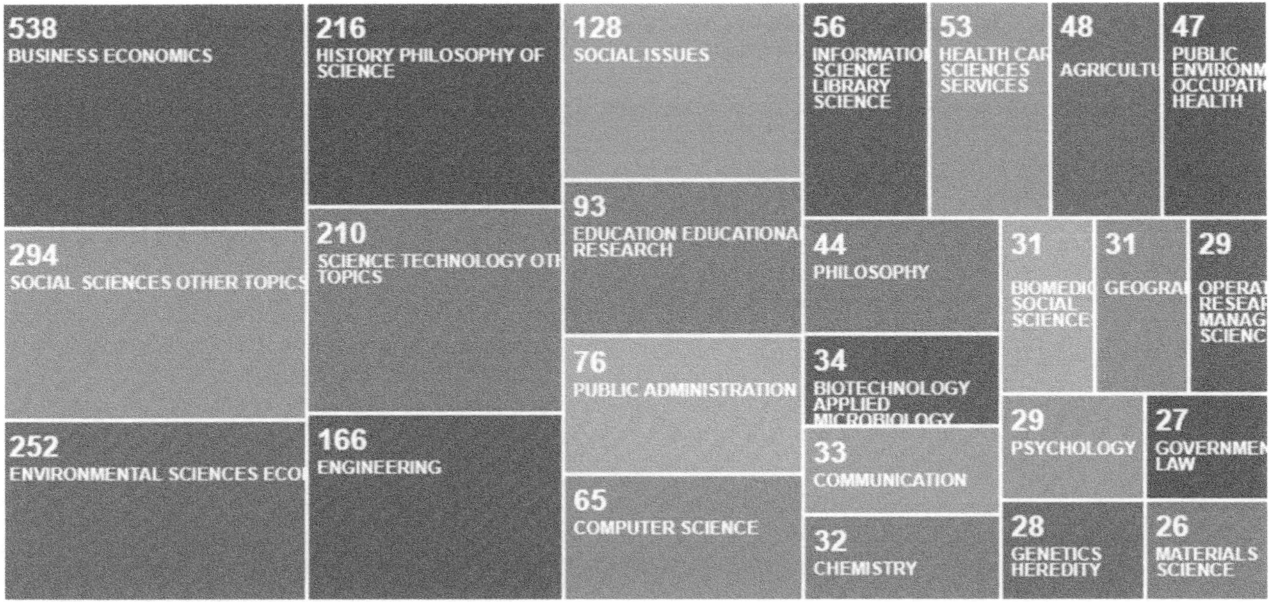

Figure 4.3. *Areas concerned by the publication of scientific results published by WoS on the theme of "responsible research innovation". For a color version of this figure, see www.iste.co.uk/aouinait/innovation.zip*

Figure 4.4. *Research funding organizations in the "responsible research innovation" theme. For a color version of this figure, see www.iste.co.uk/aouinait/innovation.zip*

The same trend was observed for the keywords "responsible innovation", with a significant growth in the early 2010s. As far as the theme of collaborative innovation is concerned, the 1990s saw the rise of researchers' attention on the subject. The beginning of the 2000s was marked by a boom in publications, in line with the new paradigm of open innovation defined by Henry Chesbrough in 2003. 2020 remains the year with the most publications listing the words "collaborative innovation" in the title, keywords and abstract. This analysis is also valid for open innovation. The results for the year 2021 cannot be interpreted because only five months were considered in the count (analysis performed at the beginning of June 2021).

Finally, collaborative innovation faces many obstacles and paradoxes that can slow it down or even stop it. The success of innovation lies not only in the successful commercialization of a product, a technology or a service, for example, but also in overcoming all these obstacles and resolving, or compromising, solutions that overcome the paradoxes of collaborative innovation. The interactions between the actors of a collaborative innovation project, between the actors who develop the innovation and those who implement it, are crucial for the success of the innovation (diffusion and adoption).

Paradoxes related to the implication of what openness implies, the use of creativity while having rigorous methodologies to select key partners and resources to get the most out of them. Similarly, coordinating actors from different backgrounds, disciplines and with divergent interests and working methods can be a significant obstacle, which can bring any collaborative project to a halt. Establishing upstream guidelines, identifying the tasks of each party, the legal aspects that affect the results of the project and the investments to be made is essential to avoid any conflict. The alliance of invention and convention, as well as the worship of "cultification", can mean progressive advanced rooted in practices in a generic way, but can mean obstacles to collaborative innovation, especially for actors who are not used to it or for actors with few resources such as small companies.

The development of public policies that support cooperation, coopetition and collaboration between several actors on an often territorial scale, which can be extended to a region, is becoming more and more frequent. Funding from the public sector should be joined by more substantial funding from the private sector to create collaborative projects with common interests. In this way, the major challenges facing our societies today can benefit from the active participation of multiple stakeholder groups, including citizens, public authorities, researchers, businesses, associations and consumers. The educational, economic, political and environmental systems and civil society must therefore work together, around the universal force of knowledge.

4.1.3. *Sectors conducive to open innovation*

According to research by Steiner (2014), open innovation is not "equal" or used in the same way in all sectors. The maturity of the technology and the maturity of the market for a research and development project are factors chosen by some authors to study which sectors are most likely to use this innovation model. Their results do not establish a significant difference between the agri-food sector, the manufacturing sector and the chemical sector. Nevertheless, 20% of the working time is allocated to cooperations and most often with universities. This figure is not negligible. Moreover, these collaborations are mainly carried out for the development of new technologies and for access to new markets. The exploration stages are therefore more prone to collaborations. Indeed, the actors not possessing the knowledge concerning new technologies, new services to be proposed and/or new markets likely to correspond to their innovations in the making, can collaborate with actors competent in these fields and having the expertise to identify all these elements. Moreover, the sector in which collaborative innovation is very strong is the high-tech sector. This sector was one of the first to use this concept (Gassman 2006; Steiner 2014). Indeed, 90.91% of the 2,500 companies surveyed by Chesbrough and Brunswicker (2013) were found to practice open innovation, as presented in Figure 4.5.

One of the reasons is the dynamics of this sector and the arrival of open source, which is conducive to collaboration. This term includes access to the source code, as well as the free redistribution of the software, without having to give feedback to anyone. The source code allows a programmer to modify a program as needed. The license must also allow for modifications and derivations while allowing for similar distribution to the original software.

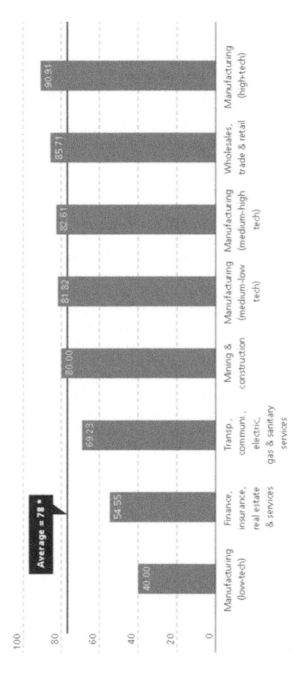

Figure 4.5. *Use of open innovation by industry sectors (Steiner 2014, based on Chesbrough and Brunswicker 2013). For a color version of this figure, see www.iste.co.uk/aouinait/innovation.zip*

On the other hand, traditional sectors such as the chemical industry are less users of innovation, possibly due to the lower qualifications of the personnel in these so-called traditional sectors. Rather conservative sectors such as the financial sector, however, have demonstrated the use of open innovation (Mention and Torkkeli 2014), especially through the diffusion of information and communication technologies. Companies in the manufacturing industry (low tech) appear to be the companies that use collaborative innovation the least, with 40% of them using it, followed by the companies in the finance, insurance and services sectors (54.55%).

4.2. Limitations of the open innovation paradigm

There are many criticisms of innovation models, including the dichotomy of open versus closed innovation (Dahlander and Gann 2010; Isckia and Lescop 2011; Loilier and Tellier 2011). This opposition and related criticisms are partly based on the degree of openness of corporate boundaries and the permeability of those boundaries. A hybridization between the closed and open form exists and is described by Loilier and Tellier (2011). According to them, this form is an "intermediate model that mixes the 'public' dimension at work in Open Source (free participation of users) and the 'private' dimension of the closed model of more traditional industries (appropriation of results by the firm)". Nevertheless, this hybrid form is not the most commonly used form by firms due to the low monetary incentive, which is more generous in other models. Capturing the rent of marketable products and innovations is one of the objectives of innovators, the economic level being underlying the mode of appropriability chosen.

4.2.1. *Actors' levels of organization, between small and large firms*

A disadvantage of collaboration is the sometimes complicated organization between the project stakeholders. The involvement of each actor is not necessarily measurable. Some of them may substitute for others, limiting their input and acting as a "stowaway" (Gangloff-Ziegler 2009). In the same sense, Guillemot et al. (2016) cite the fear of sharing of know-how as a disadvantage and an obstacle to collaborative innovation. Having to transfer and exchange our own knowledge and know-how with actors who are collaborators but who could also be competitors in another context, can negatively impact the willingness to participate in open innovation. Another disadvantage cited by Gangloff-Ziegler (2009) is the transparency or structuring of the activities involved in collaborative projects, which can slow down some actors. Moreover, collaboration implies a reduction in competition between actors. "Coopetition", a principle that allows for the combination of cooperation between actors and their competition, allows individual needs to be satisfied.

The subjectivity of stakeholders can play a role in the dissemination of information. Indeed, the stakeholder who disseminates and shares elements finds them important and interesting for them and potentially for other audiences. In addition to this notion of the importance of information, authenticity and originality "must be related to the purpose of the intended collaboration" (Gangloff-Ziegler 2009). The ability to step back from the information or knowledge collected and acquired during the project may be useful in identifying what is worth sharing and transferring to other actors.

West (2006) and Burger-Helmcehn et al. (2013) further discuss a problem at the managerial level in collaborating between structures of different sizes. Large companies do not operate in the same way as SMEs. Decision-making processes as well as time and financial constraints can diverge greatly between these actors.

Loilier and Tellier (2011) take a critical look at the new nature of the open innovation model. This model, which has been described as bringing innovation to the management of the innovation process and collaborations between partners, in particular through the multiple possibilities of collaboration, is ultimately not new in itself. Using information and knowledge coming from outside to be able to innovate by oneself is not innovative. The acquisition of licenses is an example of using internally technologies developed elsewhere.

4.2.2. Intellectual property: a sensitive point in the collaboration

Among the disadvantages of collaborative innovation, we can mention the fear of companies regarding the commitment required for the establishment of collaborative projects. Several risks are to be incurred when one actor collaborates with another, and even more so when the collaboration is not only bilateral but involves several different partners. The management of intellectual property is a sensitive subject that can slow down different actors. The management of intellectual property rights is often seen as a barrier to engaging in open innovation. Strategies regarding outside-in and inside-out processes are at the heart of this management. Ownership of results and innovation, the use of these results and their fate (e.g. assignment, exclusion or sale) are crucial aspects to be defined upstream of the initiation of the collaborative project (Burger-Helmcehn et al. 2013; Mention and Torkkeli 2014; Guillemot et al. 2016). Companies fear information and knowledge leakage, believing that revealing knowledge to partners not included in the collaborations is risky. These actors could use it and the competition (St Pierre and Hanel 2005; Khedher 2010). Moreover, intellectual property modalities such as the degree to which knowledge circulates openly and is free to use can become an element of competitiveness and subject, ultimately, to intellectual protection (Leroux et al. 2014). Furthermore, open innovation can be beneficial to value patents that are created but not used, by offering them to other companies. 20% of patents would generate 80% of the revenue. This highlights the significant amount of patents that are not used internally by firms (Isckia and Lescop 2011). This potential for dormant patents is valid for several sectors, and is not a new phenomenon. Finally, the weakness of the protection of intellectual property rights of some companies can represent a significant barrier to engaging in open innovation (Ouellet 2013).

4.2.3. *Clarification of monetary benefits*

The economic benefits and their distribution are also some of the objects to be specified, as well as the delimitations of the collaboration (e.g. who does what, from when to when), and its duration. Another theme concerns the investments that each partner must make, in terms of human resources, equipment human resources, equipment, infrastructure, as well as time (Guillemot et al. 2016). For their part, St. Pierre and Hanel (2005) cite the hesitation of private companies to collaborate with universities. Some companies prefer to collaborate with individual university actors, such as professors, on a long-term basis. This temporality is important for building trust with the researcher(s) involved in the collaboration. The reduction of costs and the establishment of a certain routine are also motivations to cooperate in this sense. The interpersonal relationships are, in this context, crucial for establishing bonds of trust and mutual exchange, which will evolve and adapt during the realization of joint projects.

4.2.4. Restricting access to protected results and impacts on science

The disadvantage in the restrictions on disclosure of results provided by collaborative projects is the barrier of access to science. The scientific field wants to provide research results, which to a certain extent can be protected. But the protection that is too much sought after by the actors hinders the missions of the scientific sector. Moreover, the technological and non-technological progress that companies could make with these results is considerably slowed down. These negative consequences also affect the university, such as weakened scientific communication, a shift from basic to applied research, deteriorated student–faculty relations and a reduction in the resources initially dedicated to teaching. All these risks are very significant and call into question the value of potential collaborations.

Khedher (2010) adds a disadvantage to those already mentioned: that of managing tasks carried out internationally. The cultural distance that can exist between partners from different countries, or even continents, implies one more variable to manage in the partnership. The habits, routines of the companies or the management methods may be divergent, increasing the risk of the collaboration's failure. Taking into account the local environment and contexts is important here. Cultural distance is not the only issue to be considered for actors wishing to collaborate with partners at an international level. The possible political, economic, administrative and societal distances are just as important.

In addition to these multiple distances with international partners, there is trust. For Zaheer and Zaheer (2006), in a context of fiduciary asymmetry, trust is all the more important because the risk involved increases. After an analysis of all these factors, the partners may decide to start a collaboration to develop innovations, which, if successful, could enter several markets and have a significant diffusion (Khedher 2010).

4.2.5. Actors' cognitive skills

The cognitive skills of the actors entering into collaborative work must be sufficient, otherwise they will not be useful elements for the collaboration. Gangloff-Ziegler (2009) talks about indispensable cognitive factors and more precisely about two types of knowledge: those related to the specialty of collaborative work and those called "procedural", which are useful when using methods and tools. A lack of training and support can then be detrimental to collaborative work and also be an obstacle to the commitment of the actors. The initial phase of identifying partners for the development of innovations is essential to maximize the chances of successful collaboration before the innovation is successfully created. The lack of user-friendliness of the innovative methods, services and tools disseminated, as well as their limited availability, restricted access and complexity of use are other obstacles (Gangloff-Ziegler 2009). A capacity of actors to be able to navigate between data collection tools, to use diverse methods and to apply their cognitive abilities is important for collaboration. Having a solid knowledge base helps to strengthen our position in increasingly competitive markets.

4.2.6. *What value does the innovation bring?*

Isckia and Lescop (2011) approach open innovation from the perspective of the value that outbound and inbound innovation bring. Indeed, inbound innovation can be seen as a process of exploring the possibilities of companies with a collection of ideas upstream of the innovation process. This exploration can lead to interesting solutions that will be developed in order to lead to a marketable innovation. For example, Procter & Gamble's (P&G) "Connect and Develop" program aims to identify and exploit internal and external innovation assets and to increase innovation capacity by soliciting several stakeholders such as suppliers, scientists, entrepreneurs and competitors. Their goal is to solve problems and answer questions that the company submits to them. P&G mobilizes its networks to seek out and identify opportunities to collaborate with innovators in all locations to find new products, technologies, packaging or business connections that will satisfy consumers in the near future. Outbound innovation, on the other hand, requires the provision of resources to external partners through contracts such as joint ventures, licenses or research and development agreements. Thus, Chesbrough defines the existence of an intermediary market, composed of these contracts resulting from outbound innovation. The latter is therefore an essential point for the collaborative innovation strategy, without which companies would be limited to carrying out exploration activities. This critical analysis of the components of open innovation paradigm developed in the early 2000s sheds light on the pitfalls that collaborative innovation can generate.

Isckia and Lescop (2011) take the case of large firms that can insert themselves into markets such as Apple in the mobile device market, Microsoft in the console market and Google in the operating system market. The competition between these multinationals is played out through the use of open innovation. The discovery and penetration of new markets, the capture of profits and the monitoring and control of the open innovation process are thus achieved by these firms. However, according to the authors, these strategies could weaken the competitive pressure due to the concentration of high value-added markets. This would destroy the incentives for innovation. The environment of the firm is therefore very important. The players present, their number and profiles, the existence of products and services that are complementary to the products of a central market (such as software being complementary to the "operating system" product), the maturity of the industry and the barriers to entry are all factors that influence open innovation.

Similarly, a relationship between the level of skills of firms and the degree of openness to innovation has been established in an OECD report (2008). Core skills are primarily developed in firms. Open innovation can concern so-called "peripheral" projects that include an exploration of development possibilities such as entering new markets. Openness thus serves to develop skills and to strengthen the position of firms on the market and to become a partner bringing added value to collaborative projects (Isckia and Lescop 2011).

According to the OECD (2008), market, industry, technology and knowledge factors can explain why open innovation is likely to work. Structural characteristics conducive to open innovation include technology life cycles (use of ICT, electronic and telecommunication tools) that tend to be short, have high intensity of knowledge and technology used, legal protection of the innovations created and identity of partners working to facilitate collaboration. Nevertheless, it can be difficult to open up to partners who are usually outside the industry such as research laboratories and academic organizations. In addition, the tacit nature of knowledge can hinder the transfer and sharing of information and knowledge, as described earlier in this book. Path dependency, which implies that future innovation depends on previous innovations, can also be an obstacle to open innovation, where creativity is limited if incentives to look outside the "comfort zone" are not in place.

In addition, Laursen and Salter (2005) are interested in the level of ownership of firms and the link with the openness of the innovation. Ownership allows the innovator to benefit from the value created by an innovation. Thus, innovators obtain a return on their internal innovations and/or an external innovation offer. The authors investigated British industries. Their results tend to support the hypothesis that open innovation is more used in industries with high ownership (such as pharmaceuticals) and less used in industries with low ownership (such as textiles).

Mention and Torkkeli (2014) discuss the limited scope of actors impacted by the innovation created through collaboration. This could be the case because of the targeted markets depending on the nature of the innovation. They can be more or less restricted if the innovation is a niche innovation, or very specific.

Table 4.2 summarizing the advantages and disadvantages of the open innovation model and the closed innovation model comes from Nunes and Abreu (2020). The authors present the independence from external partners, the non-risk of information leakage and competitive advantage, particularly in the closed innovation model. Isckia and Lescop (2011) validate the element of the table concerning the costs of research and development and other costs inherent to the innovation process, specifically the exploration and creation of innovation. These are shared among partners and can be an important motivation for companies or organizations wanting to open up their innovation model. However, the advantages of the open innovation model appear to be more numerous, including the elements described in the section above. A larger knowledge base, an increased learning capacity that will be used in future projects, access to various markets, cost reduction and other advantages quite commonly found in the literature are present in this table. Furthermore, the major drawbacks take up the sensitive subject of intellectual property and inherent rights with possible avoidance of elements of competitiveness, more difficult management and coordination with multiple partners and having different practices and environments, as well as a potential loss of control of the innovation process.

An advantage that can also be seen as a limitation of the open innovation model is the mobility of labor. Actors who change firms take with them very fundamental knowledge. Some of this knowledge is tacit and cannot be automatically transferred to the new environment. However, another part can be used in the new environment and contribute to the improvement of the position of the "new" firm on the market, for example. Important data can be better integrated (Chesbrough 2012; Aouinaït 2021).

	Advantages	Disadvantages
Closed innovation model	Overall control of the innovation process and intellectual property	Human resources (expertise and experience) are not all present within the company
	Little or no dependence on external elements	Higher levels of investment to fuel R&D departments
	No risk of leakage of confidential information	Development with a slower pace
		Limited market share gains
Open innovation model	Discovery exclusivity provides a competitive advantage in the market (earlier presence in the market)	Higher risk, as the ideas developed may not be supported by the organization
	Circulation of knowledge, ideas and technologies inside and outside the company, which increases the learning capacity	Increased process coordination and implementation costs
	Technological synergy effects	High dependence on external knowledge
	Diversification of R&D investments	Loss of control over key knowledge and flexibility, creativity and strategic power
	Intellectual property can be used as a strategic asset, bringing in new sources of revenue (copyright royalties)	
	Reduced costs of innovation initiatives (resource acquisition benefits)	Risk of leakage, confidential information
	Sharing the risks of innovation investments with other partners	Loss of overall control over the innovation process and intellectual property
	Increased differentiation of the company's products, as well as the creativity of the innovation process	

Table 4.2. *Advantages and disadvantages of open innovation (Nunes and Abreu 2020)*

Crowdlending uses the principles of crowdfunding and crowdsourcing with the participation of citizens in the financing of projects. For crowdlending, citizens can lend money in the form of micro-loans that allow very small, small and medium-sized companies to obtain financing for their projects. It is also possible to make a simple donation, a donation with repayment, an equity investment or a loan with or without interest (Ben Slimane and Rousselet 2018). In 2008, it was in the United States that this practice emerged. This digital transformation of lending is supported by the government with a decree put in place in October 2014 (Duran 2018). However, this outsourcing can lead to problems. In this case, repayment concerns and the opacity of the processes and financial information can block lenders from continuing to collaborate. In addition to the purely financial exchange, lenders may seek a social perspective in the transaction. People who decide to invest do so to support a certain sector (e.g. real estate, renewable energy) or types of firms (e.g. SMEs, VSEs, cooperative societies) and thus provide them with support. The links that are established within the lending community become multiform.

The downside of this participatory financing lies in the selection of companies for which access to such financing is very complicated. Ben Slimane and Rousselet (2018) studied 15 participatory platforms for businesses. Recently established businesses and those with low turnover (less than €100,000 per year) have difficulty accessing funding. Platforms that act as a financial intermediary between companies (borrowers) and investors (lenders) consider, in addition to the financial criteria, the project's theme in the sense of potential attractiveness. Indeed, projects that attract the attention of individual lenders are likely to have a higher probability of funding.

This analysis of crowdlending clearly shows the complexity of the collaboration between different stakeholders. Collaboration here is not understood as an interpersonal relationship established with frequent and continuous contacts between the actors, but rather as an anonymous and social relationship.

4.3. Questions related to collaborative innovation

4.3.1. *The various paradoxes inherent in collaborative innovation*

4.3.1.1. *The opening paradox*

One of the most obvious paradoxes of open innovation is the one that concerns the openness of a company to innovate and its closure to benefit from the results of this innovation process. The paradox of openness is a trade-off that companies must find between opening up to third parties to create and access knowledge and resources, while at the same time weakening their ability to use the knowledge. Arora et al. (2015) hypothesize a positive relationship between openness and patenting. Indeed, firms that protect their innovations with patents to avoid knowledge transfers that would be involuntary. However, the paradox here lies in the attractiveness of these companies as interesting partners for collaboration. The relationship between openness and patenting is negative. This dichotomy represents the paradoxes that innovation, and especially open innovation, brings with it. The relationship between openness and patenting is a function of the firm's technological position. The better the firm is positioned in the use of technology, the more likely it is to open up its innovation process. The authors do not find a generic model for this trade-off in a sample of 325 firms in the United Kingdom, but rather a case-by-case adaptation by firms. Leading firms, those that innovate and may be at the root of collaborations, would be less well situated and more vulnerable to unintended knowledge transfers that occur during collaboration. These lead firms would therefore file more patents as part of the opening. In addition, follow-on firms are more reluctant to patent because of their decreased attractiveness and potential for future collaborations.

Leveque et al. (2020) investigated the combination of spatially and temporally situated devices, to understand their complementarity by taking as examples a collaborative innovation space and a collaborative innovation event. Organizational ambidexterity could be achieved by an innovation entity in this framework. Organizational ambidexterity is defined by the authors as the balance between exploiting existing knowledge and markets, and exploring new opportunities. This organizational ambidexterity can be broken down into contextual, sequential or structural ambidexterity. Companies have the possibility to move from an exploration activity to an exploitation activity on a varied time scale throughout the project's setup.

On the one hand, collaborative innovation spaces have been studied as a context favorable to contextual ambidexterity, where improvisational and bricolage activities can be used in the creation of innovation, as in the case of the Renault FabLab. On the other hand, collaborative innovation events that include hackathons, startup weekends or learning expeditions are increasingly developed in a wide variety of sectors and by different actors. Their flexibility in terms of target audiences, formats and degree of involvement makes them increasingly interesting events for firms, and vectors of collective or collaborative innovation. Collaborative innovation spaces and collaborative innovation events are not interdependent. One can exist without the other and vice versa. However, it has been demonstrated in the study by Leveque et al. (2020) that collaborative innovation events very often take place in collaborative innovation spaces. Thus, collaborative innovation spaces and collaborative innovation events complement each other in a physical/virtual, local/global and permanent/temporary dialectic. The actors who are included in the activities developed in these environments and in these event-based projects are supported to create innovation spontaneously or in an organized way. The exploration–exploitation balance makes sense in this complementarity.

Moreover, both confidentiality and the distribution of the fruits of innovation are affected by this paradox. Servajean-Hilst and Duverdier (2015) cite the figure of 58% of companies in the open innovation scale from the MEDEF open innovation committee in 2014 that consider "the fear of intellectual property theft" as a barrier to using open innovation[1]. This barrier is modulated according to the sector concerned and the life cycle of the innovation. As described by Arora et al. (2015), openness can be positively correlated with the use of intellectual property mechanisms such as patents or trade secrets. The short life cycles of technologies are also in favor of openness in the innovation process. On the other hand, for longer life cycles, the dominance of tacit knowledge that circulates in the sector and the dependence of the innovation process on previous innovations (known as path dependence) are not in favor of openness (Isckia and Lescop 2011). Strategies to control the process of innovation openness involve identifying confidential and disclosable elements. The entrepreneurial environment and

---

1 The MEDEF (*mouvement des entreprises de France*, French business movement) created a committee dedicated to Open Innovation in April 2014. One of the activities carried out by this committee was the realization of a scale to analyze the maturity of French companies in the field of open innovation.

the culture of the organizations involved in collaborative projects are factors to be taken into account upstream of any knowledge and information diffusion and transfer activity. The "business intelligence culture" must be developed and maintained (Servajean-Hilst and Duverdier 2015).

4.3.1.2. *The paradox of using creativity in the innovation process*

Other paradoxes concern the oppositions between creativity and innovation and innovation, chance and necessity, rationality and intuition, or divergence and convergence. First of all, creativity can appear as contradictory to innovation. The former is spontaneous, whereas the latter is organized to crystallize an invention into a marketable product. The creativity of actors can be stimulated through certain activities, in order to free their imagination and stimulate capacities that will be useful to innovate. Informal interactions are increasingly important in the innovation process. It is through these interactions that ideas can emerge, and word-of-mouth circulates relevant information for a given project. The decompartmentalization of disciplines, the combination and hybridization of knowledge are then possible. Interaction between actors, mutual aid and training are exercises that can lead to collective innovation. These exercises can be encouraged through games, putting collaborators from the same company in concrete situations, for example. Favoring the conditions for the emergence of creativity can be achieved. The paradox of disorder versus method can thus be overcome by enabling the freedom to imagine, escaping the usual frameworks, comfort zones and expected paths. However, a certain methodology to be able to channel and synthesize the results of these exercises must allow for refocusing the whole to reach concrete paths to create innovation (Blandin et al. 2016).

4.3.1.3. *The time paradox*

The time paradox is an integral part of collaborative innovation. Two temporalities coexist in the innovation process. The emergence of ideas, which can be spontaneous if the conditions are met (e.g. with creativity, the diversity of actors pooling their efforts), takes place in the short-term. On the other hand, the formalization and organization of the rest of the innovation process is measured on a longer time scale. Several years can pass between the crystallization of the idea into a marketable innovation. How can we reconcile these different temporalities inherent to innovation as a whole? In the individual-collective paradox, the question is to know and understand how ideas that are mostly individual can be anchored in an innovation process that is, for its part, rather collective. This question arises in particular in open third places such as FabLabs, Living Labs and hackerspaces. What are the methods for managing the "collective" in order to integrate all the individualities and enhance them through innovative results? Another paradox studied by Blandin et al. (2016) concerns serendipity or discovery by chance. How can this serendipity be shaped and controlled to direct it towards "necessity" that would be integrated into the generation of collective innovation?

4.3.1.4. *The paradox of "cultification"*

Khan and Jospeh (2003) identified paradoxes related to innovation at the time. Three major paradoxes were cited in their article in the Stanford Social Innovation Review: i) "how to pursue innovation without falling prey to cultification", ii) "how to collaborate without being derailed by compromise" and iii) "how to scale revolutionary inventions within the established conventions of organizations". These paradoxes point to the presence of obstacles that are not dependent on the competencies of the actors acting in support of innovation. They can lead to an innovation dissonance, where a balance between uncertainty and risk related to any innovation activity and organization necessary to direct actors and their actions towards innovation.

By "cultification" the authors refer to a kind of worship that has been created around innovation. Indeed, it is very widespread in the strategies of organizations, whether in the private sector or in the public sector, by professionals or by the general public. Innovation has become almost commonplace and even basic, since incremental innovation is more accessible and easier to implement than radical innovation. Innovation is almost no longer questioned in our society. However, the incessant use of innovation and the development of multiple, related projects can be counterproductive. The example cited by Khan and Joseph (2003) of the mHealth Alliance illustrates this. This alliance aims to improve the health of the population by promoting the development of mobile technologies and their use by users. The collection of health data, its storage and processing, the development of platforms and care are activities targeted by the alliance. However, many pilot projects have emerged at the same time, considerably slowing down their simultaneous development. Many resources are needed to move from the pilot phase to the implementation phase (e.g. scale-up, marketing activities and commercialization). As a result, few projects actually result in an innovation that will be launched on the market. This phenomenon is not new and will intensify in the years to come if nothing is done, especially in terms of project management and task allocation. Delegating certain activities can be a way to optimize the time and resources of each stakeholder to collectively achieve a final product, as Switchboard has done. This non-profit organization has set itself the goal of linking health care workers between two African countries, by partnering with mobile operators already present locally. Thus, the success of this mission enables its "replicability" in other countries of the African continent.

Collaboration implies confronting different actors with divergent interests and a balance of power can be established. Competition for resources and negotiation over resource allocation and intellectual property rights can occur throughout the project. Therefore, successful and efficient collaboration requires the inclusion of actors who respect the goals of other actors, including their multiple perspectives (Khan and Joseph 2003).

4.3.1.5. *Invention versus convention*

Large companies may be confronted with another paradox, that of invention in convention. The compartmentalization of activities which are integrated in several departments, such as Research and Development, marketing, communication, purchasing, IT, among others, initially introduced to maximize the efficiency of activities, could be harmful to innovation. The invention is disconnected from its integration into the conventional system. The scaling up of the invention while preserving its particularities can pose a problem when this invention must circulate between different departments of the company, or even between the company's subsidiaries. This denaturing of the invention will have a negative impact on its qualification as an innovation (Khan and Jospeh 2003).

4.3.1.6. *Value creation and capture*

Another sensitive element of collaborative innovation lies in the common definition of value creation and the capture of this value, for example, by licensing technologies to make them profitable for the different stakeholders in the collaboration. The balance between this creation and acquisition of value is another paradox of collaborative innovation. Thus, the identification of strengths and weaknesses by the companies involved in the project is fundamental. What resources are key to the project? Who owns them? Which resources and information should remain in-house? Which ones can be shared? Are the strategies of small and medium-sized enterprises similar to or different from those of large companies? All of these questions must be answered from a value creation perspective. The distribution of responsibilities, the sharing of intellectual property and the sharing of returns and benefits from the fruits of innovation are decisive steps in establishing collaborations (Servajean-Hilst and Duverdier 2015). A contractual form between the stakeholders can be synonymous with good understanding and success of the collaborative project for open innovation.

4.3.2. Role of governance and actors

4.3.2.1. *Public policies for collective innovation*

Other types of paradoxes exist in relation to collaborative innovation. This is the case of the paradoxes generated by the public policies innovation designed in the 1990s and intensified in the 2000s. Clusters have been the center of these innovation innovation policies, generating effects at the regional level. Actors of various profiles such as universities, research laboratories and companies work in clusters to create innovation based on collaboration and geographical proximity. Cluster governance has a role to play in engaging collaborative innovation. Modifications or adaptations of this governance can be envisaged to take into account the new modalities and expectations of society and the issues at stake at the general level. The practices that are put in place to support the creation, dissemination and use of knowledge in clusters and innovative environments raise questions.

The departments or internal services of companies are all concerned by the collaborative innovation process and are impacted by its opening. The purchasing department, in connection with the supply of raw materials and equipment for production, the human resources department, which is looking for new talent to complement its in-house expertise and know-how or the Research and Development department, which is directly concerned by open innovation. How do the players in these departments organize themselves internally to optimize their position in collaborative innovation, especially in the face of partners with whom exchanges will be frequent? This organizational paradox of combining internal and external processes must be resolved in the establishment of collaborative projects.

At the enterprise level, and more specifically for small and medium-sized enterprises (SMEs), it is legitimate to ask how SMEs develop and maintain collaborative innovation networks, according to their context and limiting factors (e.g. lack of human, financial and financial and infrastructural resources)? What strategies do they use to take advantage of collaboration with actors who may be very different and belong to different sectors? These questions are part of the paradox of specific collaborative arrangements.

4.3.2.2. Involvement of actors and their environments in collaborative innovation: triple, quadruple and quintuple helix models

In the open models supporting collaboration as an axis of innovation, the triple helix (Etzkowitz and Leydesdorff 2000) has been developed and studied for several years. This model highlights the triptych of university, government and business as actors collaborating to exchange and produce knowledge and innovations. Ten years later, the quadruple and quintuple helix models complement it. For example, Carayannis et al. (2012) and Carayannis and Campbell (2017) present the new helices that reinforce the model developed in the 2000s by Etzkowith and Leydersdoff. The democratic environment and the public become inherent spheres of the innovation system. For example, culture, art, creative industries, lifestyles, media and civil society are all important contextual elements that play a more or less important role in innovation systems (Hashe et al. 2020).

On this new basis, the fifth helix that is added includes aspects related to the natural environment, societal and economic, and global challenges such as the "socio-ecological transition" and "social ecology". The authors propose to use this quintuple helix for the transdisciplinary study of social ecology and sustainable development. The interweaving of these new helices in the triple helix model is shown in Figure 4.6.

The base of the triple helix provides an archetype of trilateral networks of hybrid organizations, targeting relationships between universities, industries and governments (Carayannis et al. 2012). Thus, in the addition of the other helices to arrive at the fuller model of five helices that interlock and work together, knowledge and know-how circulate among five subsystems: (1) the educational system, (2) the economic system, (3) the natural environment, (4) the civil society and the media and cultural-based culture and (5) the political system.

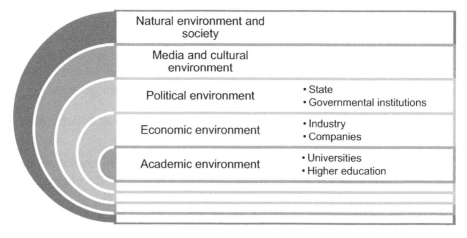

Figure 4.6. *Quintuple helix model (based on Carayannis et al. 2012). For a color version of this figure, see www.iste.co.uk/aouinait/innovation.zip*

Knowledge is the "pivotal force" (Carayannis et al. 2012) of the system. Collaborations between actors, while combining the sum of their interactions with the accumulation of knowledge and expertise, can be used to develop innovative solutions to increasingly significant problems, particularly in the area of sustainability of systems.

Advantages, Disadvantages and Issues Related to Collaborative Innovation 141

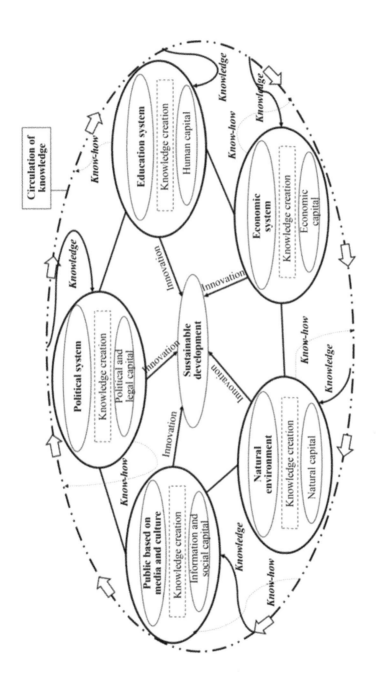

Figure 4.7. *Circulation of knowledge and know-how in the quintuple helix model (taken from Carayannis et al. 2012)*

Conclusion

Open or collaborative innovation is a widely used and studied topic in the literature related to a wide variety of disciplines. The universal nature of innovation makes it an almost commonplace topic, used in every possible way, which can lead to confusion about its definition and scope. There have been several criticisms and debates about the degree of openness that companies and organizations can achieve in innovation processes. This book has attempted to shed light on what is defined as innovation in a broad sense: product, process, organization, marketing or services. It has also presented innovation as a co-product of relationships and collaborations established between several stakeholders.

Innovation openness is no longer a new strategy. It is implemented almost systematically by large companies and is increasingly introduced in small and medium-sized enterprises (SMEs), when resources are present and supports (decision support, financial, regulatory and infrastructural support) are also present. The paradox of "cultification", as presented in Chapter 4, demonstrates this. Collaboration, which is a key factor in open innovation, helps to overcome the problems of lack of resources and capabilities necessary to innovate successfully. Companies do not always have them, especially since the more the needs and expectations of customers increase, the more the innovation intensifies. Actors try to meet the needs of customers by bringing them innovation. Therefore, multiple forms of expertise, know-how and knowledge must be accumulated to be able to use them in innovation processes. However, they are not always available in companies and cannot be easily obtained on the market.

Chapter 1 reviews the concepts of open and collaborative innovation, its emergence and characteristics, such as the absorption capacity of firms, serendipity or the role of chance in the discovery of inventions, and the balance between exploration and exploitation of resources and knowledge that must be established in any innovation process. As far as knowledge is concerned, a combination of scientific knowledge characterized as "universal, objective and decontextualized" and tacit knowledge characterized as "implicit, indigenous and context-dependent" allows actors to be in possession of sufficient capabilities to implement new technologies and management practices. Chapters 3 and 4 have shown this. Knowledge is at the heart of innovations and of any new product, organization or service developed by companies, universities, research laboratories and actors who are inclined to innovate. However, knowledge is not a traditional factor of production, as land, labor or capital can be in the agricultural sector. The relationships that are established between several actors in a network raise the question of the transparency of the information disseminated, as well as the uncertainty and asymmetry of this information and knowledge. Their transaction costs can be very high and depend in part on the type of knowledge such as the degree of codification (codified/formal or tacit/informal) and technology integration. The term "sticky knowledge" defined by von Hippel and "stickiness" by Cowan to characterize knowledge that is difficult to transfer outside its context of emergence is essential for understanding and optimizing the clarity and transfer of knowledge and innovations. Informal interactions represent an interesting channel for knowledge diffusion. Informal methods such as the transfer and use of unsystematic technology that were prevalent in some sectors can lead to the formalization of exchanges and to more structured and organized relationships later on.

Chapter 2 presents the history of the evolution of business collaboration, the top-down and bottom-up innovation models, the formation of networks of actors with the territorial dimension, as well as examples of collaboration, such as the exchange of licenses, spin-off, licensing-in, licensing-out and intellectual property rights in general. Furthermore, at the geographical level, national innovation systems promote the production of technology as well as the production of scientific results and knowledge. Their diffusion and possible use by the targeted actors, from the private or public sector, are part of the national framework in which companies can innovate. At the regional level, regional innovation systems can promote collaborative innovation at the heart of more territorialized and dispersed frameworks, which are set up in many territories in Europe. The territorial dimension of open innovation has been studied for a short time. The types of proximities coming from Ron Boschma's work have shed light on their role in the circulation of knowledge and flows of material and immaterial assets between actors involved in collaborative innovation projects. Geographical proximity enables this circulation, especially in organized ecosystems such as clusters, innovative environments and industrial districts. In such organizational arrangements, we see the creation of networks that integrate local actors who are historically present on the territory. These actors are complemented by others, who are new in the environment and identified as useful resources for a project. This is the case for innovation facilitators or intermediaries, who benefit from a physical proximity that is at the heart of the connection maintained between the actors in the network. Research centers at the local or regional level, technology transfer centers and actors located at the interface between fundamental and applied research are good examples. Another concrete example is the Italian industrial region of Emilia Romagna. This region is characterized by strong growth and low unemployment. It is home to large companies in the automotive sector (Ferrari, Maserati and Lamborghini) and in the agri-food sector (Barilla and Granarolo), as well as numerous SMEs, particularly in the world-renowned ceramics sector. A whole range of local, regional and international players are jointly involved in the projects of the districts present in the area. The cognitive proximity facilitates the understanding and the connection of the actors between them, just like the institutional proximity which establishes reference points for the actors. The organizational routines, regulations, standards and similar habits that the actors know encourage them to collaborate and understand each other. Innovation networks support businesses and can enable the emergence of innovative initiatives and links between network actors, promoting and encouraging further collaboration to deliver innovation.

Chapter 3 sets out to define the reasons for introducing collaborative innovation, the forms it takes and the actors involved. The use of ideas from the customer or user of the innovation in the innovation process originates from the beginning of the 20th century. In 1927, Michelin created the idea box so that the firm's employees could share proposals for improvements. The solutions that could improve the activities of employees in the production lines are all the more efficient if they come from these employees, on the ground, who know and understand what the problems are. After Michelin, the SNCF followed in the footsteps of the idea box in the 1930s. In the 1970s, quality approaches were introduced in large companies, which then used them in their production line improvement process. This was the beginning of the bottom-up method in which employees are a force of proposal. The idea box is gradually transformed into a participative platform where the exchange of information, ideas and the sharing of customized solutions to various problems becomes common. Collaborative innovation is born within these collaborative tools, which benefit from the expansion of information and communication technologies. In the 2000s, consumers intervened in the innovation process via product tests or consumer panels. This recourse to consumers and users of innovations reflects an element of trust. As described in Chapter 4, the trust that is established between the stakeholders of collaborative projects working for the emergence of innovation is crucial. The trust and exchanges between the actors are the basis of a "collective intelligence" that enables the best solutions to be found for the situations encountered.

The development of participatory platforms such as crowdfunding, crowdsourcing or crowdlending also testifies to the rise of the active role of various actors and users in the innovation process. Participatory financing such as crowdlending has a bright future ahead of it. In the first quarter of 2020, 40.7 million euros were raised via this participatory practice. This amount was still 6% lower than the previous year, but the platforms that allow for collecting funds are competing with each other to attract new contributors and thus develop numerous projects in support of companies seeking financing. The diversification of investments through several projects and several platforms dedicated to this practice is a model that is spreading.

Chapter 3 also presents the case of open source software, open digital platforms such as Innocentive and Yet2.com, as well as third places as open spaces for the production of science, knowledge and technologies, which can host several actors (e.g. employees of companies, entrepreneurs, students and other individuals likely to work remotely), facilitating their future collaboration. These environments are coworking spaces, Living Labs, FabLabs, hacker spaces or maker spaces. In parallel with the digital revolution that characterizes the 21st century and that is trans-sectorial, virtual platforms are developing all over the world, as are these physical spaces or third places that are also proliferating. The three characteristics of these environments are a physical location, services that are constantly being adapted and a community of diversified actors. The dynamics established in these spaces through networking and the emergence and proposal of innovative solutions have inspired private sector companies to develop their own. The characteristic of physical proximity is important for maintaining relationships between the actors who work in these spaces. Thus, the management of physical places, in order to keep them open, friendly and attractive, is crucial to catalyzing relationships based on this physical proximity. The digitization of economies leads to a structural change in the management of innovation. This is true for the European case and also for other parts of the world, where societal, economic and environmental issues are becoming increasingly important.

All kinds of innovations can be created and then deployed on the market within the third places, with a co-production of knowledge. More and more innovations are being developed for social and environmental purposes. Innovations, which have been used for a long time, have gradually moved from transition management to strategic management of niches. Traditionally, the highly institutionalized socio-technical regimes of research development and valorization of research since the second half of the 20th century are giving way to a growth of local individual and collective initiatives, based on a bottom-up structuring. The use of science with and for society is growing, with forms of innovation that include more users and clients through participatory innovation, coming from technical democracy.

Finally, Chapter 4 presents the advantages and disadvantages of collaborative innovation strategies for the actors, for the environmental and economic spheres in particular, while raising some paradoxes of this concept, which was developed almost 20 years ago. Collaborative innovation can be considered as cumbersome. The driving force of open innovation works because of the dynamism of the actors and stakeholders in innovative projects. Different forms of partnerships can follow one another throughout the innovation process, depending on the needs of the actors, the knowledge and resources required and the strategy for integrating the innovation into the business. Nevertheless, this diversity of stakeholder profiles can give rise to drawbacks and difficulties. For example, management problems, financial barriers and problems, intellectual property and data sharing obstacles, and common language concerns may arise between actors. The sharing of tasks, the dissemination of results, and the financial, human and material investments can lead to reluctance and conflict. To take advantage of collaborative innovation, changes and adaptations from different spheres may be required. In this way, a comparable culture, a similar organization and a common language are vectors of a greater probability of successful collaboration. Thus, it is important to clarify everything upstream of the partners' involvement and to define the terms of collaboration, in order to reduce the risk of collaboration failures. Another type of actor who can help in this sense is the innovation intermediary. They can connect actors, involve them and mobilize them. Their ability to make the link between actors, to translate or popularize information that would be difficult to understand and therefore usable is important in this type of configuration. The role of intermediaries is also to avoid conflicts of interest and to actively stimulate the innovation process.

Some authors make the distinction between shared invention and competitive innovation. The former concerns an invention produced by actors from divergent backgrounds, all bringing complementary knowledge, based on "shared intelligence". This production can be achieved thanks to social dynamics that support the coherence of the inventions of old techniques. The second refers to the production of innovation by actors belonging to social groups based on the experiences of actors in a social dynamic to complement existing inventions supporting their competitive strengths. These concepts have been used in local economic policies such as the metropolitan project of Grand Nancy in France. The main objective is to anticipate demographic, ecological and digital mutations at the local and global levels by bringing together different actors from civil society, political decision-makers and economic agents.

The transitional period in which we find ourselves reveals the essential importance of collaboration and social links at all levels and in all sectors. The digital revolution of the last few years is at the service of responsible innovation which is itself an integral part of entrepreneurial strategies for a successful ecological transition. Global issues such as the fight against global warming, demographic pressure on cities that spill over into so-called "peri-urban" areas, public health problems such as cardiovascular disease, obesity, pollution or the vulnerability of jobs in certain sectors weakened by public policies are also encountered by actors at the local level.

Finally, the political, cultural, economic, technological, and social context and systems must be integrated into collaborative projects to develop innovations to curb nature-related problems. Indeed, according to a 2021 United Nations Environment Programme (UNEP) report, the Earth has lost about half of its forests and coral reefs, as well as 70% of wetlands and 65% of major rivers. The organization estimates that until 2050, US$536 billion per year (equal to the US Small and Medium Business Assistance Plan after the Covid-19 pandemic) would need to be invested to fund innovative nature-based solutions. The agricultural, food and construction sectors in particular depend on nature. More than half of the world's total GDP depends in part on nature. Therefore, in order to achieve the objectives of combating global warming, land degradation and biodiversity protection, funding from the public and especially the private sectors, which have so far lagged behind with only 20% of the funding, is fundamental. Employment, education and health can be impacted by the lack of this financial support due to the weakness of countries to progress in these areas. The collaboration between several disciplines, several actors from different regions of the world or even different sectors could lead to the development of innovations for the regeneration of a greener agriculture, the preservation and restoration of forests and mangroves, for example.

References

Adams, R., Bessant, J., Phelps, R. (2006). Innovation management measurement: A review. *International Journal of Management Reviews*, 8(1), 21–47.

Afuah, A.N. and Bahram, N. (1995). The hypercube of innovation. *Research Policy*, 24(1), 51–76.

Agogué, M., Yström, A., Le Masson, P. (2013). Rethinking the role of intermediaries as an architect of collective exploration and creation of knowledge in open innovation. *International Journal of Innovation Management*, 17(02), 1–32.

Ahuja, G. (2000). Collaboration networks, structural holes and innovation: A longitudinal study. *Administrative Science Quarterly*, 45, 425–455.

Akrich, M., Callon, M., Latour, B. (1988). A quoi tient le succès des innovations. *Gérer et Comprendre Annales des mines*, 11, 4–17.

Albert-Cromarias, A. and Asselineau, A. (2013). Proximity cooperation driving innovation. The Naturopole case-file. *Problems and Perspectives in Management*, 11(3), 37–46.

Aliouat, B. and Thiaw, C. (2018). Communauté épistémique et dynamique d'innovation collaborative: L'innovation contrariée au sein des pôles de compétitivité. *Communication & Management*, 15(1), 35–59.

Almeida, P. and Kogut, B. (1999). Localization of knowledge and the mobility of engineers in regional networks. *Management*, 45(7), 905–917.

Amabile, T., Schatzel, E., Moneta, G., Kramer, S. (2004). Leader behaviors and the work environment for creativity: Perceived leader support. *The Leadership Quarterly*, 15, 5–32.

André, P., Schraefel, M., Teevan, J., Dumais, S. (2009). Discovery is never by chance: Designing for (un)serendipity. *Proceedings of the seventh ACM Conference on Creativity and Cognition (C&C '09), Association for Computing Machinery*, New York, 305–314.

Andriopoulos, C. and Lewis, M. (2009). Exploitation-exploration tensions and organizational ambidexterity: Managing paradoxes of innovation. *Organization Science*, 20, 696–717.

Aouinaït, C. (2019). Innovation capacity of the agricultural sector: Network of productive interactions, knowledge transfer and differentiation mechanisms. PhD Thesis, École Polytechnique Fédérale de Lausanne.

Aouinaït, C. (2021). Innovation collaborative et innovation ouverte: Caractéristiques de leur mise en œuvre. *Technologie et Innovation*, 6.

Aouinait, C., Jeangros, B., Nassar, V., Crole-Rees, A. (2014). Caractérisation des innovations en production végétale: L'exemple du colza HOLL. *Revue Suisse d'Agriculture*, 5, 104–111.

Arbo, P. and Benneworth, P. (2007). Understanding the regional contribution of higher education institutions: A literature review. OECD Education Working Papers, No. 9, OECD Publishing, Paris.

Arfaoui, M. (2015). La "co-création" comme dispositif. *Communication*, 33(2), 1–24. http://communication.revues.org/6013; DOI: 10.4000/communication.6013.

Argote, L., McEvily, B., Reagans, R. (2003). Managing knowledge in organizations: An integrative framework and review of emerging themes. *Management Science*, 49, 571–582.

Arora, A. and Gambardella, A. (1994). Evaluating technological information and utilizing it: Scientific knowledge, technological capability, and external linkages in biotechnology. *Journal of Economic Behavior and Organization*, 24(1), 91–114.

Arora, A. and Gambardella, A. (2010). Chapter 15: The market for technology. In *Handbook of the Economics of Innovation*, Hall, B.H. and Rosenberg, N. (eds). North-Holland, Amsterdam.

Arora, A., Athreye, S., Huang, C. (2015). The paradox of openness revisited: Collaborative innovation and patenting by UK innovators. *MERIT Working Papers 2015-031, United Nations University – Maastricht Economic and Social Research Institute on Innovation and Technology (MERIT)*.

Arundel, A. (2001). The relative effectiveness of patents and secrecy for appropriation. *Research Policy*, 30, 611–624.

Asheim, B., Boschma, R., Cooke, P. (2011). Constructing regional advantage: Platform policies based on related variety and differentiated knowledge bases. *Regional Studies*, 45(7), 893–904.

Aubouin, N. and Capdevila, I. (2019). La gestion des communautés de connaissances au sein des espaces de créativité et innovation: Une variété de logiques de collaboration. *Innovations*, 58(1), 105–134. https://doi.org/10.3917/inno.058.0105.

Audretsch, D.B. and Feldman, M.P. (1996). R&D spillovers and the geography of innovation and production. *American Economic Review*, 86(3), 630–640.

Auh, S. and Menguc, B. (2005). Balancing exploration and exploitation: The moderating role of competitive intensity. *Journal of Business Research*, 58, 1652–1661.

Aydalot, P. (ed.) (1986). *Milieux innovateurs en Europe*. GREMI, Paris.

Ayerbe, C. and Azzam, J.E. (2015). Pratiques coopétitives dans l'Open Innovation: Les enseignements des patent pools. *Management international/International Management/Gestiòn internacional*, 19(2), 95–114.

Ayerbe, C. and Chanal, V. (2011). Quel management des DPI dans les business modèles ouverts ? *Revue française de gestion*, 210, 99–115.

Bageac, D. (2013). L'innovation ouverte dans un contexte organisationnel. Gestion et management. Thesis, CERGAM – Centre d'Etudes et de Recherche en Gestion d'Aix-Marseille, Aix-Marseille University.

Balas, N. and Palpacuer, F. (2008). Les réseaux d'innovation sont-ils toujours ancrés dans les territoires ? Le cas de l'alliance crolles 2. *Entreprises et histoire*, 53.

Baldwin, C. and von Hippel, E. (2011). Modeling a paradigm shift: From producer innovation to user and open collaborative innovation. *Organization Science*, 22(6), 1399–1417, Harvard Business School Finance Working Paper No. 10-038.

Baldwin, C., Hienerth, C., von Hippel, E. (2006). How user innovations become commercial products: A theoretical investigation and case study. *Research Policy*, 35, 1291–1313.

Banker, R.D., Bardhan, I., Asdemir, O. (2006). Understanding the impact of collaboration software on product design and development. *Information Systems Research*, 17(4), 352–373.

Baregheh, A., Rowley, J., Sambrook, S. (2009). Towards a multidisciplinary definition of innovation. *Management Decision*, 47(8), 1323–1339. https://doi.org/10.1108/00251740910984578.

Barge-Gil, A. (2010). Cooperation-based innovators and peripheral cooperators: An empirical analysis of their characteristics and behavior. *Technovation*, 30, 195–206.

Barjolle, D., Quiédeville, S., Rossier, R., Stolz, H., Stolze, M. (2014). Study on investment in agricultural research: Review for Switzerland. Report, The Impact of Research on EU Agriculture, IMPRESA Project.

Barondeau, R. (2015). La collaboration wiki: Critiques, justifications et perspectives: Le cas du nouveau Centre hospitalier de l'Université de Montréal (CHUM). Administration PhD Thesis, Université du Québec à Montréal.

Béjean, M., Picard, R., Bréda, G. (2021). Living Labs, innovation collaborative et écosystèmes: Le cas de l'initiative "Concept Maturity Levels" dans les Medtech. *Innovations*, 2(2), 81–110.

Bekkers, R. and Bodas Freitas, I.M. (2011). The performance of university-industry collaborations: Empirical evidence from the Netherlands. *Druid 2011: Innovation, Strategy, and Structure – Organizations, Institutions, Systems and Regions*, Copenhagen.

Ben Slimane, F. and Rousselet, E. (2018). Le financement participatif (ou le crowlending) aux PME et TPE: Mythes et réalités d'une innovation financière. *Innovations*, 2(2), 15–39.

Benali, K., Bourguin, G., David, B., Derycke, A., Ferraris, C. (2002). Collaboration/Coopération. *Information Interaction Intelligence – Actes des 2èmes assises du GdR I3*, Gérome Canals, Nancy, 17.

Bénézech, D. (2012). The open innovation model: Some issues regarding its internal consistency. *Journal of Innovation Economics & Management*, 10(2), 145–165.

Bercovitz, J. and Feldmann, M. (2006). Entrepreneurial universities and technology transfer: A conceptual framework for understanding knowledge-based economic development. *Journal of the Technology Transfer*, 31, 175–188.

Berger-Douce, S. (2015). La performance par l'innovation responsable. *Entreprendre & Innover*, 1(1), 37–44.

Bergvall-Kåreborn, B. and Ståhlbröst, A. (2009). Living lab: An open and citizen-centric approach for innovation. *International Journal of Innovation and Regional Development*, 1, 356–370.

Berninghaus, S.K. and Schwalbe, U. (1996). Evolution, interaction, and Nash equilibria. *Journal of Economic Behavior & Organization*, 29(1), 57–85.

Biggs, S.D. and Clay, E. (1981). Sources of innovation in agricultural technology. *World Development*, 9(4), 321–336.

Blandin, C., Frugier, D., Gaujard, C., Gisselbrecht, A., Michel, D., Poste, S., Deroo, M. (2016). Surmonter les paradoxes de l'innovation collective. *Entreprendre & Innover*, 3(3), 61–71.

Blume, L.E. (1995). The statistical mechanics of best-response strategy revision. *Games and Economic Behavior*, 11(2), 111–145.

Bonnemaizon, A., Benoît-Moreau, F., Cadenat, S., Renaudin, V. (2013). Regards sur la co-production du client: Comment les entreprises nous font-elles participer ? *Décisions Marketing*, 9–24.

Boschma, R. (2005). Proximity and innovation: A critical assessment. *Regional Studies*, 39(1), 61–74.

Bottazzi, L. and Peri, G. (2003). Innovation and spillovers in regions: Evidence from European patent data. *European Economic Review*, 47(4), 687–710.

Boudreau, K. (2010). Open platform strategies and innovation: Granting access vs. devolving control. *Management Science*, 56(10), 1849–1872.

Boudreau, K. and Hagiu, A. (2009). Platform rules: Regulation of an ecosystem by a private actor. In *Platforms, Markets and Innovation; Cheltenham*, Gawer, A. (ed.). Edward Elgar, Cheltenham and Northampton, MA.

Bouncken, R.B. and Reuschl, A.J. (2018). Coworking-spaces: How a phenomenon of the sharing economy builds a novel trend for the workplace and for entrepreneurship. *Review of Managerial Science*, 12(1), 317–334.

Bouncken, R.B., Laudien, S.M., Fredrich, V., Görmar, L. (2018). Coopetition in coworking-spaces: Value creation and appropriation tensions in an entrepreneurial space. *Review of Managerial Science*, 12, 385–410.

Bourdieu, P. (1980). Le capital social. Actes de la recherche en sciences sociales. *Le capital social*, 31, 2–3.

Bourguignon, R. and Novicevic, M. (2012). Chester I. Barnard: The functions of the executive et ses prolongements. José Allouche. *Encyclopédie des Ressources Humaines*, Vuibert.

Boutillier, S. and Fournier, C. (2009). La responsabilité sociale des entreprises artisanales, innovation sociale ou néopaternalisme: Résultats d'une enquête menée dans la région du Nord/Pas de Calais (France). *Marché et organisations*, 1(1), 39–60.

Boutillier, S., Capdevila, I., Dupont, L., Morel, L. (2020). Collaborative spaces promoting creativity and innovation. *Journal of Innovation Economics & Management*, 31(1), 1–9.

Bréchet, J.-P. and Saives, A-L. (2001). De la spécificité à la compétitivité. L'exemple de la construction de la compétitivité sur une base territoriale. *Revue finance contrôle stratégie*, 4, 5–30.

Brem, A., Bilgram, V., Marchuk, A. (2019). How crowdfunding platforms change the nature of user innovation – From problem solving to entrepreneurship. *Technological Forecasting and Social Change*, 144, 348–360.

Breschi, S. and Lissoni, F. (2006). Mobility of inventors and the geography of knowledge spillovers: New evidence on US data. CESSPRI Working paper.

Buisine, S., Boisadan, A., Richir, S. (2017). L'innovation radicale par la méthode de l'utilisateur extraordinaire. *Psychologie du travail et des organisations*, 24, 374–386.

Burger-Helmchen, T., Pénin, J., Guittard, C., Schenk, E., Dintrich, A. (2013). *L'innovation ouverte: Définition, pratiques et perspectives*. Chambre de commerce et d'industrie de Paris.

Buur, J. and Matthews, B.E.N. (2008). Participatory innovation. *International Journal of Innovation Management*, 12, 255–273.

Cainelli, G., Evangelista, R., Savona, M. (2006). Innovation and economic performance in services: A firm-level analysis. *Cambridge Journal of Economics*, 30(3), 435–458.

Callon, M. (1999). Une contribution de la sociologie à l'analyse des externalités. Essai sur la notion de cadrage/débordement. *Dominique Foray et Jacques Mairesse, Innovation et performance*, EHESS, 399–432.

Capdevila, I. (2015). Les différentes approches entrepreneuriales dans les espaces ouverts d'innovation. *Innovations*, 48(3), 87–105.

Carayannis, E. and Campbell, D. (2017). Les systèmes d'innovation de la quadruple et de la quintuple hélice. *Innovations*, 3(3), 173–195.

Carayannis, E., Barth, T., Campbell, D. (2012). The Quintuple Helix innovation model: Global warming as a challenge and driver for innovation, *Journal of Innovation and Entrepreneurship*, 1(2), 1–12. https://doi.org/10.1186/2192-5372-1-2.

Cardon, D. (2006). La trajectoire des innovations ascendantes: Inventivité, coproduction et collectif sur Internet. *Innovations, usages, réseaux symposium*, Montpellier, 17–18 November.

Casadella, V. and Benlahcen-Tlemcani, M. (2006). De l'applicabilité du Système National d'Innovation dans les Pays Moins Avancés. *Innovations*, 24(2), 59.

Chabault, D. (2010). Gouvernance et trajectoire des pôles de compétitivité. *Management & Avenir*, 6(36), 130–151.

Chesbrough, H.W. (2003). *Open Innovation: The New Imperative for Creating and Profiting from Technology*. Harvard Business School Publishing, Brighton.

Chesbrough, H.W. (2006a). *Open Business Models: How to Thrive in the New Innovation Landscape*. Harvard Business School Publishing, Brighton.

Chesbrough, H.W. (2006b). *Open Innovation: A New Paradigm for Understanding Industrial Innovation. Open Innovation/Resarching a New Paradigm*. Oxford University Press.

Chesbrough, H.W. (2008) Orchestrating appropriability: Towards an endogenous view of capturing value from innovation investments. In *Handbook of Technology and Innovation Management*, Shane, S. (ed.). Wiley, Chichester.

Chesbrough, H.W. (2012). Open innovation: Where we've been and where we're going. *Research-Technology Management*, 55(4), 20–27.

Chesbrough, H.W. and Appleyard, M.M. (2007). Open innovation and strategy. *California Management Review*, 50(1), 57–76.

Chesbrough, H.W. and Brunswicker, S. (2013). Managing open innovation in large firms survey report. Executive Survey on Open Innovation, FRAUNHOFER Soc.

Chesbrough, H.W. and Rosenbloom, R.S. (2002). The role of the business model in capturing value from innovation: Evidence from Xerox Corporation's technology spin-off companies. *Industrial and Corporate Change*, 11(3), 529–555.

Chouteau, M. and Viévard, L. (2007). L'innovation, un processus à décrypter. Millénaire 3: Le centre ressources prospectives du grand Lyon.

Christensen, C.M. (1997). *The Innovator's Dilemma: When New Technologies Cause Great Firms to Fail*. Harvard Business School Press, Boston, MA.

Chung, S. and Kim, G. (2003). Performance effects of partnership between manufacturers and suppliers for new product development. *Research Policy*, 32, 587–603.

Codini, A.P. (2015). Business networks along innovation life cycle. *Journal of Business & Industrial Marketing*, 30(3/4), 329–341.

Cohen, W.M. (2010). Fifty years of empirical studies of innovative activity and performance. In *Handbook of the Economics of Innovation*, 1st edition, Hall, B.H. and Rosenberg, N. (ed.). Elsevier, Amsterdam.

Cohen, W.M. and Levinthal, D.A. (1989). Innovation and learning: The two faces of R&D. *The Economic Journal*, 99(397), 569–596.

Cohen, W.M. and Levinthal, D.A. (1990). Absorptive capacity: A new perspective on learning and innovation. *Administrative Science Quarterly*, 35, 128–152.

Cohen, W.M., Florida, R., Goe, W.R. (1994). University. Industry Research Centers in the United States. Report, Carnegie Mellon University, Pittsburgh, PA.

Cohendet, P. and Schenk, E. (1999). Irréversibilités, compatibilité et concurrence entre standards technologiques. In *Réseaux et coordination*, Callon, M., Cohendet, P., Curien, N., Dalle, J.M., Eymard-Duvernay, F., Doray, D., Schenk, E. (eds). Economica, Paris.

Cohendet, P., Kirman, A., Zimmermann, J.B. (2003). Émergence, formation et dynamique des réseaux. Modèles de la morphogenèse. *Revue d'économie industrielle*, 103(1), 15–42.

Commission de la communauté europeénne (2001). Promouvoir un cadre pour la responsabilité sociale des entreprises. CCE, Brussels, 35.

Commission mondiale sur l'environnement et le développement (1987). Notre avenir à tous. http://www.ceres.ens.fr/IMG/pdf/rapport_brundtland.pdf.

Cooke, P., Uranga, M.G., Etxebarria, G. (1998). Regional systems of innovation: An evolutionary perspective. *Environment and Planning A*, 30, 1563–1584.

Csikszentmihalyi, M. and Le Fevre, J. (1989). Optimal experience in work and leisure. *Journal of Personality and Social Psychology*, 56(5), 815–822.

Cova, B. (2008). Consumer made: Quand le consommateur devient producteur. *Décisions Marketing*, (50), 19–27. http://www.jstor.org/stable/20723307.

Cowan, R., David, P., Foray, D. (2000). The explicit economics of knowledge codification and tacitness. *Industrial and Corporate Change*, 9(2), 211–253.

Crépon, B. and Duguet, E. (1994). Innovation: Mesures, rendements et concurrence. *Économie et Statistique*, 275, 121–134.

Curien, N. (1999). Coordination et réseaux: De l'interconnexion à l'intermédiation. In *Réseau et coordination*, Callon, M., Cohendet, P., Curien, N., Dalle, J.M., Eymard-Duvernay, F., Doray, D., Schenk, E. (eds). Economica, Paris.

Daane, J.F., Oliveros, O., Bolo, M. (2009). Performance indicators for agricultural innovation systems in the ACP Region: Synthesis report. *International Expert Consultation Workshop*, Wageningen, 15–17 July.

Dahl, M.S. and Pedersen, C.Ø.R. (2004). Knowledge flows through informal contacts in industrial clusters: Myth or reality? *Research Policy*, 33, 1673–1686.

Dahlander, L. and Gann, D.M. (2010). How open is innovation? *Research Policy*, 39(6), 699–709.

Dalziel, M. (2010). Why do intermediaries exist? *DRUID Summer Conference 2010 on Opening Up Innovation: Strategy, Organization and Technology*, Imperial College London Business School, 16–18 June.

Dasgupta, P. and David, P. (1994). Towards a new economics of science. *Research Policy*, 23, 487–521.

Daumas, J.C. (2007). Districts industriels: Du concept à l'histoire: Les termes du débat. *Revue économique*, 58(1), 131–152.

Davies, A. and Tollervey, K. (2013). *The Style of Coworking: Contemporary Shared Workspaces*. Prestel Verlag, Munich.

D'Este, P. and Patel, P. (2005). University – Industry linkages in the UK: What are the factors determining the variety of university researchers' interactions with industry? *DRUID 10th Anniversary Summer Conference 2005 on Dynamics of Industry and Innovation: Organizations, Networks and Systems*, 29.

De Guzman, G.V. and Tang, A.I. (2011). *Working in the UnOffice: A Guide to Coworking for Indie Workers, Small Businesses, and Nonprofits*. Night Owls Press, Portland, OH.

Dekkers, R., Koukou, M., Mitchell, S., Sinclair, S. (2019). Engaging with open innovation: A Scottish perspective on its opportunities, challenges and risks. *Journal of Innovation Economics & Management*, 1(1), 193–226.

Delgado, L., Galvez, D., Hassan, A., Palominos, P., Morel, L. (2020). Innovation spaces in universities: Support for collaborative learning. *Journal of Innovation Economics & Management*, 1(1), 123–153.

Deltour, F. and Lethiais, V. (2014). L'innovation en PME et son accompagnement par les TIC: Quels effets sur la performance ? *Systèmes d'information & management*, 19, 45–73. https://doi.org/10.3917/sim.142.0045.

Denervaud, I., Gérardin, O., Noé, M., Souplet, C., Tartar, M. (2010). L'innovation collaborative dans tous ses états. *L'Expansion Management Review*, 138(3), 110–119.

Deskmag (2015). First results of the new global coworking survey. https://www.deskmag.com/en/coworking-news/first-results-of-the-new-global-coworking-survey-2015-16.

Docherty, M. (2006). Primer on open innovation: Principles and practice. *OECD Open Innovation in Global Networks*. http://www.oecd.org/publishing/corrigenda.

Doloreux, D. and Bitard, P. (2005). Les systèmes régionaux d'innovation: Discussion critique. *Géographie, économie, société*, 1(1), 21–36.

Doreian, P. and Stoneman, F. (eds) (1997). *Evolution of Social Networks*. Routledge, Amsterdam.

Dosi, G. and Nelson, R.R. (2010). Chapter 3: Technical change and industrial dynamics as evolutionary processes. In *Handbook of the Economics of Innovation*, Hall, B.H. and Rosenberg, N. (ed.). Elsevier, Amsterdam.

Dosi, G., Llerena, P., Sylos Labini, M. (2006). The relationships between science, technologies and their industrial exploitation: An illustration through the myths and realities of the so called "European Paradox". *Research Policy*, 35(10), 1450–1464.

Drucker, P.F. (1985). *Innovation and Entrepreneurship: Practice and Principles*. Harper & Row, London.

Drucker, P.F. (2014). *Innovation and Entrepreneurship*. Routledge, London. https://doi.org/10.4324/9781315747453.

Duc, C. (2018). La moitié des sociétés procèdent à des innovations. *Insee Première no. 1709*.

Dufeu, A. (2011). Analyse des processus d'intégration-désintégration verticales. *Cahier de recherche no. CR02*.

Dupont, L., Mastelic, J., Nyffeler, N., Latrille, S., Seulliet, E. (2019). Confiance et Technologie: Deux dimensions de l'innovation ouverte et agile appliquée à l'énergie. *Technologie et innovation*, ISTE OpenScience, L'innovation agile, 19(4), ⟨10.21494/ISTE.OP.2019.0314⟩. ⟨hal-02047441⟩.

Duran, N. (2018). Les rôles des acteurs dans la formation et le développement du crowdlending: Analyse des liens et échanges sociaux. *Innovations*, 2(2), 141–160.

Dyer, H. and Singh, H. (1998). The relational view: Cooperative advantage and sources of interorganizational competitive advantage. *Academy of Management Review*, 23, 660–679.

Edquist, C. (1997). *Systems of Innovation: Technologies, Institutions, and Organizations*. Pinter, London.

Enkel, E., Kausch, C., Gassmann, O. (2005). Managing the risk of customer integration. *European Management Journal*, 23(2), 203–213.

Enos, J.L. (1962). *Petroleum Progress and Profits: A History of Process Innovation*. MIT Press, Cambridge, MA.

Estellés-Arolas, E. and González-Ladrón-de-Guevara, F. (2012). Towards an integrated crowdsourcing definition. *Journal of Information Science*, 38(2), 189–200. https://doi.org/10.1177/0165551512437638.

Etzkowitz, H. and Leydesdorff, L. (2000). The dynamics of innovation: From national systems and "Mode 2" to a Triple Helix of University-Industry-Government Relations. *Research Policy*, 29(2), 109–123.

EU SCAR (2012). Agricultural knowledge and innovation systems in transition – A reflection paper. European Commission.

Evangelista, R., Perani, G., Rapiti, F., Archibugi, D. (1997). Nature and impact of innovation in manufacturing industry: Some evidence from the Italian innovation survey. *Research Policy*, 26, 521–536.

Fabbri, J. and Charue-Duboc, F. (2016). Les espaces de coworking: Nouveaux intermédiaires d'innovation ouverte ? *Revue française de gestion*, 254, 163–180. https://doi.org/10.3166/rfg.2016.00007.

Fagiolo, G. and Dosi, G. (2003). Exploitation, exploration and innovation in a model of endogenous growth with locally interacting agents. *Structural Change and Economic Dynamics*, 14(3), 237–273.

Faure, G., Chiffoleau, Y., Goulet, F., Temple L., Touzard, J.M. (2018). *Innovation et développement dans les systèmes agricoles et alimentaires*. Editions Quæ, Versailles.

Feldman, M.P. and Kogler, D. (2010). Stylized facts in the geography of innovation. https://EconPapers.repec.org/RePEc:eee:haechp:v1_381.

Fily, M.F. (2015). Connaitre et utiliser les licences Creative Commons, en 6 points. Montpellier (FRA): CIRAD, 11.

Foray, D. (2004). *The Economics of Knowledge*. MIT Press, Cambridge, MA.

Foray, D. (2009). Recherche, innovation et croissance économique: Qu'est-ce qui importe vraiment ? *Le Colloque 2009 Futuris. Le soutien public à l'innovation des entreprises: Quelle efficacité, quelles perspectives ?* 1–23.

Foray, D. and Lundvall, B.A. (1994). Chapter 7: The knowledge-based economy: From the economics of knowledge to the learning economy. In *The Economic Impact of Knowledge*, Neef, D., Siesfeld, G.A., Cefola, J. (eds). Taylor & Francis, London.

Forest, J. (2014). *Petite histoire des modèles d'innovation. Principes d'économie de l'innovation*. Peter Lang, Bern.

Foster, A. and Ford, N. (2003). Serendipity and information seeking: An empirical study. *Journal of Documentation*, 59(3), 321–340. https://doi.org/10.1108/00220410310472518.

Freeman, C. (1968). Chemical process plant: Innovation and the world market. *National Institute Economic Review*, 45, 29–51.

Freeman, C. (1987). *Technology and Economic Performance: Lessons from Japan*. Pinter, London.

Füller, J. (2010). Refining virtual co-creation from a consumer perspective. *California Management Review*, 52, 98–122.

Gallaud, D. and Nayaradou, M. (2012a). Open innovation and co-operation: Which choice of means of protection for innovation? *Journal of Innovation Economics*, 10(2), 167.

Gallaud, D., Martin, M., Reboud, S., Tanguy, C. (2012b). Proximités organisationnelle et géographique dans les relations de coopération: Une application aux secteurs agroalimentaires. *Géographie, économie, société*, 3(3), 261–285.

Gallini, N. and Winter, R. (1985). Licensing in the theory of innovation. *RAND Journal of Economics*, 16, 237–252.

Gandia, R., Brion, S., Mothe, C. (2011). Innovation ouverte et management de la propriété intellectuelle: Quelles stratégies dans le secteur du jeu vidéo ? *Revue française de gestion*, 210, 117–131.

Gangloff-Ziegler, C. (2009). Les freins au travail collaboratif. In *Le travail collaboratif: Une innovation générique*, Le Roux, S. (ed.). L'Harmattan, Paris ⟨hal-00550661⟩.

Garrett, L., Spreitzer, G., Bacevice, P. (2017). Co-constructing a sense of community at work: The emergence of community in coworking spaces. *Organization Studies*, 38, 821–842.

Gassmann, O. (2006). Opening up the innovation process: Towards an agenda. *R&D Management*, 36, 223–228.

Gassmann, O., Enkel, E., Chesbrough, H.W. (2010). The future of open innovation. *R&D Management*, 40(3), 213–221.

Gay, C., Liotard, I., Revest, V. (2019). Les concours d'innovation en ligne: Un instrument pertinent pour la recherche et l'innovation responsable. *Innovations*, MIT Press, 129–150.

Gershenfeld, N. (2005). *Fab: The Coming Revolution On Your Desktop – From Personal Computers to Personal Fabrication*. Basic Books, New York.

Gershenfeld, N. (2012). How to make almost anything: The digital fabrication revolution. *Foreign Affairs*, 91(6), 43–57.

Gibbons, M., Trow, M., Scott, P., Schwartzman, S., Nowotny, H., Limoges, C. (1994). *The New Production of Knowledge: The Dynamics of Science and Research in Contemporary Societies*. Sage, London, Thousand Oaks, New Delhi.

Gilbert, B.A., Audretsch, D.B., McDougall, P.P. (2004). The emergence of entrepreneurship policy. *Small Business Economics*, 22, 313–323. https://doi.org/10.1023/B:SBEJ.0000022235.10739.a8.

Gilly, J.P. and Grossetti, M. (1993). Organisations, individus et territoires. Le cas des systèmes locaux d'innovation. *Revue d'économie régionale et urbaine*, 3, 449–468.

Godin, B. (2005). The linear model of innovation: The historical construction of an analytical framework. Project on the History and Sociology of S&T Statistics, Working paper, 30, Montreal, CSIIC.

Goffin, K., Baxter, D., Szwejczewski, M., Cousens, A., van der Hoven, C. (2011). Tacit knowledge, lessons learnt, and new product development. *Journal of Product Innovation Management*, 28(2), 300–318.

Granovetter, M.S. (1973). The strength of weak ties. *The American Journal of Sociology*, 78, 1360–1380.

Grimpe, C. and Hussinger, K. (2013). Formal and informal knowledge and technology transfer from academia to industry: Complementarity effects and innovation performance. *Industry & Innovation*, 20(8), 683–700.

Grossetti, M. (2004). Concentration d'entreprises et innovation: Esquisse d'une typologie des systèmes productifs locaux. *Géographie, économie, société*, 2(2), 163–177.

Guilhon, B. (2008). Division du travail cognitif et quasi-marché de la connaissance. *Revue économique*, 59(2), 241–263.

Guillemot, G., Buisine, S., De Cagny, A., Davies, M., Humblot, B., Muller-Segard, L. (2016). Les innovations créatrices d'emplois industriels. *Conférence CESI Campus Rouen*.

Gupta, AK., Smith, K.G., Shalley, C.E. (2006). The interplay between exploration and exploitation. *Academy of Management Journal*, 49(4), 693–706. https://doi.org/10.5465/AMJ.2006.22083026.

Hafsi, T. and Martinet, A. (2007). Stratégie et management stratégique des entreprises. *Gestion*, 32, 88.

Hall, B.H., Jaffe, A., Trajtenberg, M. (2005). Market value and patent citations. *The RAND Journal of Economics*, 36(1), 16–38.

Hall, B.H., Helmers, C., Rogers, M., Sena, V. (2014). The choice between formal and informal intellectual property: A review. *Journal of Economic Literature*, 52(2), 1–50.

Hasche, N., Höglund, L., Linton, G. (2020). Quadruple helix as a network of relationships: Creating value within a Swedish regional innovation system. *Journal of Small Business & Entrepreneurship*, 32(6), 523–544. DOI: 10.1080/08276331.2019.1643134.

Henderson, R.M. and Clark, K.B. (1990). Architectural innovation: The reconfiguration of existing product technologies and the failure of established firms. *Administrative Science Quarterly*, 35(1), 9. https://doi.org/10.2307/2393549.

Henkel, J. (2006). Selective revealing in open innovation processes: The case of embedded linux. *Research Policy*, 35, 953–969.

Herstad, S., Bloch, C., Ebersberger, B., Velde, E. (2008). Open innovation and globalization; theory, evidence and implications. Vision Era Net, April.

von Hippel, E. (1976). The dominant role of users in the scientific instrument innovation process. *Research Policy*, 5(3), 212–239.

von Hippel, E. (1986). Lead users: A source of novel product concepts. *Management Science*, 32(7).

von Hippel, E. (1988). *Sources of Innovation*. Oxford University Press, New York. https://ssrn.com/abstract=2877276.

von Hippel, E. (1994). Sticky information and the locus of problem solving: Implications for innovation. *Management Science*, 40(4), 429–439.

von Hippel, E. (2001). Innovation by user communities: Learning from open-source software. *MIT Sloan Management Review*, 42, 82–86.

von Hippel, E. (2003). Open source software and the "Private-Collective" innovation model: Issues for organization science. *Organization Science*, 14(2), 208–223.

von Hippel, E. (2005). Democratizing innovation: The evolving phenomenon of user innovation. *Journal für Betriebswirtschaft*, 55, 63–78.

von Hippel, E. and Primack, J. (1971). Scientists and the politics of technology. *Applied Spectroscopy*, 25, 403–413.

von Hippel, E., de Jong, J.P.J., Flowers, S. (2012). Comparing business and household sector innovation in consumer products: Findings from a representative study in the United Kingdom. *Management Science*, 58, 1669–1681.

Hoang, H. and Rothaermel, F. (2005). The effect of general and partner-specific alliance experience on Joint R&D project performance. *The Academy of Management Journal*, 48, 332–345.

Howe, J. (2006). The rise of crowdsourcing. *Wired*, 14.

Howells, J. (1996). Tacit knowledge. *Technology Analysis & Strategic Management*, 8(2), 91–106.

Howells, J. (2006). Intermediation and the role of intermediaries in innovation. *Research Policy*, 35(5), 715–728.

Huizingh, E.K.R.E. (2011). Open innovation: State of the art and future perspectives. *Technovation*, 31, 2–9.

Iansiti, M. and Levien, R. (2004). Strategy as ecology. *Harvard Business Review*, 82(3), 68–78, 126.

Ingram, J. (1985). Farmer-scientist knowledge exchange: An essay. *Encyclopedia of Food and Agricultural Ethics*, p. 9.

Institut d'aménagement et d'urbanisme de la région d'Ile-de-France (2008). Clusters Mondiaux: Regards croisés sur la théorie et la réalité des clusters. Identification et cartographie des principaux clusters internationaux. https://halshs.archives-ouvertes.fr/halshs-00412049/documents.

Isckia, T. (2011). Ecosystèmes d'affaires, stratégies de plateforme et innovation ouverte: Vers une approche intégrée de la dynamique d'innovation. *Management & Avenir*, 46(6), 157–176, INSEEC/Management Prospective Editions ⟨10.3917/mav.046.0157⟩. ⟨hal-02435338⟩.

Isckia, T. and Lescop, D. (2011). Une analyse critique des fondements de l'innovation ouverte. *Revue française de gestion*, 37(210), 87–98.

Jaffe, A.B. (1989). Real effects of academic research. *The American Economic Review*, 79(5), 957–970.

Johnsen, T., Phillips, W., Caldwell, N., Lewis, M. (2006). Centrality of customer and supplier interaction in innovation. *Journal of Business Research*, 59(6), 671–678.

Jones, A.M. (2013). *The Fifth Age of Work*. Night Owls Press, Portland, OH.

Jones, D., Sundsted, T., Bacigalupo, T. (2009). *I'm Outta Here: How Coworking is Making the Office Obsolete*. Not an MBA Press, Austin, TX.

Kaine, G., Hill, M., Rowbottom, B. (2008). Types of agricultural innovations and the design of extension programs. Working paper, September.

Kakko, I. and Inkinen, S. (2009). Homo creativus: Creativity and serendipity management in third generation science and technology parks. *Science and Public Policy*, 36(7), 537–548, August.

Karlsson, C. (1988). Innovation adoption and the product life cycle. *Umeå Economic Studies*, 185, 232.

Katz, R. and Allen, T.J. (1988). Organizational issues in the introduction of new technologies. In *Managing Professionals in Innovative Organizations*, Katz, R. (ed.). Ballinger, Cambridge, MA, 442456.

Katz, M. and Shapiro, C. (1985). On the licensing of innovations. *The RAND Journal of Economics*, 16(4), 504–520.

Kemmis, S. and McTaggart, R. (2007). Chapter 10: Participatory action research. Communicative action and the public sphere. In *Strategies of Qualitative Inquiry*, Denzin, N.K. and Lincoln, Y.S. (eds). SAGE Publications, Thousand Oaks, CA.

Khan, Z. and Joseph, K. (2003). Embracing the paradoxes of innovation. *Innovation for a Complex World*, Supplement to Stanford social innovation review, 21–23.

Khedher, S. (2010). L'écosystème d'une firme: Une stratégie de gestion de l'innovation ouverte. Thesis, Université du Québec à Montréal.

Kindermann, R.P. and Snell, J.L. (1980). On the relation between Markov random fields and social networks. *Journal of Mathematical Sociology*, 7(1), 1–13.

King, S. (2017). Coworking is not about workspace: It's about feeling less lonely, *Harvard Business Review*. https://hbr.org/2017/12/coworking-is-not-about-workspace-its-about-feeling-less-lonely.

Kirman, A.P. (1993). Ants, rationality and recruitement. *Quarterly Journal of Economics*, 108, 137–56.

Kirman, A.P. (1998). Economies with interacting agents. In *The Economics of Networks*, Cohendet, P., Llerena, P., Stahn, H., Umbhauer, G. (eds). Springer Verlag, Berlin.

Klerkx, L. and Leeuwis, C. (2008). Matching demand and supply in the agricultural knowledge infrastructure: Experiences with innovation intermediaries. *Food Policy*, 33(3), 260–276.

Klevorick, A.K., Levin, R.C., Nelson, R.R., Winter, S.G. (1995). On the sources and significance of interindustry differences in technological opportunities. *Research Policy*, 24(2), 185–205.

Klewitz, J., Zeyen, A., Hansen, E.G. (2012). Intermediaries driving eco-innovation in SMEs: A qualitative investigation. *European Journal of Innovation Management*, 15(4), 442–467.

Kline, S. and Rosenberg, G. (1986). An overview of innovation. In *The Positive Sum Strategy: Harnessing Technology for Economic Growth*, Landau, R. and Rosenberg, N. (eds). National Academy Press, Washington, DC.

Knickel, K., Brunori, G., Rand, S., Proost, J. (2009). Towards a better conceptual framework for innovation processes in agriculture and rural development: From linear models to systemic approaches. *The Journal of Agricultural Education and Extension*, 15(2), 131–146. DOI: 10.1080/13892240902909064.

Koenig, G. (2012). Le concept d'écosystème d'affaires revisité. *Management*, 15(2), 209–224.

Kongsted, H.C., Tartari, V., Cannito, D., Norn, M.T., Wohlert, J. (2017). University researchers' engagement with industry, the public sector and society: Results from a 2017 survey of university researchers in Denmark. DEA. https://dea.nu/sites/dea.nu/files/cbs_dea_survey_of_researchers_external_engagement.pdf.

Krauz, A. (2016). Transition management in Montreuil: Towards perspectives of hybridisation between "Top-Down" and "Bottom-Up" transitions. In *Governance of Urban Sustainability Transitions: European and Asian Experiences*, Loorbach, D., Wittmayer, J., Shiroyama, H., Fujino, J., Mizuguchi, S. (eds). Springer, Japan.

Krupicka, A. and Coussi, O. (2017). Compréhension d'un cas d'innovation institutionnelle au travers de la théorie de la traduction éclairée par les proximités de ressources. *Gestion et Management Public*, 5(3), 5–25.

Kwiatkowski, A. and Buczynski, B. (2011). *Coworking: Building Community as a Space Catalyst*. Cohere Coworking, Fort Collins, CO.

Lacoste, S. and Pardo, C. (2016). Les pratiques conjointes de responsabilité sociale de l'entreprise (RSE) au sein d'un écosystème d'affaires. Une étude de cas. *Management & Avenir*, 3(3), 35–55.

Lakhani, K.R., Jeppesen, L.B., Lohse, P.A., Panetta, J.A. (2006). The value of openness in scientific problem solving. Working Paper Number: 07–050, Harvard Business School.

Langlois, R.N. (2003). Schumpeter and the obsolescence of the entrepreneur. Koppl, R., Birner, J., Kurrild-Klitgaard, P. (eds). *Austrian Economics and Entrepreneurial Studies*, Advances in Austrian Economics, Vol. 6, Emerald Group Publishing Limited, Bingley. https://doi.org/10.1016/S1529-2134(03)06018-6.

Laperche, B. and Uzunidis, D. (2007). Le Système national d'innovation russe en restructuration: Réformes institutionnelles et politique industrielle. *Innovations*, 2(2), 69–94.

Laperche, B., Lima, M., Seuillet, E., Trousse, B. (eds) (2019). Les écosystèmes d'innovation: Regards croisés des acteurs clés, L'esprit économique, Economie et Innovation, Paris, l'Harmattan, 321. *Innovations*, 61, 201–204.

Laursen, K. and Salter, A.J. (2005). My precious technology: The role of legal appropriability strategy in shaping innovative performance. Working Paper, Tanaka Business School, Imperial College London.

Laursen, K. and Salter, A.J. (2006). Open for innovation: The role of openness in explaining innovation performance among UK manufacturing firms. *Strategic Management Journal*, 27, 131–150.

Lave, J. and Wenger, E. (1991). *Situated Learning: Legitimate Peripheral Participation*. Cambridge University Press, Cambridge.

Lawson, C. and Lorenz, E. (1999). Collective learning, tacit knowledge and regional innovative capacity. *Regional Studies*, 33(4), 305–317.

Le Bas, C. and Torre, A. (1993). Études empiriques – Survey sur les surveys d'innovation – Une première évaluation des enquêtes d'innovation européennes. *Revue d'économie industrielle*, 65(1), 80–95.

Le Roy, F., Robert, M., Lasch, F. (2013). Coopérer avec ses amis ou avec ses ennemis: Quelle stratégie pour l'innovation produit ? *Revue française de gestion*, 3(3), 81–100.

Lebraty, J.F. (2007). Vers un nouveau mode d'externalisation: Le crowdsourcing. 12th AIM Conference, Lausanne, June.

Leeuwis, C. (ed.) (2004). Chapter 2: From extension to communication for innovation. In *Communication for Rural Innovation: Rethinking Agricultural Extension*, 3rd edition. Wageningen Academic Publishers, Wageningen.

Leeuwis, C. and Aarts, N. (2011). Rethinking communication in innovation processes: Creating space for change in complex systems. *The Journal of Agricultural Education and Extension*, 17(1), 21–36. DOI: 10.1080/1389224X.2011.536344.

Lelong, B. and Gayoso, É. (2010). Innovation avec l'usager et plateformes collaboratives: Des modes d'engagement hétérogènes. *Réseaux*, 164(6), 97–126.

Leminen, S. (2013). Coordination and participation in living lab network. *Technology Innovation Management Review*, 3, 5–14.

Leroux, I., Muller, P., Plottu, B., Widehem, C. (2014). Innovation ouverte et évolution des business models dans les pôles de compétitivité: Le rôle des intermédiaires dans la création variétale végétale. *Revue d'économie industrielle*, 146, 115–151.

Lessig, L. (2004). *Free Culture: The Nature and Future of Creativity*. Penguin Books, New York.

Lethiais, V., Deltour, F., Le Gall, S. (2015). Le rôle des TIC et du territoire dans la capacité d'innovation des PME: Une étude empirique. *ASRDLF 2015: 52ème Colloque de l'Association de Sciences Régionales de Langue Française*, Montpellier, July.

Leveque, J., Ben Mahmoud-Jouini, S., Fabbri, J. (2020). Espace et événement collaboratifs d'innovation, deux dispositifs complémentaires pour l'ambidextrie. Synergies entre Innovation Lab et Innovation Challenge. *Finance contrôle stratégie*, 23(Special edition), 89–115.

Levitt, B. and March, J.G. (1988). Organizational learning. *Annual Review of Sociology*, 14. 319–340.

Lévy, P. (1994). *L'intelligence collective: Pour une anthropologie du cyberspace*. La Découverte, Paris.

Levy, R. and Woessner, R. (2006). Le territoire français en tant que Système Régional d'Innovation. BETA working document no. 2006-24.

Leydersdorff, L. and Etzkowitz, H. (2000). Le "Mode 2" et la globalisation des systèmes d'innovation "nationaux": Le modèle à Triple hélice des relations entre université, industrie et gouvernement. *Sociologie et sociétés*, 32(1), 135–156.

Lichtenthaler, U. and Ernst, H. (2007). External technology commercialization in large firms: Results of a quantitative benchmarking study. *R&D Management*, 37(5), 383–397.

Liénart, S. and Castiaux, A. (2012). Innovation et respect environnemental sont-ils compatibles ? Le cas du secteur des TIC. *Reflets et perspectives de la vie économique*, LI(4), 77–96. https://doi.org/10.3917/rpve.514.0077.

Likert, R. (1961). *New Patterns of Management*. McGraw Hill, New York.

Likert, R. (1974). *Le gouvernement participatif de l'entreprise*. Gauthier-Villard, Paris.

Liotard, I. (1999). Les droits de propriété intellectuelle, une nouvelle arme stratégique des firmes. *Revue d'économie industrielle*, 89(1), 69–84.

Liotard, I. (2010). Crowdsourcing et plateforme Internet: Le cas de Innocentive. Open source innovation (beyond software), Strasbourg, 1–21, February.

Liotard, I. and Revest, V. (2015). Innocentive un modèle hybride d'innovation basé sur l'appel à la foule et l'Innovation Ouverte. In *Le retour des communs: La crise de l'idéologie propriétaire*, Coriat, B. (ed.). Les Liens qui libèrent, Paris.

Lissoni, F. (2001). Knowledge codification and the geography of innovation: The case of Brescia mechanical cluster. *Research Policy*, 30, 1479–1500.

Lo, A. (2014). Fab Lab en entreprise: Proposition d'ancrage théorique. *XXIIIème conférence annuelle de l'Association Internationale de Management Stratégique*.

Loilier, T. and Tellier, A. (2011). Que faire du modèle de l'innovation ouverte ? *Revue française de gestion*, 37(210), 69–85.

Lundvall, B.Å. (ed.) (1992). *National Innovation Systems: Towards a Theory of Innovation and Interactive Learning*. Pinter, London.

Lundvall, B.Å. (2005). National innovation systems – Analytical concept and development tool. *DRUID 10th Anniversary Summer Conference 2005 on Dynamics of Industry and Innovation: Organizations, Networks and Systems*.

Lundvall, B.Å. (2007). National systems of innovation: Analytical concept and development tool. *Industry and Innovation*, 14(1), 95–119.

Lundvall, B.Å. (2008). From the economics of knowledge to the learning economy why focus on economics of knowledge? *Proceedings of the 5th International, Ph.D. School on Innovation and Economic Development*, Globelics Academy.

Lüthje, C. (2002). Characteristics of innovating users in a consumer goods field: An empirical study of sport-related product consumers. *Technovation*, 24, 683–695.

Mahdad, M., Minh, T.T., Bogers, M.L.A.M., Piccaluga, A. (2020). Joint university-industry laboratories through the lens of proximity dimensions: Moving beyond geographical proximity. *International Journal of Innovation Science*, 12(4), 433–456.

Mansfield, E., (1985). How rapidly does new industrial technology leak out? *Journal of Industrial Economics*, 34(2), 217–223.

March, J.G. (1991). Exploration and exploitation in organizational learning. *Organization Science*, 2(1), 71–87.

Marinos, C. (2018). Espaces collaboratifs de travail et clubs d'entreprises: Des réseaux au cœur des dynamiques collaboratives d'innovation. *Innovations*, 1(1), 119–141.

Martin, L. and Nguyen-Thi, T.U. (2015). The relationship between innovation and productivity based on R&D and ICT use. An empirical analysis of firms in Luxembourg. *Revue économique*, 66, 1105–1130.

Mendez, A. and Mercier, D. (2006). Compétences-clés de territoires: Le rôle des relations interorganisationnelles. *Revue française de gestion*, 164(5), 253–275.

Mention, A.L. (2011). Co-operation and co-opetition as open innovation practices in the service sector: Which influence on innovation novelty? *Technovation*, 31, 44–53.

Mention, A.L. and Torkkeli, M. (eds) (2014). *Innovation in Financial Services: A Dual Ambiguity*. Cambridge Scholars Publishing.

Metcalfe, S. (1995). The economic foundations of technology policy: Equilibrium and evolutionary perspectives. In *Handbook of the Economics of Innovation and Technological Change*, Stoneman, P. (ed.). Blackwell Publishers, Oxford.

Meyers, P.W. and Athaide, G.A. (1991). Strategic mutual learning between producing and buying firms during product innovation. *Journal of Product Innovation Management*, 8, 155–169.

Micaëlli, J., Forest, J., Coatanéa, É., Medyna, G. (2014). How to improve Kline and Rosenberg's chain-linked model of innovation: Building blocks and diagram-based languages. *Journal of Innovation Economics & Management*, 3(3), 59–77.

Mignon, S. and Laperche, B. (2018). La connaissance: Matrice de l'innovation ouverte. *Innovations*, 1(1), 5–12.

Mikhak, B., Lyon, C., Gorton, T., Gershenfeld, N., McEnnis, C., Taylor, J. (2002). Fab Lab: An alternate model of ICT for development. *2nd International Conference on Open Collaborative Design for Sustainable Innovation*.

Mintzberg, H. (1979). *The Structuring of Organizations*. Prentice-Hall, Englewood Cliffs, NJ.

Mintzberg, H. (1982). *Structure et dynamique des organisations*. Les Éditions d'Organisation, Paris.

Moore, J.F. (1993). Predators and prey: A new ecology of competition. *Harvard Business Review*, 71(3), 75–86.

Morgan, K. and Murdoch, J. (2000). Organic vs. conventional agriculture: Knowledge, power and innovation in the food chain. *Geoforum*, 31(2), 159–173.

Muller, P. (2021). La production des innovations sociale: Une analyse par le modèle de l'écologie créative. *Technologie et Innovation*, 6.

Murray, F. and O'Mahony, S. (2007). Exploring the foundations of cumulative innovation: Implications for organization science. *Organization Science*, 18(6), 1006–1021.

Nambisan, S. (2013). Information technology and product/service innovation: A brief assessment and some suggestions for future research. *Journal of the Association for Information Systems*, 14(4), 215–226.

Nelson, R. (ed.) (1993). *National Innovation Systems. A Comparative Analysis.* Oxford University Press, New York/Oxford.

Nieto, M. and Santamaría, L. (2007). The importance of diverse collaborative networks for the novelty of product innovation. *Technovation*, 27, 367–377.

Nunes, M. and Abreu, A. (2020). Managing open innovation project risks based on a social network analysis perspective. *Sustainability*, 12, 3132.

Nuvolari, A., (2004). Collective invention during the British industrial revolution: The case of the Cornish pumping engine. *Cambridge Journal of Economics*, 28, 347–363.

OECD (2008). *Open Innovation in Global Networks*. OECD, Paris.

OECD/Eurostat (2005). *Oslo Manual. Guidelines for Collecting and Interpreting Innovation Data*. OECD, Paris.

OECD/Eurostat (2019). *Manuel d'Oslo 2018: Lignes directrices pour le recueil, la communication et l'utilisation des données sur l'innovation*, 4th edition. Mesurer les activités scientifiques, technologiques et d'innovation. OECD, Paris.

Önday, Ö. (2016). National and regional innovation systems, industrial policies and their impacts on firm innovation strategies and performance-economic role of knowledge. *International Journal of Contemporary Applied Sciences*, 3(2), 1–35.

Orléan, A. (1998). The evolution of imitation. In *The Economics of Networks*, Cohendet, P., Llerena, P., Stahn, H., Umbhauer G. (eds). Springer, Berlin Heidelberg. https://doi.org/10.1007/978-3-642-72260-8_16.

Ouellet, M. (2013). *Du chercheur innovateur au client co-créateur ou l'apport d'un nouveau paradigme de l'innovation collaborative: Cadre conceptuel*. Université du Québec à Montréal. https://irec.quebec/repertoire/fiche/du-chercheur-innovateur-au-client-cocreateur-ou-lapport-dun-nouveau-paradigme-de-linnovation-collaborative-un-cadre-conceptuel.

Pakes, A. and Griliches, Z. (1980). Patents and R&D at the firm level: A first report. *Economics Letters*, 5(4), 377–381.

Parrilli, M.D. and Heras, H.A. (2016). STI and DUI innovation modes: Scientific-technological and context-specific nuances. *Research Policy*, 45(4), 747–756.

Patel, P. and Pavitt, K. (1994). The nature and economic importance of national innovation systems. *STI Review*, no. 14, OECD, Paris.

Patris, C., Warrant, F., Valenduc, G. (2001). L'innovation technologique au service du développement durable. Working paper, FTUNamur, Programme "Leviers du développement durable". Research contract no. HL/DD/020.

Paus, M. and Réviron, S. (2010). Mesure de l'impact territorial d'initiatives agroalimentaires. Enseignement de deux cas suisses. *Économie rurale*, 315, 28–45.

Pavitt, K. (1984). Sectoral patterns of technical change: Towards a taxonomy and a theory. *Research Policy*, 13(6), 343–373.

Pecqueur, B. and Zimmermann, J.B. (2004). *Les fondements d'une économie de proximité*. Hermes-Lavoisier, Paris.

Pelissier, C. (2008). Le crowdsourcing, une intermédiation hybride du marché: De nouvelles formes d'organisation innovante pour une articulation entre logiques marchandes et dynamiques communautaires. 5e doctoriales du GDR TIC & Sociétés, Rennes.

Pelissier, C. (2015). Les plateformes Internet comme intermédiaires hybrides du marché. Thesis, Université Grenoble Alpes.

Pénin, J. (2008). More open than open innovation? Rethinking the concept of openness in innovation studies, BETA. Working document no. 2008-18.

Pirola-Merlo, A. (2010). Agile innovation: The role of team climate in rapid research and development. *Journal of Occupational and Organizational Psychology*, 83(4), 1075–1084.

Polenske, K. (2004) Competition, Collaboration and cooperation: An uneasy triangle in networks of firms and regions. *Regional Studies*, 38(9), 1029–1043.

Poncet, J., Kuper, M., Chiche, J. (2002). Wandering off the paths of planned innovation: The role of formal and informal intermediaries in a large-scale irrigation scheme in Morocco. *Agricultural Systems*, 103(4), 171–179.

Porter, M.E. (1990). The Competitive Advantage of Nations. *Harvard Business Review*, 68(2) (March–April), 73–93.

Porter, M.E. (2007). Clusters and economic policy: Aligning public policy with the new economics of competition. ISC white paper, Harvard Business School, Institute for Strategy and Competitiveness.

Powell, W.W., Koput, K., Smith-Doerr, L. (1996). Interorganizational collaboration and the locus of innovation: Networks of learning in biotechnology. *Administrative Science Quarterly*, 41, 116–145.

Rallet, A. (2002). L'économie de proximités: Propos d'étape. *Études et recherches sur les systèmes agraires et le développement*. INRA Editions, 11–25.

Rallet, A. and Torre, A. (1998). On geography and technology. The case of proximity relations in localised innovations networks. In *Clusters and Regional Specialisation*, Steiner, M. (ed.). Pion Publication, London.

Rallet, A. and Torre, A. (2004). Proximité et localisation. *Économie rurale*, 280(1), 25–41.

Raveyre, M.-F. and Saglio, J. (1984). Les systèmes industriels localisés: Éléments pour une analyse sociologique des ensembles de PME industriels. *Sociologie du travail*, 2, 157–175.

Rayna, T. and Striukova, L. (2010). Large-scale open innovation: Open source vs. patent pools. *International Journal of Technology Management*, 3–4, 477–496.

Reason, P. and Bradbury, H. (eds) (2008). *The Sage Handbook of Action Research: Participative Inquiry and Practice*. Sage, CA.

Remer, T.G. (ed.) (1965). *Serendipity and the Three Princes, from the Peregrinaggio of 1557*. University of Oklahoma Press.

Rodié, I. (2007). Responsabilité sociale des entreprises. Le développement d'un cadre européen Thesis, Institut Européen de l'université de Genève, Geneva.

Rosenberg, N. (ed.) (1976). Technological change in the machine tool industry, 1840–1910. *Perspectives on Technology*, Cambridge University Press, Cambridge.

Rossi, F. and Rosli, A. (2013). Indicators of university–industry knowledge transfer performance and their implications for universities: Evidence from the UK's HE-BCI survey (No. 13), July.

Roy, S., Sivakumar, K., Wilkinson, I. (2004). Innovation generation in supply chain relationships: A conceptual model and research propositions. *Journal of the Academy of Marketing Science*, 32(1), 61–79.

Russell, J., Greenhalgh, T., Boynton, P., Rigby, M. (2004). Soft networks for bridging the gap between research and practice: Illuminative evaluation of CHAIN. *British Medical Journal*, 328, 1–6.

Ruttan, V. (2002). Controversy about agricultural technology: Lessons from the green revolution. University of Minnesota, Department of Applied Economics, Staff Papers.

Sachwald, F. (2008). Réseaux mondiaux d'innovation ouverte, systèmes nationaux et politiques publiques. Ministère de l'Enseignement supérieur et de la Recherche. https://www.enseignementsup-recherche.gouv.fr/cid28373/-reseaux-mondiaux-d-innovation-ouverte-systemes-nationaux-et-politiques-publiques.html.

Sakkab, N.Y. (2002) Connect & develop complements research & develop at P&G. *Research-Technology Management*, 45(2), 38–45.

Sandulache, C.E. (2019). Comment appréhender les nouvelles formes d'organisation du travail au service de l'innovation collaborative dans le cadre des territoires inscrits dans une démarche de stratégie intelligente? – Cas des tiers – lieux collaboratifs. Gestion et management. Université de la Réunion ⟨NNT: 2019LARE0006⟩. ⟨tel-02172252⟩.

Santamaría, L., Jesús, M., Rodríguez, A. (2021). Failed and successful innovations: The role of geographic proximity and international diversity of partners in technological collaboration. *Technological Forecasting & Social Change*, 166, 1–13.

Sapienza, H.J., Parhankangas, A., Autio, E. (2004). Knowledge relatedness and postspin-off growth. *Journal of Business Venturing*, 19(6), 809–829

Sarasvathy, S. (2001). Toward causation and effectuation: A theoretical shift from inevitability to economic entrepreneurial contingency. *The Academy of Management Review*, 26(2), 243–263.

Sawhney, M., Gianmario, V., Prandelli, E. (2005). Collaborating to create: The internet as a platform for customer engagement in product innovation. *Journal of Interactive Marketing*, 19, 4–17.

Saxenian, A.L. (1994). *Regional Advantage: Culture and Competition in Silicon Valley and Route 128*. Harvard University Press, Cambridge, MA.

Schartinger, D., Rammer, C., Fischer, M.M., Fröhlich, J. (2002). Knowledge interactions between universities and industry in Austria: Sectoral patterns and determinants. *Research Policy*, 31, 303–328.

Schelling, T. (1978). *Micromotives and Macrobehavior*. Norton, New York.

Schmalensee, R. and Evans, D.S. (2007). Industrial organization of markets with two-sided platforms. *Competition Policy International*, 3(1). https://ssrn.com/abstract=987341.

Schumpeter, J.A. (1934). *The Theory of Economic Development: An Inquiry into Profits, Capital, Credits, Interest, and the Business Cycle*. Transaction Publishers, Piscataway, NJ.

Scotchmer, S. (1991). Standing on the shoulders of giants: Cumulative research and the patent law. *Journal of Economic Perspectives*, 5, 29–41.

Servajean-Hilst, R. and Duverdier, O. (2015). Les grands paradoxes de l'Open Innovation: Gérer l'ouverture et le partage dans les projets d'innovation collaboratifs. *Journal des Sociétés*, 130, 13–15.

Seyfang, G., Park, J.J., Smith, A. (2013) A thousand flowers blooming? An examination of community energy in the UK. *Energy Policy*, 61, 977–989.

de Silva, M., Howells, J., Meyer, M. (2018). Innovation intermediaries and collaboration: Knowledge-based practices and internal value creation. *Research Policy*, 47(1), 70–87.

Shah, S.K. (2000). Sources and patterns of innovation in a consumer products field: Innovations in sporting equipment. Sloan School Working Paper 4105, Massachusetts Institute of Technology, Cambridge, MA.

Shah, S.K. and Tripsas, M. (2007). The accidental entrepreneur: The emergent and collective process of user entrepreneurship. *Strategic Entrepreneurship Journal*, 1, 123–140.

Shah, S.K. and Tripsas, M. (2012). When do user innovators start firms? A theory of user entrepreneurship. In *Revolutionizing Innovation: Users, Communities and Open Innovation*, Harhoff, D. and Lakhani, K.R. (eds). MIT Press, Cambridge, MA.

Shapiro, C. and Varían, H.R. (1998). Information rules: A strategic guide to the network economy. *The Journal of Technology Transfer*, 25, 250–252.

Spielman, D.J. and Birner, R. (2008). How innovative is your agriculture? Using innovation indicators and benchmarks to strengthen national agricultural innovation systems. Agriculture and rural development discussion paper, no. 41 Washington, D.C. World Bank Group. http://documents.worldbank.org/curated/en/696461468316131075/How-innovative-is-your-agriculture-Using-innovation-indicators-and-benchmarks-to-strengthen-national-agricultural-innovation-systems.

Spinuzzi, C., Bodrožić, Z., Scaratti, G., Ivaldi, S. (2019). Coworking is about community: But what is "community" in coworking? *Journal of Business and Technical Communication*, 33(2), 112–140.

St-Pierre, M. and Hanel, P. (2005). La collaboration entre les universités et les entreprises du secteur manufacturier canadien. *Cahiers de recherche sociologique*, 40, 69–109.

Steiner, A. (2014). Élaboration et mise en œuvre d'un modèle organisationnel favorisant l'open innovation: Contribution à l'innovation collaborative. *Revue française de gestion*, 71–84.

Swedberg, R. (1990). *Economics and sociology: Redefining their boundaries: Conversations with Economists and Sociologists*. Princeton University Press, NJ.

Szostak, B., Muller, P., Fagbohoun, S., Yahiaoui, S. (2018). Caractériser la gouvernance d'un éco-système d'innovation ouverte fondé sur des communs. Exploration du cas du transport et de la mobilité en France. *9èmes Journées du GT Innovation de l'AIMS*, Montreal, 17–19 October.

Teece, D.J. (1986). Profiting from technological innovation – Implications for integration, collaboration, licensing and public-policy. *Research Policy*, 15(6), 285–305.

Teece, D.J. (2007). Explicating dynamic capabilities: The nature and microfoundations of sustainable enterprise formation. *Strategic Management Journal*, 28(13), 1319–1350.

Tether, B.S. (2002). Who co-operates for innovation, and why: An empirical analysis. *Research Policy*, 31, 947–967.

Thagard, P. and Croft, D. (1999). Scientific discovery and technological innovation: Ulcers, dinosaur extinction, and the programming language java. In *Model-Based Reasoning in Scientific Discovery*, Magnani, L., Nersessian, N.J., Thagard, P. (eds). Springer, Boston, MA.

Thiaw, C.A.L. (2013). Innovation collaborative et orientation client/marché au sein des Pôles de compétitivité: Analyse empirique des dynamiques de projets/ acteurs (Cas des Réseaux d'innovation en Région PACA). Management Sciences PhD Thesis, Université Nice-Sophia Antipolis, April.

Thiaw, C.A.L. (2021). Orientation marché et innovation collaborative par les interactions université-industrie. *Technologie et innovation*, 6, 1–13.

Tidd, J. (1995). Development of novel products through intraorganizational and interorganizational networks. *Journal of Product Innovation Management*, 12(4), 307–322.

Torre, A. (2016). La figure du réseau: Dimensions spatiales et organisationnelles. *Géographie, économie, société*, 18, 455–469.

Tripsas, M. (1997). Surviving radical technological change through dynamic capability: Evidence from the typesetter industry. *Industrial & Corporate Change*, 6(2), 341–377.

Trott, P. and Hartmann, D. (2009). Why Open Innovation is old wine in new bottles. *International Journal of Innovation Management*, 13(4), 715–736.

Uzunidis, D. (2008). Milieux innovateur et gestation d'un entrepreneuriat innovant. *Marché et organisations*, 1(1), 119–145.

Uzunidis, D. (2010). Innovation et proximité: Entreprises, entrepreneurs et milieux innovateurs. *La Revue des Sciences de Gestion*, 1(1), 13–22.

Uzzi, B. (1996). The sources and consequences of embeddedness for the economic performance of organizations: The network effect. *American Sociological Review*, 61, 674–698.

Vall, E., Chia, E., Blanchard, M., Koutou, M., Coulibaly, K., Andrieu, N. (2016). La co-conception en partenariat de systèmes agricoles innovants. *Cahiers Agricultures*, 25(1), 15001.

Vanhaverbeke, W.W., Van de Vrande, V., Chesbrough, H. (2008). Understanding the advantages of open innovation practices in corporate venturing in terms of real options. *Creativity and Innovation Management*, 17(4), 253–254.

Vrande, V.V.D., Jong, J.P.J., Vanhaverbeke, W., Rochemont, M. (2009). Open innovation in SMEs: Trends, motives and management challenges. *Technovation*, 29, 423–437.

Wang, Y., Roijakkers, N., Vanhaverbeke, W. (2011). Linking open innovation to national systems of innovation: A coevolutionary perspective. *International Journal of Innovation and Regional Development*, 3(5), 446.

Watts, D. and Strogatz, S. (1998). Collective dynamics of "small-world" networks. *Nature*, 393, 440–442.

Weitzman, J. (2004). Open access and creative common sense. *The Scientist*, 18(9), A2+.

West, J. (2006). Does appropriability enable or retard open innovation? *Open Innovation: Researching a New Paradigm*, 109–133.

White, H. (1992). *Identity and Control: A Structural Theory of Social Action*. Princeton University Press, NJ.

Whitley, R. (2002). Developing innovative competences: The role of institutional frameworks. *Industrial and Corporate Change*, 11, 497–528.

Wood, B.A., Blair, H.T., Gray, D.I., Kemp, P.D., Kenyon, P.R., Morris, S.T., Sewell, A.M. (2014). Agricultural science in the wild: A social network analysis of farmer knowledge exchange. *PLoS ONE*, 9(8), e105203.

Younes, D., Jacob, M.-R., Marti, I. (2019). L'innovation sociale sur les territoires – Comment passer de l'intervention exogène à la communauté innovante ? *Revue française de gestion*, 280, 75–90.

Zacklad, M. (2020). Les enjeux de la transition numérique et de l'innovation collaborative dans les mutations du travail et du management dans le secteur public. In *Travailler dans les services publics la nouvelle donne*, Gillet, A. (ed.). Presses de l'EHESP, Rennes.

Zaheer, S. and Zaheer, A. (2006). Trust across borders. *Journal of International Business Studies*, 37, 21–29.

Zainal Abidin, S.B., Mokhtar, S.S., Yusoff, R.Z. (2011). A systematic analysis of innovation studies: A proposed framework on relationship between innovation process and firm's performance. *The Asian Journal of Technology Management*, 4(2), 65–83.

Index

A, B

acquisition
  of commercial contracts, 103
  of inputs, 60
  of knowledge, 20, 22, 24, 103
  of licenses, 125
  of resources, 26
  of technologies, 48
  value, 137
activities, 16, 31, 33, 34, 40, 70, 72, 73, 76, 78, 79, 82, 84, 87, 100, 101, 113, 114, 135, 137
  collaborative, 6
  commercial, 86, 112
  commercialization, 16
  exploration, 23, 128
  imitation, 23
  improvisational, 134
  innovation, 76, 115
  networking, 87
  open innovation, 12
  R&D, 4, 9, 17, 24, 86, 99
  research, 9, 41, 43
  technology development, 87
added value, 15, 20, 67, 71, 73, 77, 81, 105, 129
agriculture/farming, 19, 57, 70

approach
  bottom-up, 37–39, 66, 73
  participatory, 16, 40
  top-down, 38, 72
appropriation, 51, 57, 60, 82, 124
bottom-up, 38, 65, 66, 73, 90, 96, 146
boundaries, 10, 23, 31, 47, 51, 56, 67, 100
business ecosystem, 38, 42, 54

C, D

capabilities/abilities/capacities, 20, 23, 24, 58, 65, 86, 87, 109, 135
  cognitive, 91, 128
  dynamic, 43
  innovation, 81
  motor, 91
  necessary, 141
  organizational, 82
  sensory, 91
  specific, 94
capacity/ability/capability, 81, 104, 113, 146
  absorption, 4, 16, 75, 101, 144
  evaluation, 17
  innovation, 16, 37, 92, 110, 116
  of actors, 25, 83, 101, 128
  of firms, 4, 17

to acquire, 18
to innovate, 25
to recognize, 17
to undertake, 12
circulation of knowledge, 35, 73, 143
closed innovation, 9, 12, 49, 124, 130
clusters, 38, 61, 76, 77, 79, 80, 96, 138, 143
co-creation, 60, 87, 94, 106
co-location, 76
cognitive proximity, 66, 74, 75, 83, 143
collaborative innovation, 7, 10, 37, 49, 51, 55, 65, 66, 81, 99–102, 106–108, 116, 121, 124, 125, 128, 135, 137, 138, 143, 144, 147
collective intelligence, 95, 96, 146
communication, 43, 44, 47, 51, 68, 79, 81, 88, 94, 96, 101, 103, 104, 108, 109, 111, 124, 127, 137, 146
competition, 54, 81, 102, 126, 129
competitiveness, 42, 51, 57, 60, 83, 84, 126
clusters, 38, 80
consumer
behavior, 19, 41
panels, 146
cooperation, i, iv, v, 9, 10, 31, 33–35, 43, 60, 113, 116, 121, 122, 125
corporate social responsibility, 111, 112
creative commons, 51, 61, 62
creativity, 15, 16, 61, 82, 121, 135
crowdsourcing, 56, 59, 110, 132, 146
cultural distance, 127
cycle
innovation, 29, 91
life, 5, 6, 134
degree
of codification, 142
of innovation, 4
of novelty, 18, 83

of openness, 13, 23, 25, 28, 51, 60, 124, 143
development, 68, 96
economic, 68
research, 145
diffusion, 4, 6, 12, 31, 38–40, 42, 56, 62, 84, 92, 121, 127, 142
of innovation, 4
diversity of partners, 60, 61

E, F

ecological transition, iv, 148
ecosystem
innovation, 82, 83, 96, 105, 107
entrepreneurs, 48, 67, 73, 92, 102, 128, 146
environment, 4, 13, 15, 17, 37, 43, 46, 47, 81, 101, 102, 109, 113, 114
academic, 30
business, 42, 43, 60, 76, 86, 129
collaborative, 31, 44
competitive, 77
entrepreneurial, 134
local, 108
research, 86
virtuals, 56
work, 34
exchange
environment, 93
financial, 132
of knowledge, 106
of licences, 51, 144
exchanges
between actors, 73, 105
codified, 57
informal, 69
of experiences, 96
of information, 72, 146
expectations
client, 41
of players, 40
of society, 138

feedback loop, 3, 36
flows
  information, 10, 107
  of assets, 145
  of knowledge, 10, 57, 88, 101, 106, 107
funding/lending, 87, 115, 118, 146, 147
  crowd, 110, 132, 146

G, I

geographical proximity, 42, 74–76, 80, 83, 138
global warming, 114, 146
ICT, 31, 44, 47, 108–110, 129
incremental innovations, 4
industrial districts, 38, 80–82, 96, 145
innovation
  incremental, 4, 11, 19, 20, 22, 80, 91, 136
  responsible, 111, 114–116, 118, 146
inside-out, 56
institutional proximity, 52, 53, 75, 83, 143
intellectual property rights, 12, 28, 49–51, 58, 59, 61, 126, 137, 144
intermediary, 28, 36, 55, 58, 84, 86, 87, 89, 105, 132, 145, 148

K, L

know-how, 4, 16, 17, 20, 29, 47, 48, 51, 66, 69, 104, 107, 124, 138, 139
knowledge, 4, 5, 10, 12, 13, 16, 18–20, 22, 24, 26, 28, 29, 34, 37, 41–43, 45, 47, 48, 51, 54, 56, 57, 59, 65–69, 71, 74–76, 82, 86–89, 93, 96, 97, 99, 101, 103, 104, 106, 107, 122, 125, 126, 129, 130, 134, 135, 139, 144, 146, 148
  accumulated, 18
  codified, 106, 107
  economic, 113
  external, 17, 60
  internal, 60
  new, 31
  scientific, 113, 144
  sensitive, 26
  social, 113
  synthetic, 42
  tacit, 73, 77, 79, 82, 106, 130
  technical, 17, 113
learning-through-doing, 72, 82
local distribution channels, 108
location, 15, 42, 70, 73, 96, 146

M, N

management
  chance, 15
  community, 59
  innovation, 145
  knowledge, 5, 109
  of ideas, 102
  of intellectual property, 84, 126
  of the innovation process, 43, 51
  of the process, 4
  of trust, 15
  progress, 16
  project, 34, 137
markets, 6, 10, 19, 23, 28, 36, 43, 44, 50, 51, 59, 60, 65, 73, 77, 79, 81, 87, 89, 90, 97, 110, 116, 129, 131, 137, 146
  access to, 99
  competitive, 76
  diversity of, 101
  governance of, 102
  innovations, 92
  intermediary, 58, 128
  maturity of the, 122
  R&D, 89
  segment, 48
  strategic, 28

media, 72, 139
National Innovation System, 82
needs
 companies, 80, 95
 consumers, 41
 customer, 23, 40, 41, 101
 local, 39
 stakeholders, 38, 89
 users, 4, 91
networks, 7, 20, 29, 31, 39, 41, 42, 45, 47, 52, 56, 58, 67, 68, 73, 76, 77, 79, 82–84, 87, 89, 92, 101, 104, 128, 139, 144, 145
 collaborative, 104
 infrastructure, 45
 innovation, 77, 84
 social, 46, 110
 sociotechnical, 107

O, P

open
 innovation, 5, 7, 9–11, 13, 23, 25, 28, 35, 42, 44, 47–50, 52, 56–61, 65, 67, 73, 75, 76, 82, 89, 95–97, 99–102, 105, 116, 121, 122, 124–126, 128–130, 133, 134, 138, 143, 145, 147
 source, 12, 50, 51, 60, 61, 68
organizational proximity, 53, 76, 83
organized proximity, 53
outside-in, 56
paradox, 116, 121, 133–135, 137, 145
path dependency, 42
policies
 innovation, 111, 138
 local, 86, 146
 public, 80, 82, 138
positive externalities, 20, 52, 109
purpose, 37, 66, 94, 128
 social and environmental, 147

R, S

radical innovation, 4
Regional Innovation System, 82
relational capital, 104
relationships/relations
 common, 76
 cooperative, 34
 economic, 53
 formal, 73, 107
 horizontal, 61
 informal, 73, 107
 inter-organizational, 77
 interpersonal, 47, 57, 69, 71, 74, 79, 82, 107, 126, 132
 marchandes, 132
 of collaboration, 43
 of proximity, 77
 social, 53, 77, 132
 virtual, 110
resources, 4, 5, 19, 23, 24, 26, 31, 35, 37, 39, 43, 44, 54, 56, 60, 61, 73, 77, 99, 109, 133, 137, 143, 145
 available, 50
 between partners, 45
 common use, 68
 community, 105
 external, 109
 financial, 28, 55, 71, 93, 94, 139
 firm's, 24
 human, 69, 71, 89, 105, 126
 intangible, 67, 69, 76
 interesting, 51
 internal, 60, 102
 mobilized, 94
 necessary, 49, 55, 92, 115, 136, 145
 sought, 28
 specific, 29, 69
 tangible, 81
risk, 23, 26, 45, 55, 57, 103, 116, 125, 127, 136, 148
serendipity, 13, 14, 136

sharing
  a common language, 107
  experiences, 107
  intellectual property rights, 69, 105
  know-how, 124
  knowledge, 75, 78
  resources, 69, 76
social
  proximity, 76, 96
  responsibility, 112
societal transformations, 101
sources
  of funding, 118
  of ideas, 10, 61
  of information, 45, 47, 100
  of innovation, 3, 13, 16, 90

strategic management, 77, 145
strength/force, 33, 46, 53, 73, 81, 100, 105, 122, 137, 146, 148
sustainability, 140

T, V

technological change, 4
territories, 31, 39, 53, 54, 76, 80, 145
top-down, 37, 38, 66, 72, 96, 144
triple helix, xv, 30, 139
value
  chain, 4, 20, 22, 66, 70, 88
  creation, 42, 137, 138

Other titles from

in

Innovation, Entrepreneurship and Management

2022

BOUCHÉ Geneviève
Productive Economy, Contributory Economy: Governance Tools for the Third Millennium (Innovation and Technology Set – Volume 15)

HELLER David
Valuation of the Liability Structure by Real Options (Modern Finance, Management Innovation and Economic Growth Set – Volume 5)

MATHIEU Valérie
A Customer-oriented Manager for B2B Services: Principles and Implementation

NOËL Florent, SCHMIDT Géraldine
Employability and Industrial Mutations: Between Individual Trajectories and Organizational Strategic Planning (Technological Changes and Human Resources Set – Volume 4)

DE SAINT JULIEN Odile
The Innovation Ecosystem as a Source of Value Creation: A Value Creation Lever for Open Innovation (Diverse and Global Perspectives on Value Creation Set – Volume 4)

SALOFF-COSTE Michel
Innovation Ecosystems: The Future of Civilizations and the Civilization of the Future (Innovation and Technology Set – Volume 14)

VAYRE Emilie
Digitalization of Work: New Spaces and New Working Times (Technological Changes and Human Resources Set – Volume 5)

ZAFEIRIS Konstantinos N, SKIADIS Christos H, DIMOTIKALIS Yannis, KARAGRIGORIOU Alex, KARAGRIGORIOU-VONTA Christina
Data Analysis and Related Applications 1: Computational, Algorithmic and Applied Economic Data Analysis (Big Data, Artificial Intelligence and Data Analysis Set – Volume 9)
Data Analysis and Related Applications 2: Multivariate, Health and Demographic Data Analysis (Big Data, Artificial Intelligence and Data Analysis Set – Volume 10)

2021

ARCADE Jacques
Strategic Engineering (Innovation and Technology Set – Volume 11)

BÉRANGER Jérôme, RIZOULIÈRES Roland
The Digital Revolution in Health (Health and Innovation Set – Volume 2)

BOBILLIER CHAUMON Marc-Eric
Digital Transformations in the Challenge of Activity and Work: Understanding and Supporting Technological Changes (Technological Changes and Human Resources Set – Volume 3)

BUCLET Nicolas
Territorial Ecology and Socio-ecological Transition (Smart Innovation Set – Volume 34)

DIMOTIKALIS Yannis, KARAGRIGORIOU Alex, PARPOULA Christina, SKIADIS Christos H
Applied Modeling Techniques and Data Analysis 1: Computational Data Analysis Methods and Tools (Big Data, Artificial Intelligence and Data Analysis Set - Volume 7)
Applied Modeling Techniques and Data Analysis 2: Financial, Demographic, Stochastic and Statistical Models and Methods (Big Data, Artificial Intelligence and Data Analysis Set – Volume 8)

DISPAS Christophe, KAYANAKIS Georges, SERVEL Nicolas, STRIUKOVA Ludmila
Innovation and Financial Markets
(Innovation between Risk and Reward Set – Volume 7)

ENJOLRAS Manon
Innovation and Export: The Joint Challenge of the Small Company
(Smart Innovation Set – Volume 37)

FLEURY Sylvain, RICHIR Simon
Immersive Technologies to Accelerate Innovation: How Virtual and Augmented Reality Enables the Co-Creation of Concepts
(Smart Innovation Set – Volume 38)

GIORGINI Pierre
The Contributory Revolution (Innovation and Technology Set – Volume 13)

GOGLIN Christian
Emotions and Values in Equity Crowdfunding Investment Choices 2: Modeling and Empirical Study

GRENIER Corinne, OIRY Ewan
Altering Frontiers: Organizational Innovations in Healthcare (Health and Innovation Set – Volume 1)

GUERRIER Claudine
Security and Its Challenges in the 21st Century (Innovation and Technology Set – Volume 12)

HELLER David
Performance of Valuation Methods in Financial Transactions (Modern Finance, Management Innovation and Economic Growth Set – Volume 4)

LEHMANN Paul-Jacques
Liberalism and Capitalism Today

SOULÉ Bastien, HALLÉ Julie, VIGNAL Bénédicte, BOUTROY Éric, NIER Olivier
Innovation in Sport: Innovation Trajectories and Process Optimization (Smart Innovation Set – Volume 35)

UZUNIDIS Dimitri, KASMI Fedoua, ADATTO Laurent
Innovation Economics, Engineering and Management Handbook 1: Main Themes
Innovation Economics, Engineering and Management Handbook 2: Special Themes

VALLIER Estelle
Innovation in Clusters: Science–Industry Relationships in the Face of Forced Advancement (Smart Innovation Set – Volume 36)

2020

ACH Yves-Alain, RMADI-SAÏD Sandra
Financial Information and Brand Value: Reflections, Challenges and Limitations

ANDREOSSO-O'CALLAGHAN Bernadette, DZEVER Sam, JAUSSAUD Jacques, TAYLOR Robert
Sustainable Development and Energy Transition in Europe and Asia (Innovation and Technology Set – Volume 9)

BEN SLIMANE Sonia, M'HENNI Hatem
Entrepreneurship and Development: Realities and Future Prospects (Smart Innovation Set – Volume 30)

CHOUTEAU Marianne, FOREST Joëlle, NGUYEN Céline
Innovation for Society: The P.S.I. Approach (Smart Innovation Set – Volume 28)

CORON Clotilde
Quantifying Human Resources: Uses and Analysis
(Technological Changes and Human Resources Set – Volume 2)

CORON Clotilde, GILBERT Patrick
Technological Change
(Technological Changes and Human Resources Set – Volume 1)

CERDIN Jean-Luc, PERETTI Jean-Marie
The Success of Apprenticeships: Views of Stakeholders on Training and Learning (Human Resources Management Set – Volume 3)

DELCHET-COCHET Karen
Circular Economy: From Waste Reduction to Value Creation
(Economic Growth Set – Volume 2)

DIDAY Edwin, GUAN Rong, SAPORTA Gilbert, WANG Huiwen
Advances in Data Science
(Big Data, Artificial Intelligence and Data Analysis Set – Volume 4)

DOS SANTOS PAULINO Victor
Innovation Trends in the Space Industry
(Smart Innovation Set – Volume 25)

GASMI Nacer
Corporate Innovation Strategies: Corporate Social Responsibility and Shared Value Creation
(Smart Innovation Set – Volume 33)

GOGLIN Christian
Emotions and Values in Equity Crowdfunding Investment Choices 1: Transdisciplinary Theoretical Approach

GUILHON Bernard
Venture Capital and the Financing of Innovation
(Innovation Between Risk and Reward Set – Volume 6)

LATOUCHE Pascal
Open Innovation: Human Set-up
(Innovation and Technology Set – Volume 10)

LIMA Marcos
Entrepreneurship and Innovation Education: Frameworks and Tools
(Smart Innovation Set – Volume 32)

MACHADO Carolina, DAVIM J. Paulo
Sustainable Management for Managers and Engineers

MAKRIDES Andreas, KARAGRIGORIOU Alex, SKIADAS Christos H.
Data Analysis and Applications 3: Computational, Classification, Financial, Statistical and Stochastic Methods
(Big Data, Artificial Intelligence and Data Analysis Set – Volume 5)
Data Analysis and Applications 4: Financial Data Analysis and Methods
(Big Data, Artificial Intelligence and Data Analysis Set – Volume 6)

MASSOTTE Pierre, CORSI Patrick
Complex Decision-Making in Economy and Finance

MEUNIER François-Xavier
Dual Innovation Systems: Concepts, Tools and Methods
(Smart Innovation Set – Volume 31)

MICHAUD Thomas
Science Fiction and Innovation Design (Innovation in Engineering and Technology Set – Volume 6)

MONINO Jean-Louis
Data Control: Major Challenge for the Digital Society
(Smart Innovation Set – Volume 29)

MORLAT Clément
Sustainable Productive System: Eco-development versus Sustainable Development (Smart Innovation Set – Volume 26)

SAULAIS Pierre, ERMINE Jean-Louis
Knowledge Management in Innovative Companies 2: Understanding and Deploying a KM Plan within a Learning Organization
(Smart Innovation Set – Volume 27)

2019

AMENDOLA Mario, GAFFARD Jean-Luc
Disorder and Public Concern Around Globalization

BARBAROUX Pierre
Disruptive Technology and Defence Innovation Ecosystems
(Innovation in Engineering and Technology Set – Volume 5)

DOU Henri, JUILLET Alain, CLERC Philippe
Strategic Intelligence for the Future 1: A New Strategic and Operational Approach
Strategic Intelligence for the Future 2: A New Information Function Approach

FRIKHA Azza
Measurement in Marketing: Operationalization of Latent Constructs

FRIMOUSSE Soufyane
Innovation and Agility in the Digital Age
(Human Resources Management Set – Volume 2)

GAY Claudine, SZOSTAK Bérangère L.
Innovation and Creativity in SMEs: Challenges, Evolutions and Prospects
(Smart Innovation Set – Volume 21)

GORIA Stéphane, HUMBERT Pierre, ROUSSEL Benoît
Information, Knowledge and Agile Creativity
(Smart Innovation Set – Volume 22)

HELLER David
Investment Decision-making Using Optional Models
(Economic Growth Set – Volume 2)

HELLER David, DE CHADIRAC Sylvain, HALAOUI Lana, JOUVET Camille
The Emergence of Start-ups
(Economic Growth Set – Volume 1)

HÉRAUD Jean-Alain, KERR Fiona, BURGER-HELMCHEN Thierry
Creative Management of Complex Systems
(Smart Innovation Set – Volume 19)

LATOUCHE Pascal
Open Innovation: Corporate Incubator
(Innovation and Technology Set – Volume 7)

LEHMANN Paul-Jacques
The Future of the Euro Currency

LEIGNEL Jean-Louis, MÉNAGER Emmanuel, YABLONSKY Serge
Sustainable Enterprise Performance: A Comprehensive Evaluation Method

LIÈVRE Pascal, AUBRY Monique, GAREL Gilles
Management of Extreme Situations: From Polar Expeditions to Exploration-Oriented Organizations

MILLOT Michel
Embarrassment of Product Choices 2: Towards a Society of Well-being

N'GOALA Gilles, PEZ-PÉRARD Virginie, PRIM-ALLAZ Isabelle
Augmented Customer Strategy: CRM in the Digital Age

NIKOLOVA Blagovesta
The RRI Challenge: Responsibilization in a State of Tension with Market Regulation
(Innovation and Responsibility Set – Volume 3)

PELLEGRIN-BOUCHER Estelle, ROY Pierre
Innovation in the Cultural and Creative Industries
(Innovation and Technology Set – Volume 8)

PRIOLON Joël
Financial Markets for Commodities

QUINIOU Matthieu
Blockchain: The Advent of Disintermediation

RAVIX Joël-Thomas, DESCHAMPS Marc
Innovation and Industrial Policies
(Innovation between Risk and Reward Set – Volume 5)

ROGER Alain, VINOT Didier
Skills Management: New Applications, New Questions
(Human Resources Management Set – Volume 1)

SAULAIS Pierre, ERMINE Jean-Louis
Knowledge Management in Innovative Companies 1: Understanding and Deploying a KM Plan within a Learning Organization
(Smart Innovation Set – Volume 23)

SERVAJEAN-HILST Romaric
Co-innovation Dynamics: The Management of Client-Supplier Interactions for Open Innovation
(Smart Innovation Set – Volume 20)

SKIADAS Christos H., BOZEMAN James R.
Data Analysis and Applications 1: Clustering and Regression, Modeling-estimating, Forecasting and Data Mining
(Big Data, Artificial Intelligence and Data Analysis Set – Volume 2)
Data Analysis and Applications 2: Utilization of Results in Europe and Other Topics
(Big Data, Artificial Intelligence and Data Analysis Set – Volume 3)

UZUNIDIS Dimitri
Systemic Innovation: Entrepreneurial Strategies and Market Dynamics

VIGEZZI Michel
World Industrialization: Shared Inventions, Competitive Innovations and Social Dynamics
(Smart Innovation Set – Volume 24)

2018

BURKHARDT Kirsten
Private Equity Firms: Their Role in the Formation of Strategic Alliances

CALLENS Stéphane
Creative Globalization
(Smart Innovation Set – Volume 16)

CASADELLA Vanessa
Innovation Systems in Emerging Economies: MINT – Mexico, Indonesia, Nigeria, Turkey
(Smart Innovation Set – Volume 18)

CHOUTEAU Marianne, FOREST Joëlle, NGUYEN Céline
Science, Technology and Innovation Culture
(Innovation in Engineering and Technology Set – Volume 3)

CORLOSQUET-HABART Marine, JANSSEN Jacques
Big Data for Insurance Companies
(Big Data, Artificial Intelligence and Data Analysis Set – Volume 1)

CROS Françoise
Innovation and Society
(Smart Innovation Set – Volume 15)

DEBREF Romain
Environmental Innovation and Ecodesign: Certainties and Controversies
(Smart Innovation Set – Volume 17)

DOMINGUEZ Noémie
SME Internationalization Strategies: Innovation to Conquer New Markets

ERMINE Jean-Louis
Knowledge Management: The Creative Loop
(Innovation and Technology Set – Volume 5)

GILBERT Patrick, BOBADILLA Natalia, GASTALDI Lise,
LE BOULAIRE Martine, LELEBINA Olga
Innovation, Research and Development Management

IBRAHIMI Mohammed
Mergers & Acquisitions: Theory, Strategy, Finance

LEMAÎTRE Denis
Training Engineers for Innovation

LÉVY Aldo, BEN BOUHENI Faten, AMMI Chantal
Financial Management: USGAAP and IFRS Standards
(Innovation and Technology Set – Volume 6)

MILLOT Michel
Embarrassment of Product Choices 1: How to Consume Differently

PANSERA Mario, OWEN Richard
Innovation and Development: The Politics at the Bottom of the Pyramid
(Innovation and Responsibility Set – Volume 2)

RICHEZ Yves
Corporate Talent Detection and Development

SACHETTI Philippe, ZUPPINGER Thibaud
New Technologies and Branding
(Innovation and Technology Set – Volume 4)

SAMIER Henri
Intuition, Creativity, Innovation

TEMPLE Ludovic, COMPAORÉ SAWADOGO Eveline M.F.W.
Innovation Processes in Agro-Ecological Transitions in Developing Countries
(Innovation in Engineering and Technology Set – Volume 2)

UZUNIDIS Dimitri
Collective Innovation Processes: Principles and Practices
(Innovation in Engineering and Technology Set – Volume 4)

VAN HOOREBEKE Delphine
The Management of Living Beings or Emo-management

2017

AÏT-EL-HADJ Smaïl
The Ongoing Technological System
(Smart Innovation Set – Volume 11)

BAUDRY Marc, DUMONT Béatrice
Patents: Prompting or Restricting Innovation?
(Smart Innovation Set – Volume 12)

BÉRARD Céline, TEYSSIER Christine
Risk Management: Lever for SME Development and Stakeholder Value Creation

CHALENÇON Ludivine
Location Strategies and Value Creation of International Mergers and Acquisitions

CHAUVEL Danièle, BORZILLO Stefano
The Innovative Company: An Ill-defined Object
(Innovation between Risk and Reward Set – Volume 1)

CORSI Patrick
Going Past Limits To Growth

D'ANDRIA Aude, GABARRET Inés
Building 21st Century Entrepreneurship
(Innovation and Technology Set – Volume 2)

DAIDJ Nabyla
Cooperation, Coopetition and Innovation
(Innovation and Technology Set – Volume 3)

FERNEZ-WALCH Sandrine
The Multiple Facets of Innovation Project Management
(Innovation between Risk and Reward Set – Volume 4)

FOREST Joëlle
Creative Rationality and Innovation
(Smart Innovation Set – Volume 14)

GUILHON Bernard
Innovation and Production Ecosystems
(Innovation between Risk and Reward Set – Volume 2)

HAMMOUDI Abdelhakim, DAIDJ Nabyla
Game Theory Approach to Managerial Strategies and Value Creation
(Diverse and Global Perspectives on Value Creation Set – Volume 3)

LALLEMENT Rémi
Intellectual Property and Innovation Protection: New Practices and New Policy Issues
(Innovation between Risk and Reward Set – Volume 3)

LAPERCHE Blandine
Enterprise Knowledge Capital
(Smart Innovation Set – Volume 13)

LEBERT Didier, EL YOUNSI Hafida
International Specialization Dynamics
(Smart Innovation Set – Volume 9)

MAESSCHALCK Marc
Reflexive Governance for Research and Innovative Knowledge
(Responsible Research and Innovation Set – Volume 6)

MASSOTTE Pierre
Ethics in Social Networking and Business 1: Theory, Practice and Current Recommendations
Ethics in Social Networking and Business 2: The Future and Changing Paradigms

MASSOTTE Pierre, CORSI Patrick
Smart Decisions in Complex Systems

MEDINA Mercedes, HERRERO Mónica, URGELLÉS Alicia
Current and Emerging Issues in the Audiovisual Industry
(Diverse and Global Perspectives on Value Creation Set – Volume 1)

MICHAUD Thomas
Innovation, Between Science and Science Fiction
(Smart Innovation Set – Volume 10)

PELLÉ Sophie
Business, Innovation and Responsibility
(Responsible Research and Innovation Set – Volume 7)

SAVIGNAC Emmanuelle
The Gamification of Work: The Use of Games in the Workplace

SUGAHARA Satoshi, DAIDJ Nabyla, USHIO Sumitaka
Value Creation in Management Accounting and Strategic Management: An Integrated Approach
(Diverse and Global Perspectives on Value Creation Set –Volume 2)

UZUNIDIS Dimitri, SAULAIS Pierre
Innovation Engines: Entrepreneurs and Enterprises in a Turbulent World
(Innovation in Engineering and Technology Set – Volume 1)

2016

BARBAROUX Pierre, ATTOUR Amel, SCHENK Eric
Knowledge Management and Innovation
(Smart Innovation Set – Volume 6)

BEN BOUHENI Faten, AMMI Chantal, LEVY Aldo
Banking Governance, Performance And Risk-Taking: Conventional Banks Vs Islamic Banks

BOUTILLIER Sophie, CARRÉ Denis, LEVRATTO Nadine
Entrepreneurial Ecosystems (Smart Innovation Set – Volume 2)

BOUTILLIER Sophie, UZUNIDIS Dimitri
The Entrepreneur (Smart Innovation Set – Volume 8)

BOUVARD Patricia, SUZANNE Hervé
Collective Intelligence Development in Business

GALLAUD Delphine, LAPERCHE Blandine
Circular Economy, Industrial Ecology and Short Supply Chains
(Smart Innovation Set – Volume 4)

GUERRIER Claudine
Security and Privacy in the Digital Era
(Innovation and Technology Set – Volume 1)

MEGHOUAR Hicham
Corporate Takeover Targets

MONINO Jean-Louis, SEDKAOUI Soraya
Big Data, Open Data and Data Development
(Smart Innovation Set – Volume 3)

MOREL Laure, LE ROUX Serge
Fab Labs: Innovative User
(Smart Innovation Set – Volume 5)

PICARD Fabienne, TANGUY Corinne
Innovations and Techno-ecological Transition
(Smart Innovation Set – Volume 7)

2015

CASADELLA Vanessa, LIU Zeting, DIMITRI Uzunidis
Innovation Capabilities and Economic Development in Open Economies
(Smart Innovation Set – Volume 1)

CORSI Patrick, MORIN Dominique
Sequencing Apple's DNA

CORSI Patrick, NEAU Erwan
Innovation Capability Maturity Model

FAIVRE-TAVIGNOT Bénédicte
Social Business and Base of the Pyramid

GODÉ Cécile
Team Coordination in Extreme Environments

MAILLARD Pierre
Competitive Quality and Innovation

MASSOTTE Pierre, CORSI Patrick
Operationalizing Sustainability

MASSOTTE Pierre, CORSI Patrick
Sustainability Calling

2014

DUBÉ Jean, LEGROS Diègo
Spatial Econometrics Using Microdata

LESCA Humbert, LESCA Nicolas
Strategic Decisions and Weak Signals

2013

HABART-CORLOSQUET Marine, JANSSEN Jacques, MANCA Raimondo
VaR Methodology for Non-Gaussian Finance

2012

DAL PONT Jean-Pierre
Process Engineering and Industrial Management

MAILLARD Pierre
Competitive Quality Strategies

POMEROL Jean-Charles
Decision-Making and Action

SZYLAR Christian
UCITS Handbook

2011

LESCA Nicolas
Environmental Scanning and Sustainable Development

LESCA Nicolas, LESCA Humbert
Weak Signals for Strategic Intelligence: Anticipation Tool for Managers

MERCIER-LAURENT Eunika
Innovation Ecosystems

2010

SZYLAR Christian
Risk Management under UCITS III/IV

2009

COHEN Corine
Business Intelligence

ZANINETTI Jean-Marc
Sustainable Development in the USA

2008

CORSI Patrick, DULIEU Mike
The Marketing of Technology Intensive Products and Services

DZEVER Sam, JAUSSAUD Jacques, ANDREOSSO Bernadette
Evolving Corporate Structures and Cultures in Asia: Impact of Globalization

2007

AMMI Chantal
Global Consumer Behavior

2006

BOUGHZALA Imed, ERMINE Jean-Louis
Trends in Enterprise Knowledge Management

CORSI Patrick *et al.*
Innovation Engineering: the Power of Intangible Networks